"A Reliable Car and a Woman Who Knows It"

"A Reliable Car and a Woman Who Knows It"

The First Coast-to-Coast Auto Trips by Women, 1899–1916

by

CURT McCONNELL

McFarland & Company, Inc., Publishers
Jefferson, North Carolina, and London

Library of Congress Cataloguing-in-Publication Data

McConnell, Curt, 1959–
    "A reliable car and a woman who knows it" : the first coast-
to-coast auto trips by women, 1899–1916 / by Curt McConnell.
       p.   cm.
    Includes bibliographical references (p.) and index.
    ISBN 0-7864-0970-3 (softcover : 50# alkaline paper) ∞
    1. Automobile travel — United States — History.   2. Women
automobile drivers — United States — Biography.   I. Title: First
coast-to-coast auto trips by women, 1899–1916.   II. Title.
GV1021.M24   2000
796.7'082 — dc21   00-56059

British Library cataloguing data are available

Front cover: *(Top)* Alice Ramsey's friend, Hermine Jahns, in
motoring garb. *(Bottom)* Blanche Stuart Scott coming down into
Hanna, Wyoming, in her white Overland. *(Both photographs
courtesy of the National Automotive History Collection)*

Manufactured in the United States of America

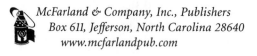

*McFarland & Company, Inc., Publishers
Box 611, Jefferson, North Carolina 28640
www.mcfarlandpub.com*

Acknowledgments

For their help editing drafts, I'd like to thank my father, Campbell R. McConnell, and my sisters, Lauren McConnell Davis and Beth McConnell. My special thanks go to Marilyn McConnell, Aiyana and Mariah McConnell-Beepath, Ben and Holly Davis and Stephen and Audrey Broll.

For general research assistance or help with specific questions on a number of chapters, I gratefully acknowledge the contributions of David L. Cole, Ralph Dunwoodie, Beverly Rae Kimes, David Smith and Karl S. Zahm, as well as:

• Kim Miller of the Antique Automobile Club of America's Library & Research Center, Hershey, Pennsylvania.
• Peggy Dusman, Dan Kirchner and Karen Prymak of the American Automobile Manufacturers Association, Detroit.
• Louis G. Helverson, Stuart McDougall and Bob Rubenstein of the Automobile Reference Collection, Free Library of Philadelphia.
• Serena Gomez and Mark Patrick of the National Automotive History Collection, Detroit Public Library, and Tom Sherry, the collection's contract photographer.
• The staffs of Bennett Martin Public Library, Lincoln, Nebraska, and Love Library, University of Nebraska–Lincoln.

Among those who made vital contributions to specific chapters are these helpful persons:

Chapter One, "Ring the Curtain Down on This Farce!": Roger Allison, David L. Cole, Karl Kabelac, Carl F.W. Larson, Terry Martin, Richard P. Scharchburg, Marilyn Vogt and Jim Winton.

Chapter Three, "The Car, the Girl and the Wide, Wide World": Dorothy Cochrane, National Air and Space Museum, Smithsonian Institution, Washington, D.C.; and Robert L. Taylor, Antique Airplane Association, Ottumwa, Iowa.

Chapter Four, "King Kruises 'Koast to Koast in a KisselKar'": Dale Anderson, Hartford (Wisconsin) Heritage Auto Museum; Ben Brewster, Wisconsin Center for Film and Theater Research, Madison; Walt Jayroe; Kristine Krueger, National Film Information Service, Beverly Hills, California; and Val V. Quandt.

Chapter Five, "Just a Matter of Good Driving, Coolness and Nerve": Helen J. Earley and James R. Walkinshaw, Oldsmobile History Center, Lansing, Michigan; and Elizabeth Norris, YWCA of the U.S.A., New York City.

Photo Credits

AAMA   Reprinted with permission of the American Automobile Manufacturers Association, Detroit

AMP   Courtesy of the Academy of Motion Picture Arts and Sciences, Beverly Hills, California

FLP   Automobile Reference Collection, Free Library of Philadelphia

HHAM   Hartford (Wisconsin) Heritage Auto Museum

NAHC   National Automotive History Collection, Detroit Public Library

NASM   National Air and Space Museum, Archives Division, Smithsonian Institution, Washington, D.C.

OHC   Oldsmobile History Center, Lansing, Michigan

SAMCC   Sacramento (California) Archives & Museum Collection Center, Eleanor McClatchy Collection

UMSC   University of Michigan Special Collections, Ann Arbor

URL   Department of Rare Books & Special Collections, University of Rochester (New York) Libraries

WCF   Wisconsin Center for Film and Theater Research of the University of Wisconsin-Madison and State Historical Society of Wisconsin

Table of Contents

Introduction

In the late 1800s and early 1900s, women wore long skirts, kept house and turned up their noses at noisy, oil-spewing motor cars. Women did nothing to help prove the utility of an invention that revolutionized transportation in the 20th century.

Is this your view of history? If so, the accounts that follow will surprise and educate you.

This book focuses on five trend-setting women. **Louise Hitchcock Davis**, with her husband John, made the first serious attempt to cross the continent by auto. The year was 1899. Ten years later, **Alice Ramsey**, at the wheel of a Maxwell touring car, became the first woman to drive across America. In 1910, **Blanche Stuart Scott** drove a toilet-equipped Overland from New York City to San Francisco, demonstrating that Ramsey's accomplishment was well within the grasp of ordinary women. Silent-film star **Anita King** generated an avalanche of publicity — for her movie studio, the KisselKar and the cause of women in general — when, in 1915, she became the first person to complete a solo transcontinental trip. Although King's leisurely jaunt spanned 48 days, **Amanda Preuss** in 1916 drove her V-8 Oldsmobile coast to coast in a time rivaling the men's speed record.

Despite the hazards, these women who set off to drive across America between 1899 and 1916 earned themselves a place in the history books for their automotive and iconoclastic achievements. For at least four reasons they left the world richer for their experiences. First, by joining a number of male drivers in proving that an automobile could safely travel long distances, they simultaneously demonstrated the utility of automobiles and fueled the public's demand for them. Long-distance treks inspired Americans to see the automobile as less of a toy and more of a tool — a necessary tool, at that. Second, the female coast-to-coast drivers freely and graphically described the poor roads they encountered, giving ammunition to political factions (automakers, farmers and ordinary citizens among them) that were agitating for highway improvements. Third, they demonstrated what many men doubted: Women made competent drivers. And fourth, they signaled to manufacturers that women joined men as potential purchasers of automobiles.

Just as the automobile liberated its driver from the tedium of horse-drawn travel, so did the early accomplishments of Davis, Ramsey, Scott, King and Preuss begin the slow and continuing process of liberating women from the chafing confines of sexual stereotypes. "Good driving has nothing to do with sex," Ramsey declared. "It's all above the collar."

American women at the time had relatively few opportunities open to them.

1

Only a small proportion of women worked outside the home; an even smaller proportion owned and drove automobiles. It is difficult, perhaps impossible, to gauge how these five heroic undertakings may have influenced American girls and women of that time. Did Ramsey's unheard-of feat inspire other women to challenge convention by becoming physicians, lawyers, college professors? Did Scott's adventures (first on land, later in the air) inspire other adventure-seeking females to follow her example? Did Preuss' rigorous training regimen inspire other women to set lofty goals and then work to achieve them?

This much is certain: the stories of the first five coast-to-coast auto treks by women make for gripping reading. Fortunately, each coast-to-coast adventurer provided plenty of commentary about her experiences, revealing her secret fears as well as her likes, dislikes and other impressions regarding the long, difficult and often dangerous overland journey.

Read on, then, in a spirit of adventure and discovery, knowing that never again will a coast-to-coast auto trip require the courage shown a century or so ago by the five drivers to whom this volume is dedicated: Louise, Alice, Blanche, Anita and Amanda.

Chapter One

"Ring the Curtain Down on This Farce!"

Louise Hitchcock Davis in a National Duryea, 1899

The automobile is as yet imperfect in many ways. Few women have the strength to manage one over the wretched country roads. Still fewer have the mechanical knowledge necessary to care for one, even exclusive of accidents.
— Louise Hitchcock Davis

In the closing months of the 1800s, two decades before American women won the right to vote, a woman assisted in the first attempt to drive across the United States by automobile. Louise Hitchcock Davis, a young reporter, left the driving to her husband, John D. Davis. (She declared in print that most women were incapable of operating the finicky, embryonic self-propelled machines of the day.) Yet by vividly describing her auto's breakdowns and shortcomings, she inspired pioneer automakers to design rugged, reliable vehicles that could easily be handled by anyone. Her thrilling, often humorous, newspaper dispatches instigated one further change by nurturing the view that the auto—widely considered a novelty—was potentially a useful means of transport, a future rival to the railroads.

Louise and John Davis, piloting a fragile machine that looked more like a buggy than an automobile, caused a near riot during their July 13, 1899, appearance on the streets of New York City. Hundreds of people in a densely packed crowd dashed toward the auto as it pulled to the curb in front of the *New York Herald* building, Broadway at 35th Street. "For a few moments there was danger of the carriage being overwhelmed," according to a reporter trapped in the surging, late-morning throng. "The police eventually succeeded in clearing a small space."[1]

It was not the automobile itself that caused the sensation. Though still a technological wonder during the last year of the 19th century, automobiles were by no means new. Dozens of makers already had a variety of steam, electric and gasoline autos on the market. By 1899, the U.S. auto industry was in its fourth year, according to historians who believe that the Duryea Motor Wagon Company of Springfield, Massachusetts, became the first American automaker to begin the systematic production of a standard design in 1896. Yet it remained for the automobile to prove its superiority over the horse.

A Monumental Moment

No, it was not the machine itself that the agitated New Yorkers pushed forward to examine. Instead, the spectators focused their wonder, adulation, reverence — and perhaps even morbid curiosity — on the occupants of the self-propelled machine. For the Davises had used the pages of the *New York Herald* to declare their intention of becoming the first persons to travel coast to coast by driving the 3,700 miles between New York City and San Francisco.

As the excited spectators realized, the Davises' departure from New York City was a monumental moment — the first time that many Americans had considered the automobile as anything more than a toy. The public's reaction to their announced trip exhibited a wonderful blend of prognostication, provincialism and ignorance. "Alas, poor horse!" exclaimed a visionary West Coast writer, accurately forecasting that the rise of the automobile meant the decline of the horse.[2] (The fulfillment of that prophecy was years away, however.)

Other observers cited various reasons for supporting the undertaking. "No new motive agency for travel by land or water can consider its reputation firmly established until a test has been made of its powers in a tour across country from New York Bay to the Golden Gate," *Leslie's Weekly* asserted. Earlier adventurers had walked, ridden horses, pushed wheelbarrows and even pedaled bicycles across the continent. "None of these trips meant anything special to the world in general," noted the *San Francisco Call*, which joined the *New York Herald* in sponsoring the Davis journey. "The undertaking of Mr. and Mrs. Davis means ... a revolution in our entire system of locomotion and burden-bear-

ing — a changing of Things as They Are into Things as They Ought to Be." Though doubting a successful outcome, the *Chicago Times-Herald*, nonetheless, believed the Davises "will perform a public service in giving a new impulse to the agitation for better roads."[3]

Bad roads would defeat the Davises, many newspapers predicted. Curiously, these newspapers, each ignorant of the roads outside its province but betting they were worse than local roads, disagreed on exactly where the worst obstacles would appear. According to the *Chicago Daily Tribune*, the old post roads along the Union Pacific tracks through the Rocky Mountains "were never much more than trails, and since the coming of the railroad they have depended chiefly upon the grizzlies to keep them in repair." But because the old post roads ran over well-worn granite, the *Denver Times* shot back, "the automobile riders will not know what good roads are until [they] leave the clingy clay of Illinois and the gumbo [mud] of Iowa behind them."[4]

As writers, the Davises planned to chronicle their adventures in daily articles written for a number of periodicals, including the *New York Herald* and *San Francisco Call*. Before marrying, Louise Hitchcock, a "talented young newspaper writer," spent four years as a reporter for her hometown *New Haven (Conn.) Palladium*. Married, working in a new city (New York) and writing under a new byline (Louise Hitchcock Davis), she sold her articles to "nearly all of the big New York papers and magazines," according to one source.[5] She reportedly contracted to write articles for six magazines based on the detailed journal she planned to keep. Press accounts neglected to name these magazines, an unfortunate omission because these articles could contribute new insights into the challenges the Davises faced.

Louise Davis was about 24 years old,

according to the *Cleveland Plain Dealer* (which declined to estimate the age of her husband). John Davis, who wrote voluminously during the journey, provided few biographical details. But the journal *Autocar* said that Davis, a former *New York Herald* reporter, "was advised to try the climate of the Pacific coast for his health." His physician "has ordered him to keep out of doors a year or more," another source added.[6]

Speaking of doctors, the spindly auto that riled the crowd gathered in Herald Square on July 13, 1899, "would have passed for a physician's gig," the *New York Herald* observed—except for the

John D. Davis grips the automobile's steering tiller in his right hand and a gearshift lever in his left. Two horseshoes adorn the headlamp. (July 22, 1899, *Harper's Weekly*)

pneumatic bicycle tires on steel-spoke rims, and the missing horse. Like a carriage, the light auto had high-backed, well-cushioned seats and a buggy top. Yet a closer inspection revealed other features, most notably control levers, that distinguished the car from a horse-drawn vehicle. "The driver sits on the left side, with his right hand on a nickel plated steering lever. Two shorter levers are within reach of his left hand. These control the speed gears. One of them moved forward gives a speed up to ten miles, a second increases the speed to twenty miles, and thrown back to thirty-five miles an hour." The gas engine "is concealed in the box beneath the seat."[7]

Photographs reveal that the National Duryea carried two horseshoes—"tokens

of good luck"—on its single headlamp. "Mr. Davis explained that he had picked them up on the road, and was not carrying them to conciliate horse owners."[8] The car's headlamp and two side-mounted carriage lamps all burned acetylene, permitting Davis to drive in the cool of the night if he desired.

From Herald Square, I Sally

A smartly dressed Louise Davis "wore a hat of drab felt with a long feather in the band," noted the *New York Tribune*. "She had on a drab jacket and a blue skirt." Her appearance received even greater attention in the *Herald*. The small car allowed Louise

Davis to carry just one change of clothes to supplement her automobile outfit — "a short skirt, bicycle boots, shirt waist and a soft gray felt hat adorned with an eagle's feather. The hat has a very wide brim, and is known in the shops as an 'automobile.' Mrs. Davis' skirt is of the length approved by the Rainy Day Club — six inches clear of the ground." John Davis wore what the *Tribune* termed an "ordinary costume," evidently unworthy of further description.[9]

At 11:02 A.M., John Davis started the car, receiving for his trouble a lusty cheer from a thousand throats. An inexperienced driver, he nevertheless displayed great skill in dodging small boys as he worked through the crowd, which, in addition to boys, included many women.[10] Among the spectators were Frank Duryea in a new Duryea surrey and Arthur S. Winslow, secretary of the National Motor Carriage Company, makers of the Davises' National Duryea automobile.

The Davises' start from New York City was "an animated and really dramatic picture,"[11] gushed the *San Francisco Call*, which printed H.F. Rodney's poetic tribute to the two overland explorers:

> I take my argonautic spree,
>   From Herald square, I sally,
> By Riverside and Tappan Zee,
>   And through the Mohawk Valley,
> With here and there a little stop
>   To tinker up a puncture,
> And here and there a little flop
>   At some unlucky juncture.
> Yet in my epoch-making race,
>   With gusto and devotion,
> I'm out to make the record pace
>   To the Pacific Ocean.[12]

The start of the San Francisco–bound auto gave the *New York Herald* the distinction of becoming the first American newspaper to sponsor a transcontinental automobile trip. (The *Call* promoted the trip only after the *Herald* organized it.) More to the point, the *Herald* bested the two scandal sheets that *Herald* editors regarded as their main rivals — Joseph Pulitzer's *New York World* and William Randolph Hearst's *New York Evening Journal*. In 1924, the *Herald* merged with the *New York Tribune*, whose colorful editor, Horace Greeley, in the 1850s had encouraged the settlement of the American West. Greeley popularized the catch phrase "Go West, young man, and grow up with the country."[13] In 1899, the Davises heeded Greeley's advice.

'Frisco or Bust

The Davis auto, joined by bicyclists, led a parade of automobiles of various makes along Fifth Avenue. At 11:46 A.M., upon reaching Central Bridge and the Harlem River, the Davises spent an hour or more saying good-bye to their friends and escorts, according to press accounts. "When a parting toast was offered, Mr. Davis replied: — 'This is to 'Frisco or Bust!'"[14]

His prophetic "bust" reference suggests that John Davis, self-described as a capable mechanic, had considered the possibility — indeed, the likelihood — of mechanical failures. His attitude was refreshingly pragmatic:

> I look for all kinds of mishaps, from punctured tires to breaks in parts of the machinery due to rapid running on rough roads. I shall carry such duplicate parts as are not too heavy, and will have a kit of tools to tighten up nuts that rack loose or to make any other repairs that are necessary. Every part of the motor is easily accessible, and I have watched the workmen put the machine together, so that I think I can adjust anything that gets out of order and overcome any ordinary difficulty. Of course if we meet with a serious accident we will depend upon

A supporting cast of automobilists and bicyclists escort the Davises, far left, through New York City after their departure from the Herald building. (AAMA)

the nearest machine shop to fix up things.[15]

Confident that he and his wife could reach San Francisco in little more than a month, Davis hoped to cover the 175 miles to Albany on their first day of travel. Yet when they arrived in Albany, following a series of breakdowns and other accidents, it was nearly midnight on Day 4. One of the accidents injured John Davis. Striking a patch of soft dirt at Red Hook, New York, on Day 3, the car pitched violently, wrenching the tiller and giving Davis a severe case of "automobile arm," a painful condition of the muscles similar to rheumatism.[16] This malady was common until 1903, when most American automakers adopted the steering wheel.

At Stuyvesant, New York, south of Al-

bany, Louise Davis proved her resourcefulness as a motorist. While waiting for the car to be repaired, she found a nickel slot machine at a local hotel. "They finally had to drag me away from it, but not until I had won enough money to pay our expenses for the day and come out ninety cents on top," she told the *Albany Times-Union.* The newspaper supplied an additional biographical tidbit on "John Dyre Davis," reporting that he "has a collection of good stories, having been in the army, and being a brother of Col. Davis of the commissory [*sic*] department of the army."[17]

In Albany on Day 5, John Davis had a machinist make duplicates of some engine parts and other pieces that had broken and delayed the car between New York City and Albany. The fortified National Duryea left Albany late in the day as a consequence,

The Davises' proposed route from New York City to Chicago. (July 13, 1899, *New York Herald*)

though John Davis reported that the cause of the nearly day-long delay was that "Mrs. Davis was thoroughly fatigued." Later, however, he asserted that "Mrs. Davis keeps up her courage wonderfully and is determined to make the Golden Gate successfully."[18]

Indeed, Louise Davis described herself as having the "constitution of iron and nerves of steel" required by early female motorists. Despite her own stellar performance, she called it "thoroughly impracticable" for women to attempt a long-distance drive alone in 1899. "The automobile is as yet imperfect in many ways. Few women have the strength to manage one over the wretched country roads. Still fewer have the mechanical knowledge necessary to care for one, even exclusive of accidents."[19]

From Albany, the Davises would travel west to Buffalo, New York, and then pass through Erie, Pennsylvania, Cleveland and Toledo, Ohio, and northern Indiana to reach Chicago, according to published reports. Westward from Chicago, they would traverse Illinois, Iowa and Nebraska, penetrate the Rocky Mountains in Colorado and Wyoming to eventually reach Ogden, Utah.

From the Rockies on west, the Davises were trusting to good luck and providence. Their only road map was one published by a bicycling group, the League of American Wheelmen, which warned that its map

contained "no official information whatever about roads between Denver and San Francisco." Fortunately, John Davis "has spent several years on the plains, and is more or less familiar with the country between Denver and San Francisco," said the *New York Herald*.[20] The newspaper indicated that the Davises would cross northern Nevada to reach San Francisco through Sacramento, California.

"Mr. Fisher" and the Breakdown Bugaboo

Even before the Davis expedition left New York state, it became evident that breakdowns would become an everyday feature of the trip. A rash of trivial but annoying mishaps frustrated the intrepid couple's early progress. This prompted John Davis to hire a mechanic — identified only as "Mr. Fisher"— to accompany the car from Peekskill (just north of New York City) all the way across New York state. A newspaper in Toledo reported that Mr. Fisher remained on duty as far west as that city.[21] His services were urgently required when serious breakdowns halted the car on days 6, 9, 18 and 20.

On Day 6, July 18, the right rear wheel collapsed at Little Falls, New York, a mishap blamed on a flaw in the metal-spoke rim.[22] John Davis traveled to nearby Utica, where the Weston-Mott Company made him a new set of heavier rear wheels on which tires three inches in diameter replaced the original two-and-a-half-inch tires. With new wheels and tires on their transcontinental machine, John and Louise Davis left Utica on Day 9, July 21. A 54-mile run took them to Syracuse, some 350 miles northwest of New York City.

At Syracuse, "the bolt connecting the piston between the two cylinders snapped and the forward piston tore a big hole in the casing of the cylinder and bent the cam shaft." The resulting delay consumed eight days: five days for a new cylinder to reach Syracuse and three days for rebuilding and testing the engine. During his forced stay in Syracuse, John Davis replaced the car's springs. "Truly, it is 'Frisco or bust,' but so far there has been more 'bust' than we like," he conceded.[23] To further underscore the car's abysmal performance, a one-armed transcontinental bicycle rider who left New York City ten days behind the Davises passed them at Syracuse on his fifth day of pedaling.[24]

The Davises left Syracuse on July 29, Day 17. They spent the following afternoon in a repair shop when an engine valve broke. Later, in Rochester, Davis had stronger valves made. On Day 20, August 1, in Bergen, New York, John Davis damaged the auto by hitting "a stone flagging over the gutter." A blacksmith heated and straightened the car's front axle, which was evidently removed from and replaced on the car by Mr. Fisher.[25]

The National Duryea's poor showing led Louise Davis to conclude that the automobile "is a treacherous animal for a long trip." The coast-to-coast car "has an antipathy for cities," she contended. "As soon as one looms up before us, and we shake off the dust, straighten ourselves and try to make a fine appearance, then snap, some part of the mechanism divorces itself from the whole and we are stranded on the busiest corner until some friendly truck hauls the vehicle away to the nearest machine shop for repairs."[26]

The Davises' $1,250 National Duryea "touring cart" was a product of the National Motor Carriage Company, which had recently begun producing Duryea autos under license in Stamford, Connecticut. Weighing about 850 pounds unloaded, the car carried ten gallons of gas and eight gallons of cooling water. Including the Davises and the small trunk and suitcase strapped on behind, the chain-driven car weighed approximately 1,200 pounds. To propel this weight, the National Duryea used an opposed two-cylinder engine (its cylinders were on the same axis with both pistons firing in toward the shared crankshaft) that reportedly developed five to seven horsepower.[27]

The Duryea was "Not an Experiment," the National company insisted. Indeed, brothers Charles E. and J. Frank Duryea of Chicopee, Massachusetts, began constructing their first auto in 1893.[28] But if the Duryea itself was no longer an experiment, crossing the continent in one undoubtedly was. Seeking to make the car as staunch as possible, National specially prepared the little coast-to-coast vehicle by improving its engine, transmission and brakes.

For instance, the three-speed transmission received "special gears which will enable it to climb mountains of quite a steep grade." Also for mountain driving, National workmen added a "plain old fashioned hand brake" to the Duryea's standard brakes. As on horse-drawn wagons, the extra brake on the National Duryea "would clutch the tires and assure safety going down any hill."[29] The car received a non-stock "roadometer," a combined speedometer and odometer. These various modifications delayed the scheduled July 1, 1899, start of the Davis journey by nearly two weeks.

Louise Davis (left) and husband John in their automobile. Modifications to the standard National Duryea included "a plain old fashioned hand brake" positioned ahead of each rear tire. (July 29, 1899, *Scientific American*)

Rambunctious Rustics

Despite such preparation, the car proved to be unreliable. In addition to the troubles already related, Davis and his hired mechanic struggled with a twice-broken cylinder petcock, an overheating engine, disabled transmission gear and broken warning bell. A methodical planner, John Davis packed "a supply of arnica [a tinc-

ture applied to sprains and bruises] for people who get in the way of the machine," according to *Leslie's Weekly*.[30] But the car inflicted no damage on pedestrians. Quite the opposite: John and Louise Davis reported at least three instances in which the onlookers damaged the auto—an unlikely man-bites-dog turn of events. "We have found it impossible to keep crowds away from the carriage," Davis complained, "and while we are watching one part[,] curious and mischievous persons toy with whatever is in sight."[31] Fumbling, furtive spectators ruined the "sparking brushes," for instance, and snapped a clutch piece by tugging on a shifting lever.

If given the chance, rural New Yorkers would strip the car of its nuts and bolts as souvenirs, one newspaper reported. John Davis himself related that the very sound of the Duryea's "gong" would instantly empty a country church: "People would go to church under protest, fearing they would miss the machine while at their devotions and the moment its approach was heralded they were ready to leave the minister at any stage of his prayer." Unceasing crowds wearied Louise Davis, who chaffed at having "to bear with the rural idea of wit, to smile benignly upon the idle curiosity of unthinking persons to whom you bear something [of] the relation of a dime museum freak whose mission is to amuse the public."[32]

One reporter implied that John Davis was an incompetent mechanic and thus partly to blame for the frustrating delays due to breakdowns. Davis called the cylinder petcock a "pettycock" and often used convoluted terms to describe other broken parts, noted Hugh Dolnar in *Autocar*, which used British spellings. "Evidently Mr. Davis has not yet learned the names of the parts of his waggon motor, but he will probably become quite familiar with the appearance of his machine elements before he reaches San Francisco."[33]

Davis in turn assigned the blame elsewhere. "The accidents we have had are of a minor kind. They were not great or disabling, but simply annoying — what might be expected, in fact, when new machinery is used." Davis in reality proved to be an astute mechanic in discovering why the engine frequently broke its intake, or inlet, valves. As he revealed to the *Erie Morning Dispatch*, he spent two hours listening and watching while the parked car's engine ran at a constant speed. It performed flawlessly. "Then I put it going in rough fashion, just as on roadways met often, and in throttling it found that the [valve] nut struck on the side of the controller and snapped the spindle [valve stem]. By means of an angle iron I secured an equal distribution in working the inlet valve. Since then I have had no trouble whatever."[34]

Yet trouble of another sort threatened the Davis journey: bad press. In a way, John Davis brought it upon himself by announcing at the outset that his National

The Davis auto often received unwanted — and destructive — attention. (July 30, 1899, *San Francisco Call*)

Duryea would outperform foreign automobiles. This ensured that the eyes of the world were upon him, even when he might have wished for the comforting cloak of obscurity. Americans came to regard the transcontinental crossing as an "us" versus "them" proposition. On Day 2, the Reverend Michael Powers of Wappingers Falls, New York, "stepped up to the automobile and gave Mr. and Mrs. Davis his blessing, adding, 'Now go in and beat the French!'"[35]

Despite encountering rough cobblestone paving, the National Duryea was running smoothly when the Davises reached what is believed to be Palmyra, New York, 20 miles southeast of Rochester. (URL)

The French, however, soon came to regard the Davises and their automobile as a source of merriment. Two weeks into the trip, the *San Francisco Call* ran a dispatch from Paris: "The American colony here is constantly twitted by French automobilists on the grotesque picture of Mr. and Mrs. Davis crawling wearily from village to village in the Empire State, not conspicuous for bad roads." Even *Automobile* acknowledged: "The Frenchman evidently knew what he was talking about who, in speaking of Davis' proposed transcontinental trip, said: In planning a trip here we look out for a place for a good dinner. In the United States you seem to have to look out for a place where you can get your automobile repaired."[36]

The Davises attributed at least some of the criticism to their own candor in reporting the automobile's shortcomings. "Other pioneers have had trouble on the road but have kept the facts out of the newspapers," the *Rochester (N.Y.) Democrat and Chronicle* reported in its paraphrased account of an interview with John Davis. "Mr. Davis said they were not keeping their mishaps from the public, for by them they hoped to show to manufacturers of horseless carriages where the greatest liability to breakage was."[37]

Louise: Auto No "Docile Donkey"

At last, after three weeks of misadventures, the Davises on August 2 reached Buffalo, which the *New York Herald* called "the old home of Mr. Davis." According to John Davis, he paid from four to 22 cents per gallon of gasoline and the car averaged about 14 miles per gallon in covering the 486½ miles from New York City. His average speed to Buffalo was 9.9 mph.[38] Undoubtedly to rest and perhaps to visit old friends, the Davises spent the following day in Buffalo. Louise Davis used some of her leisure time to write a dispatch for the *Cleveland Plain Dealer.* "I am beginning to enjoy this trip," she announced, sounding calm, cool and collected as she delicately deflected the published criticism that she and her husband had received:

It would be monotonous to go speeding across the continent without accident or mishap of any kind. One might as well fall back in the cushioned chair of a Pullman [railroad] car. But the joy of being thrown into a ditch, of having cylinders break while the motor is running at top speed, of having a wheel come off [collapse], letting you gently down to earth, and of all sorts and conditions of mishaps, is something too exhilarating for words.

You will bear in mind, gentle reader, that this trip is largely in the nature of an experiment. It might have been made in less time had we waited for the manufacturers of horseless carriages to get the machine down so fine that it would be unbreakable, but that would have withheld from you the pleasure of reading about this trip for so long that it would have lost its charm. Besides, there would be no special credit in a trip in a carriage that was guaranteed not to break, not to buck or behave itself unseemly or give any more trouble than a docile donkey.[39]

On August 6, Louise and John Davis scored a modest success, for by reaching Cleveland they tied a Winton automobile's Cleveland–New York City distance record set just two months previously. According to the *Cleveland Plain Dealer,* "Mr. Davis paid a high compliment to Mr. Alexander Winton of Cleveland, who made a trip to New York for the *Plain Dealer* to establish a record.... He said: 'Mr. Winton performed a wonderful feat and deserves great credit. No other man in the world could beat his record.'"[40] Davis, of course, had just equaled Alexander Winton's distance: He was referring to Winton's speed. Winton, president of the Winton Motor Carriage Company, covered the distance with far fewer delays than the Davises endured. Winton's running time was 47 hours, 34 minutes over just five days, beginning May 22, 1899.

By contrast, John and Louise Davis spent 25 days plying the roads between Cleveland and New York City, covering no more than 65 miles a day. During that time, their auto was laid up for ten days, including five days spent awaiting the arrival of the new cylinder. Accidents and breakdowns during many of the remaining 15 travel days meant the car was often able to run only three or four hours a day. Between the July 13 start and August 8, the Davis car broke down or received repairs at least 20 times, according to reports. The number of breakdowns soon rose to 25, *Scientific American* reported in early September. Press interest waned as breakdowns and repairs left newspapers with nothing exciting to write about, as revealed by these *Call* and *Herald* headlines over eight days in late July:

"Cannot Proceed Without New Cylinder" (July 23)

"Automobile Nearly Ready to Start Again" (July 25)

"Automobile Expected to Resume Trip To-Day" (July 26)

Reporters documented every mishap as the Davis auto inched westward toward the *San Francisco Call* building.

"Automobile Is Ready to Start" (July 27)

"To 'Frisco on Saturday" (July 28)

"Automobile Ready for Fresh Start" (July 29)

"Davis Resumes Westward Trip" (July 30)

Sponsors Abandon Davises, Who Press On

In a final trip dispatch, on August 8, the *New York Herald* reported that the National Duryea had its front axle strengthened in Cleveland. And then the *Herald* and *San Francisco Call*, without explanation, abruptly ended their coverage of the Davis transcontinental trip. The *Call* broke its silence on August 14 in an editorial mentioning both the Davis auto and the post office department's experiments with automobile mail delivery. The San Francisco newspaper adroitly avoided mentioning the *New York Herald's* co-sponsorship of the car, and that both newspapers had disowned the Davises:

> The action of the Government will of course be widely commended. It is well known the transcontinental automobile is *The Call's* automobile, and the people are always well pleased to see the Government follow the leadership of *The Call* and profit by it....
>
> In one respect the [transcontinental] undertaking has been successful. It has verified the predictions of *The Call*. When the automobile started *The Call* said the experiment would test the mechanism and show where it is defective, and the results have been even so. There has been revealed every defect in the machine from the cylinders to the nut washers.
>
> It was said the trip would test the country roads, and it has shown that some roads are rough, some are muddy, and some have ditches, and that the ma-

chine can break on the rough places, stick in the muddy places and run into the ditches with the greatest facility.

> It was pointed out that the appearance of the vehicle on rural roads would prove whether people took an interest in it and whether cattle were scared of it, and so it did. It was an object of more popular interest than a circus; it was as startling to animals as a yellow journal freak to humanity, and it once chased a cow for half a mile and would have caught her if a valve hadn't broken.
>
> The automobile is coming.... If the [Davis auto] do[es] not reach here in time for exhibition as a specimen of successful mechanism at the Mechanic's Institute Fair, it will still serve an exposition purpose. It will be hauled to Chicago and placed on a monument in front of the Art Gallery of that city as the bust of the century.[41]

The *Call*, however, was premature in writing off its wayward prodigy. After an overhauling at Cleveland, the car continued west to Toledo, *Horseless Age* reported.[42] By traveling 857 miles in 80½ hours of actual running time, the National Duryea reached Toledo on Thursday, August 17, John Davis told the *Toledo Blade*. Though the car's average speed from New York City to Toledo was a lackluster 10.6 mph, the distance "is the greatest ever accomplished by any woman in an automobile," the *Blade* said.[43]

"One thing that I have learned about automobile touring," John Davis commented, "is that a man must have plenty of pluck, patience and profanity, and I think that I am becoming proficient." Yet repairs and modifications to the National Duryea led the Davises to believe "the worst is over," according to the *Blade*. "They expect to make good time for the remainder of the way."[44]

But the worst lay ahead for them — on the road, in the halls of justice and in the automobile trade press. By and large,

Date	City to City	Distance
1 — July 13 Thu	New York City — Tarrytown, N.Y.	37/ 37
2 — July 14 Fri	Tarrytown, NY — Poughkeepsie, N.Y.	53/ 90
3 — July 15 Sat	Poughkeepsie, NY — Hudson, N.Y.	57/147
4 — July 16 Sun	Hudson, NY — Albany, N.Y.	37/184
5 — July 17 Mon	Albany, NY — Amsterdam, N.Y.	33/217
6 — July 18 Tue	Amsterdam, NY — Utica, N.Y.	42/259
7 — July 19 Wed	*repairs in Utica, N.Y.*	—/259
8 — July 20 Thu	*repairs in Utica, N.Y.*	—/259
9 — July 21 Fri	Utica, N.Y. — Syracuse, N.Y.	54/313
10 — July 22 Sat	*waiting for parts in Syracuse, N.Y.*	—/313
11 — July 23 Sun	*waiting for parts in Syracuse, N.Y.*	—/313
12 — July 24 Mon	*waiting for parts in Syracuse, N.Y.*	—/313
13 — July 25 Tue	*waiting for parts in Syracuse, N.Y.*	—/313
14 — July 26 Wed	*install new cylinder, Syracuse, N.Y.*	—/313
15 — July 27 Thu	*modify, test cylinder, Syracuse, N.Y.*	—/313
16 — July 28 Fri	*test new cylinder, Syracuse, N.Y.*	—/313
17 — July 29 Sat	Syracuse, NY — Auburn, N.Y.	32/345
18 — July 30 Sun	Auburn, NY — Newark, N.Y.	35/380
19 — July 31 Mon	Newark, NY — Rochester, N.Y.	—/—
20 — Aug. 1 Tue	Rochester, NY — Bergan, N.Y.	—/—
21 — Aug. 2 Wed	Bergen, NY — Buffalo, N.Y.	56/486
22 — Aug. 3 Thu	*rest day in Buffalo, N.Y.*	—/486
23 — Aug. 4 Fri	Buffalo, NY — Fredonia, N.Y.	65/551
24 — Aug. 5 Sat	Fredonia, NY — Erie, PA	49/600
25 — Aug. 6 Sun	Erie, PA — Cleveland	96/696
26 — Aug. 7 Mon	*repairs in Cleveland*	—/696
27 — Aug. 8 Tue	Cleveland — ?*	—/—

* * * * * * * * *

36 — Aug. 17 Thu	Milan Ohio — Toledo Ohio	—/857

*The *San Francisco Call* ended its trip coverage on Aug. 7, followed a day later by the *New York Herald*. Last reports said the Davises would leave Cleveland Aug. 8.

Sources: New York Herald, San Francisco Call and local newspapers.

The Davis Itinerary Westward to Toledo, Ohio, 1899

the trade journals overlooked the opportunity to discuss an obvious need for stronger autos and better roads and instead merely voiced an increasingly hostile opposition to the run. Foremost among such journals was *Horseless Age*:

The adventurous couple who are endeavoring to make "San Francisco or bust" in a motor carriage have apparently taken the latter alternative. At the rate at which they are traveling they could not reach San Francisco in less than five months from the date of setting out, and at the rate at which they are "busting" they would have an entirely different carriage if they ever reached the Pacific Coast. An immediate termination of the journey would be welcome by the motor vehicle industry of the United States.[45]

In a later account, *Horseless Age* gave up any pretense of reasonableness by snarling, "Ring the curtain down on this farce!" The announcement of the Davis trip sent the characteristically unflappable *Scientific American*, which closely followed automobile developments, into a poetic ecstasy: "There is no more delightful way of seeing the country than to view it from the comfortably cushioned seats of an automobile vehicle, which is never tired, and knows neither hunger nor thirst." Sadder but wiser about an automobile's appetites, *Scientific American* later advised that "all value to the industry of a trip of this kind is taken out of it by the long delays and the many breakdowns."[46]

A few reporters were more generous, however. A writer in the general-circulation *Harper's Weekly* observed that "the real contest lies between the enduring quality of the American-built machinery and the destructive energy of the awful American highways. If Mr. Davis gets to San Francisco at all, that will be record enough in itself."[47]

Of Axles and Attachments

On Friday, August 18, 1899, one day after the Davises arrived in Toledo, their chances of reaching San Francisco dimmed considerably. Late that afternoon, John and Louise Davis steered their National Duryea west out of town toward Bryan, Ohio. They did not even reach Toledo's city limits. "On Newberry street, near South, the rear axle broke squarely in two, the accident being caused by a flaw in the steel."[48]

A local foundry began the two-day job of building a new axle. While the Davises waited, a legal problem arose that was potentially much more serious than a broken axle. On Saturday, August 19, a dry goods firm in Stamford, Connecticut, seeking payment of a $60.52 bill for "furniture and furnishings," filed an attachment warrant on the automobile. A court date set for August 30, two weeks away, assured Louise and John Davis a long and profitless stay in Toledo.

It is nearly impossible today to understand the legal basis for the attachment action because it is unclear who owned the auto. Various sources said the owner was "the Akron Rubber tire company" (the Davises, to a reporter), John Davis (*New York Herald, Rochester [N.Y.] Herald* and *Autocar*) and Louise Davis (*Toledo Blade*).[49] It is more likely that the car belonged to the National Motor Carriage Company, and that the legal proceedings against the Davises in Toledo stemmed from the factory's own financial problems, as this *Motor Vehicle Review* article strongly implies:

> STAMFORD, Ct., Aug. 28 [1899] — The stock here of the National [Motor] Carriage Company, in one of whose automobiles John D. Davis and wife recently began a trip across the continent, was attached today by various creditors, including a number of the employees.
>
> The exact amount of the claims against the company are not known, but they are believed to aggregate about $10,000. Supt. T.G. Graham stated this afternoon that the difficulties were due to a reorganization of the company and that all claims will soon be paid.[50]

A search of Toledo newspapers failed to uncover the means by which the Davises resolved their legal dispute, though they did so clearly, for several brief reports tell of their departure from Toledo on a date unspecified. When did they leave and where did they go from Toledo? That all depends on which source you choose to believe. On August 19, the Davises reached Detroit, "and the trip has been abandoned," *Scientific American* reported.[51] Detroit is just 50 miles north of Toledo, adding credence to this account. Yet the credible *Toledo Blade* article said August 19 was the day a lawsuit halted the car for at least two weeks in Toledo. Further, a search of the *Detroit Free Press* from mid–August through the end of October 1899 turned up no mention of the Davises' arrival. In a Toledo article dated September 30, 1899, *Motor Age* acknowledged that after a month-long stay in Toledo the auto had left Ohio and entered Michigan. The auto journal did not name Detroit as the destination, and, cu-

riously, ignored the Davises' legal problems: "For nearly a month the Davises have been trying to get out of Toledo, but without success. Repair work on their machine kept them here for three weeks. A week ago Sunday [September 24] they broke away from the city, but their tour was short-lived for in Michigan, less than a score of miles from here [Toledo], they broke down again and are stalled."[52]

Automobile Review, Horseless Age and *Motor Age* all reported that the Davises reached Chicago on an unspecified date during the first half of October, more than two-and-a-half months after starting. An energetic hiker could have walked from New York to Chicago at a brisker pace. Did the Davises actually reach Chicago? If so, the city's big daily newspapers either did not know about it or did not care. From late September through mid–October of 1899, the *Chicago Times-Herald* made no mention of the coast-to-coast auto. Nor does the *Chicago Daily Tribune* mention the trip from late September through late October 1899.

Automobile Review, however, reported that not only did John D. and Louise Davis arrive in Chicago, they announced plans to reach Denver by the end of October. *Motor Age* said they planned to drive on to San Francisco.[53]

One automotive-history book quite literally dispenses with John and Louise Davis, contending that, after leaving Detroit, "neither the Davises nor their machine were ever seen again"![54] Truly, the best indications are that the Davises reached Chicago.

The Davises' triumphant arrival at the *San Francisco Call* building occurred only in the vivid imagination of a newspaper artist. (July 2, 1899, *San Francisco Call*)

ACROSS THE CONTINENT IN AN AUTOMOBILE

San Francisco to
Be the Objective
Point of a Race
That Fills With
Wonder the Eyes
of the Civilized
Nations.

LEAVING THE NEW YORK HERALD.

MRS. JOHN D. DAVIS OUTLINES HER WORK FOR THE SUNDAY CALL

A DANGEROUS CROSSING

MostRemarkable
Trip the World
Has Known. It
May Revolu-
tionize the En-
tire System of
Locomotion.

Though it initially supported the Davis venture, the *San Francisco Call* later suspended its coverage of the "bust of the century." (July 2, 1899, *San Francisco Call*)

And while they may have dropped out of the news columns there, it was not because they vanished without a trace. After all, such a disappearance would have been front-page news!

Rather, their paper trail and quite likely their overland trail ended at Chicago, under circumstances that are not so mysterious after all. Stung by press criticism, without sponsors and therefore lacking financial support, and with winter storms already descending upon the Rocky Mountains, the Davises could not finish their trip in 1899. Hence they had little choice but to quit, at least until the following summer. And it is no great surprise that they ended their trip quietly, with none of the pomp and circumstance that had heralded its beginning. Presumably, the first two people to launch a coast-to-coast motor trip used some other means to reach San Francisco. Or perhaps they returned home to New York City. What became of their 1899 National Duryea? The answer to that question is lost to history.

The Value of a Lesson

The participants had expressed various and disparate reasons for embarking on a transcontinental auto trip. John Davis needed fresh air to cure unspecified health problems. Quite likely, he and his wife also relished the adventure, novelty and notoriety of the undertaking.

The *Call* and *Herald* sponsored the trip for the same reason newspapers of that age sponsored any other stunt: to boost circulation. The papers never said as much, however. Instead, they gave four reasons for their sponsorship:

1. To prove the superiority of American autos over French and English makes.
2. To open "a new epoch in the history of transportation" by subjecting an automobile to the severest of tests.
3. To determine the cost of driving across the country.
4. To report on road conditions.[55]

Obviously, the Davises' transcontinental attempt failed to achieve these four goals, though they were able to report on road conditions as far west as Toledo. Of the three other goals:

• Rather than proving American autos were better than their European counterparts, the trip strongly hinted at the opposite.

• Instead of opening "a new epoch in the history of transportation," the Davis journey perhaps delayed the coming new epoch by discouraging similar trips until more reliable automobiles were available.

• The cost of a traveling across the

One cartoon indicates that Louise Davis hired a blacksmith to repair the auto. (July 22, 1899, *San Francisco Call*)

continent — undoubtedly higher than the participants and their sponsors anticipated — remained guesswork in the wake of the Davis attempt.

By merely attempting the daunting journey, however, the visionary Davises at least demonstrated the possibilities of the automobile. Their example, flawed though it was, undoubtedly also encouraged observers to consider the automobile's potential for moving people and cargo from place to place. John and Louise Davis, it appears, also set an American — possibly a world's — distance record for a one-way trip. The *New York Herald* predicted that the Davises would travel 1,030 miles by their 1899 route. Detours and side trips ran the Davises' odometer well beyond that figure, however. The Davises reported traveling 857 miles between New York City and Toledo. Even by the mid–1920s, the shortest route from Toledo on to Chicago was about 275 miles, meaning that the Davises traveled approximately 1,132 miles to reach the Windy City.[56]

Consequently, they easily bettered the 1,050 miles that Elwood Haynes and E.L. Apperson recorded on a drive from Kokomo, Indiana, to New York City. The two men, who reached New York City before the Davises reached Chicago, drove a Haynes-Apperson car at an average speed of 20 mph.[57] Their car performed the better of the two; the Davises simply drove theirs farther.

Though they failed in their grand scheme of driving their automobile across the continent, the Davises contributed more to the development of the automobile industry than many of their critics realized at the time. One great value of the trip was in demonstrating that, to prosper, American automakers needed to build more rugged, dependable autos and support better roads for their use. American autos "are too light for the rough service which is entailed and the badness of many of our roads," observed *Scientific American*, one of the few observers to appreciate this lesson.[58]

John Davis condemned rural New York roads as "a disgrace to an unexplored region, let alone a thickly populated country.... Grades have never been cut, rocks are left to roll about under foot and wheel, ruts to run deeper, and things have been left generally to care for themselves." Ultimately, the Davises' trip would inspire a public cry for better roads by "jolting a complacent conservatism with facts, figures and humiliating comparisons," the *Chicago Times-Herald* predicted.[59]

Did Louise Davis act as navigator and help maintain and repair the troublesome National Duryea auto? We do not know specifically all of the ways in which she assisted her husband, who did all of the driving on the first attempt to drive across America. But by simply reporting her experiences, Louise Davis helped promote the idea that ordinary people (men and women alike), neither engineers, inventors nor machinists, could travel long distances in an automobile. This idea was crucial to the rapid growth of the automotive industry in the early 1900s, because engineers, inventors and machinists represented a very limited market. Of course, Louise

Davis' message was a mixed one: she freely observed that the automobile of 1899 was still imperfect in many ways, and difficult for women to operate. Given the Davises' experiences, the *San Francisco Call's* inspirational poem must be rewritten:

I take my argonautic spree,
    From Herald square, I sally,
By Riverside and Tappan Zee,
    And through the Mohawk Valley,
With here and there a little stop
    To tinker up a puncture,
And here and there a little flop
    At some unlucky juncture.
Before I know it fall has come
    And that means ice and snow,
But we're flat-broke, dressed up like bums,
    And stuck in Chi-ca-go.

Louise Davis overcame the frequent breakdowns and other hardships. Thus, she demonstrated what many men of the era — and women, as well — may have doubted: that a woman could ride for weeks at a time in an automobile and actually enjoy the experience. And her experiences speeded the arrival of the day when a woman could strike out across the continent not merely as a passenger in an automobile — but as the driver.

Chapter Two

"A Reliable Car and a Woman Who Knows It"

Alice Ramsey in a Maxwell, 1909

Women can handle an automobile just as well as men.
— Alice Ramsey

Alice Ramsey, a 22-year-old mother from Hackensack, New Jersey, drove a Maxwell and three female friends 3,800 miles across the country in 1909, becoming the first woman to drive the distance.

After just a few months' practice behind the wheel of her new 1908 Maxwell runabout, Ramsey entered the two-day September 1908 Montauk Point endurance contest. Her driving skill impressed Carl W. Kelsey, Maxwell's shrewd sales manager, who conceived her coast-to-coast Maxwell trip as good publicity for the automaker.

Some early articles claim Ramsey used her own 1908 Maxwell, a runabout too small to carry four long-distance travelers. In reality, the Maxwell-Briscoe Motor Company of Tarrytown, New York, donated a 30-horsepower 1909 touring car and also promised tires, parts and other assistance along the route. In addition, the automaker supplied a traveling publicity man — John D. Murphy, the *Boston Herald's* automobile editor.

Assisted by Murphy's daily dispatches, the automobile journals and many newspapers followed her 59-day adventure.

Spring floods turned the trip across Iowa into a "terrible ordeal," forcing the four women to sleep one night in their car beside rain-swollen Weasel Creek, as Ramsey describes in her 1961 book, *Veil, Duster, and Tire Iron.* As tight-lipped as Murphy about the Maxwell's mechanical failings, Ramsey's testimonial prompted a Cheyenne, Wyoming, newspaper to claim that the car "has not given them the least bit of trouble."[1]

More than a half-century after the fact, however, Ramsey revealed that the Maxwell needed a new ignition coil early in the trip and broke axle shafts in western Iowa and central Nebraska — all before reaching Cheyenne. The car also broke a front-axle spring seat in western Utah and chewed up as many as 11 tires. But "that motor surmounted more difficulties than a modern driver can dream of — and never coughed," Ramsey declared. "I'm still proud of that Maxwell engine!"[2]

On Wyoming's confusing trails, Ramsey and her pilot car followed telegraph poles from town to town. She crossed the North Platte River at Fort Steele, Wyoming, by bumping over the Union Pacific's trestle, and completed her journey from New York City to San Francisco on August 7, 1909, three weeks behind the original schedule published in auto journals at the start. As the Maxwell company envisioned the trip:

> From start to finish Mrs. Ramsey will do the driving and will have to make all tire repairs, tire changes and such, for she will be unaccompanied by men. It will be the first time that a woman has ever attempted the long journey between the two oceans under these conditions. Unassisted, she will have to pick the route, guide the car across the Rocky Mountains and in fact will travel over roads and routes that would tax an expert male driver.[3]

Ramsey also cleaned spark plugs, scraped carbon from the combustion chambers, tightened bolts and made several emergency repairs en route. The roads were as bad as the company suggests. But through its account, which overlooked a 1908 all-woman transcontinental attempt, the automaker created an impression that persists among some modern-day automotive historians — that Ramsey and her three companions, nearly defenseless, fought their way unaided across an uncharted wilderness. Ramsey's book dispels this myth.

Like other early transcontinental drivers, she sought help from men as she needed it: a Syracuse, New York, mechanic who replaced a bad coil; Maxwell mechanics who replaced broken rear-axle shafts in the Midwest; a Callao, Utah, blacksmith who repaired the front axle; a Nebraska farmer whose horse pulled the car from two mudholes. To arrange lodging and promote the trip, Murphy traveled ahead by train and sometimes traveled with the car, which he helped push on occasion. According to Ramsey, from New York City to the Missouri River she used Blue Book maps and directions; farther west she used highly detailed Clason maps. In Omaha, Nebraska, one of Ramsey's traveling companions met a group of San Francisco men driving east, "who gave us some very valuable information as to what to expect from here to San Francisco."[4]

Ramsey also took on local guides or followed pilot cars in every state but New York and Pennsylvania, receiving uninterrupted assistance from central Nebraska to San Francisco, and got help and advice from a nearly unbroken string of Maxwell dealers from coast to coast. Following closely the route that in 1913 became the Lincoln Highway, Ramsey traveled across or through parts of New York, Pennsylvania, Ohio, Indiana, Illinois, Iowa, Nebraska, Colorado, Wyoming, Utah, Nevada and California.

Ramsey: An Experienced Tourist

Alice Huyler Ramsey, as she was later known, was born November 11, 1886, in Hackensack, to John Edwin and Ada Mumford (Farr) Huyler. Her father was a lumber and coal dealer. When she entered Vassar College at Poughkeepsie, New York, in the fall of 1903, she was already engaged to John Rathbone Ramsey. She left Vassar after two years to marry Ramsey, who, in his 40s, was "more than twice my age and with many years of experience as a counselor-at-law and county official." They had a son, John, in 1907 and a daughter, Alice, in 1910. John Ramsey was Bergen County clerk in 1909, when his wife made her historic trip. From 1917 to 1921 he was a U.S. representative from New Jersey.[5]

Ramsey got her automobile runabout after an unexpectedly exciting trip she took in a runabout carriage behind her husband's powerful bay horse, Duke. After two years of marriage, she had finally worked up the courage to take out Duke alone:

> Suddenly behind us, I heard an approaching automobile. This was the spring of 1908 and there were probably not a half dozen motor vehicles in Hackensack.... Duke began laying back his ears as the sound of the motor came nearer. I wasn't exactly scared, but I realized I better be prepared for some sort of crisis. *And it happened!* Just as the monster overtook us there was a loud *Honk! Honk!* and George Johnson in his new Pierce-Arrow runabout flew by at a 30-mile clip. That was all Duke needed to display what *his* speed was! He gave one snort, and put out for parts unknown.

Assuming automobiles were safer than horses, her husband bought her a red 1908 Maxwell runabout from the Hackensack agency, which provided driving lessons. Though he never learned to drive and felt uncomfortable riding in an auto, her husband encouraged her budding interest, Ramsey said. "I was now completely enamored of this modern form of transportation and during the summer months I ticked off 6000 miles of pleasure driving, with my friends. We explored the highways around New Jersey, most of which were in the dirt stage or, in some cases, bound with crushed stone into macadam." In the year preceding her long trip, Ramsey became "an experienced tourist, the president of the Women's Motoring Club of New York, and of the women's section of the Maxwell-Briscoe Motor Club," the journal *Automobile* said.[6]

Her experience included driving in two endurance contests. The first was the Montauk Point mechanical-reliability run of September 16 and 17, 1908. On the first morning, Ramsey drove her runabout from Hackensack into New York City, accompanied by Berry Lewis, the Hackensack Maxwell agent, and her husband's sisters, Margaret Atwood and Nettie Powell. They met other competing cars at Columbus Circle and drove in a group to Lynbrook, Long Island, the starting point. "Considerable attention had been paid to Mrs. Joan Newton Cuneo who was to drive a 50-horsepower Rainier, and to me with my smaller Maxwell, for we were the only women to attempt the run," Ramsey recalled. Maxwell-Briscoe publicity man Carl Kelsey drove one of the two other Maxwells entered in the approximately 200-mile trip from Lynbrook, through Blue Point, Southampton and Amagansett to the lighthouse at Montauk Point, and back.

Apparently to see how she would handle the difficult drive ahead, Kelsey asked Ramsey to lead the three Maxwells during the afternoon run. "Rough surfaces made me fight the wheel continually. We stopped but a moment at Southampton and put out on the final lap. Suddenly we came to the dunes after a few miles of fairly good road, and just two sandy ruts lay ahead.... The route now became a natural roller coaster, a bit too scary to be much fun. First up sandy inclines, then down long slopes...." That description may be too tame, as "this stretch of sand drifts, mud sloughs, and chuck holes racked every car severely," the *New York Times* said. "Those who have had experience with several Glidden tours are agreed that the driving over this stretch is as trying as anything ever encountered in the big touring contest," the newspaper said, referring to the annual long-distance reliability tour sponsored by the American Automobile Association.[7]

A Transcontinental Proposition

Pleased by Ramsey's performance, Kelsey used that evening's dinner for the Maxwell participants to suggest a transcontinental trip. "I was flabbergasted by the proposition," Ramsey said later. "This

Date	Ramsey's City to City Progress, 1909
1 — June 9 Wed	New York City — Poughkeepsie, N.Y.
2 — June 10 Thu	Poughkeepsie, N.Y. — Amsterdam, N.Y.
3 — June 11 Fri	Amsterdam, N.Y. — Auburn, N.Y.
4 — June 12 Sat	Auburn, N.Y. — Buffalo, N.Y.
5 — June 13 Sun	*idle day in Buffalo, N.Y.*
6 — June 14 Mon	*idle day at Buffalo, N.Y., Niagara Falls*
7 — June 15 Tue	Buffalo, N.Y. — Cleveland
8 — June 16 Wed	Cleveland — Toledo, Ohio
9 — June 17 Thu	Toledo, Ohio — Goshen, Ind.
10 — June 18 Fri	Goshen, Ind. — Chicago
11 — June 19 Sat	*attend auto races, Crown Point, Ind.*
12 — June 20 Sun	*idle day in Chicago*
13 — June 21 Mon	*idle day in Chicago*
14 — June 22 Tue	Chicago — Rochelle, Ill.
15 — June 23 Wed	Rochelle, Ill. — Mechanicsville, Iowa
16 — June 24 Thu	Mechanicsville, Iowa — Cedar Rapids, Iowa
17 — June 25 Fri	Cedar Rapids, Iowa — flooded Weasel Creek
18 — June 26 Sat	Weasel Creek — Boone, Iowa
19 — June 27 Sun	Boone, Iowa — Jefferson, Iowa*
20 — June 28 Mon	Jefferson, Iowa — Vail, Iowa
21 — June 29 Tue	*to Omaha, Neb. by train to plan new route*
22 — June 30 Wed	Vail, Iowa — breakdown 3 miles SW of Vail
23 — July 1 Thu	*idle day: repairs at breakdown site*
24 — July 2 Fri	3 miles SW Vail, Iowa — Sioux City, Iowa
25 — July 3 Sat	*rest day in Sioux City, Iowa*
26 — July 4 Sun	*rain delay in Sioux City, Iowa*
27 — July 5 Mon	*rain delay in Sioux City, Iowa*
28 — July 6 Tue	Sioux City, Iowa — Jackson, Neb.
29 — July 7 Wed	Jackson, Neb. — Wisner, Neb.
30 — July 8 Thu	Wisner, Neb. — Leigh, Neb.
31 — July 9 Fri	Leigh, Neb. — Grand Island, Neb.
32 — July 10 Sat	Grand Island, Neb. — breakdown 4 miles west
33 — July 11 Sun	*idle day: repairs at breakdown site*
34 — July 12 Mon	Grand Island, Neb. — Overton, Neb.
35 — July 13 Tue	Overton, Neb. — Ogallala, Neb.
36 — July 14 Wed	Ogallala, Neb. — Cheyenne, Wyo.
37 — July 15 Thu	*idle day in Cheyenne, Wyo.*
38 — July 16 Fri	Cheyenne, Wyo. — Rock River, Wyo.
39 — July 17 Sat	Rock River, Wyo. — Rawlins, Wyo.
40 — July 18 Sun	Rawlins, Wyo. — Rock Springs, Wyo.
41 — July 19 Mon	Rock Springs, Wyo. — Opal, Wyo.
42 — July 20 Tue	Opal, Wyo. — Salt Lake City
43 — July 21 Wed	*idle day in Salt Lake City*
44 — July 22 Thu	*idle day in Salt Lake City*
45 — July 23 Fri	*idle day in Salt Lake City*
46 — July 24 Sat	Salt Lake City — E Fish Springs, Utah
47 — July 25 Sun	E Fish Springs, Utah — stranded W Callao, Utah

Date	Ramsey's City to City Progress, 1909
48 — July 26 Mon	*repairs at Callao, Utah*
49 — July 27 Tue	*repairs at Callao, Utah*
50 — July 28 Wed	*repairs at Callao, Utah*
51 — July 29 Thu	Callao, Nev.— Ibapah, Utah
52 — July 30 Fri	Ibapah, Nev.— Ely, Nev.
53 — July 31 Sat	Ely, Nev.— Eureka, Nev.
54 — Aug. 1 Sun	Eureka, Nev.— Pat Walsh ranch W Austin, Nev.
55 — Aug. 2 Mon	Pat Walsh ranch — Rawhide, Nev.
56 — Aug. 3 Tue	Rawhide, Nev.— Reno, Nev.
57 — Aug. 4 Wed	Reno, Nev.— Lakeside Park, Calif.
58 — Aug. 5 Thu	Lakeside Park, Calif.— Sacramento, Calif.
59 — Aug. 6 Fri	Sacramento, Calif.— Hayward, Calif.
60 — Aug. 7 Sat	Hayward, Calif.— San Francisco, Calif.

* * * * * * * *

*Ramsey's book neglects to name the overnight stop between Boone and Vail, Iowa. The evidence suggests it was Jefferson.

Sources: Auto journals, newspapers and Alice Huyler Ramsey, *Veil, Duster, and Tire Iron*.

was a challenge if I ever had one."[8] For receiving a perfect score in the Montauk Point reliability test, Ramsey won the bronze medal that she wore on her motoring cap during the transcontinental trip.

Ramsey did well in her second contest four months later. Ten cars started and finished a two-day endurance contest that Ramsey's Women's Motoring Club of New York organized for January 11–12, 1909. The drivers navigated the approximately 100 miles between New York to Philadelphia on Monday and back again on Tuesday. The rules allowed each driver to take a female passenger, supposedly a mechanic, but Ramsey invited her young friend Hermine Jahns, who later joined her on the cross-country trip (see photograph, page 30). Joan Newton Cuneo of Jamaica, Long Island, New York, drove a Lancia runabout in the contest. Also entered were a Cadillac, Franklin, Renault and six Maxwells, including Ramsey's.

During much of the run, Cuneo led all others, though the contest was one of reliability, not of speed. Yet Ramsey led the pack into Trenton, New Jersey, on the first day, the *New York Times* reported. Cuneo and Ramsey were among four women who were "especial rivals," the *Times* said. "Each drove her car with all the skill she could command, and neither would yield an inch to her opponents. The pace was maintained at high speed all the time, and the men drivers of the escorting cars were put to it to keep up with the women."[9] With her perfect score, Ramsey won the "Benjamin Briscoe trophy," given in honor of the Maxwell-Briscoe namesake "to the driver of the Maxwell car making the best showing."[10]

As related in Chapter 1, Louise Hitchcock Davis and her husband, John D. Davis, in 1899 made the first serious attempt to cross the United States by auto. Four years

Wearing her Montauk Point medal on her cap, Ramsey (left) and Cuneo pose during a later endurance contest. (NAHC)

later, Dr. H. Nelson Jackson and Sewall K. Crocker became the first drivers to complete the journey by guiding their 1-cylinder Winton from San Francisco to New York City in slightly more than 63½ days. In a 4-cylinder Franklin runabout, Lester L. Whitman and Clayton S. Carris halved that time to 32½ days in 1904. Joined by three relief drivers in 1906, Carris and Whitman lowered the crossing time to just 15 days.

Setting a different sort of record, Pennsylvania lumberman Jacob M. Murdock in 1908 became the first person to drive his family across the country. Murdock's passengers included his wife, Anna, and two daughters, Florence Lillian, 16, and Alice, 14, who became the first females to cross the United States in an automobile as passengers. Yet it remained for a woman

to hazard the trek at the wheel of an automobile.

Maxwell's Golden Opportunity

The Maxwell-Briscoe company saw Ramsey's coast-to-coast trip in a Maxwell as a chance to make some splashy headlines. To make sure it got them, the automaker hired Murphy to precede the car, line up newspaper interviews and supply lively copy to the newspapers and auto journals. Though it was not her idea to have an advance man, Ramsey said, "the Maxwell firm insisted that the spectacle of four women driving across the country over practically uncharted wilderness was a golden opportunity for building up their own prestige in the automobile industry." Murphy performed his job admirably, as *Motor World* attested:

His chief duties, in addition to seeing that no harm befalls the ladies, is to make sure that proper notice is taken of them and their car by the newspapers of the cities at which they arrive. Mr. Murphy is loaded with facts and fancies regarding the trip and no newspaper men go hungry for want of material concerning the expedition when they seek for information. In consequence, the enterprise is receiving publicity by the yard.[11]

The company furnished the car and paid expenses, said Ramsey. "Its officers also instructed their agents to keep on hand tires, gasoline and spare parts in case of any breakdowns, and asked that their

Ramsey and her Maxwell on the New York–Philadelphia run. (NAHC)

representatives give us every possible attention."

For her part, "Mrs. Ramsey is an ardent automobile enthusiast, who believes in the driving of cars by women just as much as by men," *Automobile* said in 1909. As a Salt Lake City newspaper reported it at the time, Ramsey set out "to demonstrate that women are independent of mere men and that they can and dare brave the wilds of various parts of the country, overcome many difficulties and take care of themselves."[12]

Murphy's hand — or handwriting — in promoting the Maxwell is evident in an *Automobile* dispatch from Nebraska, reporting (with emphasis added) that "so far

the trip has proven Mrs. Ramsey's contention, that *in the right car* a woman can make the trip without trouble." Ramsey told an interviewer in 1975: "I did it because it was a challenge, and because I knew it would be fun…. Good driving has nothing to do with sex. It's all above the collar."[13]

The Maxwell DA

A Detroit manufacturer of sheet metal, Benjamin Briscoe raised the money to create the Maxwell-Briscoe Motor Company. Jonathan D. Maxwell, formerly an engineer with Olds Motor Works (maker of the

Ramsey's friend Hermine Jahns in motoring garb. (NAHC)

Oldsmobile), designed the 2-cylinder auto bearing his name, and the factory produced the first Maxwells in 1904, calling them 1905 models. Though the company introduced a 4-cylinder engine for the 1906 model year, it continued making 2-cylinder cars through 1912.[14]

For Ramsey, the factory prepared a five-passenger 1909 Model DA touring car. The machine's 104-inch wheelbase (the distance separating the front wheels from the rear) and 56-inch tread (the distance between the left-side and right-side wheels) made it, in its day, a medium-sized vehicle. Using cylinders cast individually, rather than in a block, the DA's 4-cylinder engine of 4¼-inch bore (the cylinder diameter) and stroke (the up-and-down distance each piston traveled in its cylinder) developed 30 horsepower. The factory substituted a special 20-gallon gas tank under the front seat for the standard 14-gallon tank and mounted a luggage rack behind

the car. Otherwise, it was the company's standard $1,750 touring car, painted dark green, Ramsey said. The car had acetylene headlamps, covered with "pantasote 'raincoats'" to keep off mud and dust when not in use. Its Ajax tires measured 32 × 4 inches.

An acetylene generator and metal tool box occupied the left running board. The generator mixed carbide crystals and water to produce acetylene gas; the tool box was large enough for carrying a hand pump and other tools. The cowl lights and taillight burned kerosene. The car had a fabric top, roll-up side curtains and a celluloid windshield. Equipped with a three-speed transmission and a sheet-metal pan beneath it to protect the engine, the Maxwell weighed 2,100 pounds empty. Loaded, it weighed 3,500 pounds, Powell told a reporter in Sioux City, Iowa. The *Salt Lake (City) Herald*, however, maintained "the car with its passengers, camping outfit, shovels, axes, etc., weighs more than 3,800 pounds."[15] The Maxwell had two sets of brakes on the rear wheels — an internal, expanding set and an external, contracting set — and a sight-feed glass tube on the dash for monitoring the engine's oil level. The driver dipped a ruled stick into the tank to gauge the gas level.[16]

Nettie, Maggie and Hermine

At John Ramsey's urging, Ramsey invited her husband's two sisters along as companions. Margaret Atwood and Nettie Powell, both living in Hackensack, had ridden with Ramsey during the Montauk Point endurance run and on many other occasions. "Nettie and Maggie were well into their forties, Nettie the older by several years," Ramsey, 22 at the time, recalled years later. She also invited Hermine Jahns,

From left to right: Atwood, Ramsey (at wheel), Jahns and Powell pose for a publicity photo in the Maxwell. The "MBMC" on the pennant stands for Maxwell-Briscoe Motor Company. (AAMA)

reportedly 19, an unattached friend and both the youngest and tallest of the four women. Jahns had recently moved from Wisconsin to live with her sister in Hackensack.

Ramsey had some initial doubts about her two sisters-in-law:

> The "girls," as we referred to my husband's sisters, well-groomed and dressed in the daintiest of French-heel footgear, were conservative and reserved to the nth degree. Nettie assumed a sort of dominance in decisions; Maggie was the more submissive and sensitive type. Nettie would pursue her show of authority as far as she could maintain it.... Could such dressy and fastidious women manage with little in the way of fancy clothes for so long a period?

Yes, concluded Ramsey, who learned that "my husband's two sisters were anxious to participate for the fun of it." A highlight of the trip for Powell, a sports fan, was the chance to meet prize fight promoter Tex Rickard, who stayed at their Ely, Nevada, hotel.

Following the advice of highway mapper A.L. Westgard — who worked for the Automobile Club of America, Touring Club of America, and later the American Automobile Association — Ramsey traveled without guns for protection, she said in her book. "A dog, yes, if you like; but no guns," he told her. "We prized his counsel highly as he and his wife had had extensive practical experience and knew whereof they spoke," Ramsey said. This was perhaps a last-minute decision: Newspapers as far west as Utah, evidently drawing on Maxwell press releases in preparing articles on Ramsey's arrival, mention guns on board. "The firearms, Mrs. Ramsey explained, 'are to scare away any over-curious wild animals,'" according to the June 17 *Automobile*.[17]

Did You Pack the Wind Matches?

For equipment, Ramsey said, the travelers took spare inner tubes and a tire-repair kit, stowed in a "tire drum," a round trunk in the center of the spare tires. Other equipment included tire chains, tire irons, a tire pump, a jack, one or more axes and the unspecified tool kit, all kept in a tool box on the running board. They always carried at least two spare tires, according to Ramsey.

She brought a picnic basket "with a minimum of good rations and eating equipment"; a camping outfit; "and a camera which took photos of post-card size." For lighting the lamps, Ramsey carried "wind matches which would keep burning in any gale until they burned themselves out." In Chicago, she added "a stout towing rope, a block and tackle, and a short shovel," she reported. "We had a tank of compressed air for supplying air to the tires in emergency," she said in describing tire repairs her first day beyond Chicago, "but we all

agreed it should be saved for flats on the desert or in the rain."

The car arrived in Cedar Rapids, Iowa, equipped with "long strips of canvas, which will be used along the way on the sandy roads, in order to give the wheels a purchase when the shifting sands become so bad that the tires will not grip," the *Cedar Rapids Daily Republican* observed. Her plan, evidently, was to spread out the canvas for her wheels to follow, as did Jacob M. Murdock in 1908. Other supplies included a roll of wire for emergency repairs, a "little Sterno outfit" for heating food, two extra leaf springs bolted to a running board, and other unspecified spare parts. In the West, "I carried a two-quart emergency supply of oil and a five-gallon can of gasoline lashed to the running board."[18]

She was carrying neither extra gas nor extra water in Iowa when she ran out of gas once and cooling water several times. Before crossing the southwest desert, however, she bought a canvas South African water bag to hang from the moving auto. The "gradual seepage of the moisture through the canvas cools the contents by its evaporation," she explained in her 1961 book. "These are in common use in desert sections of our country to this day, but they were new to *us*."

Each woman packed one suitcase. "Nettie and Maggie both owned beautiful traveling luggage, fitted with cut-glass containers with silver tops for toilet articles." Ramsey and Jahns had more Spartan grips:

Into the cases went our "city duds"— dressy suits with pretty blouses, an extra pair of good-looking shoes, and the usual change of underwear and overnight necessities. Dresses were long and full in that era, so this amount just about filled a case.... For day-by-day wearing we had chosen suits of tan covert cloth as being most practical as far as dust and light rain were concerned.

In the West, the Maxwell carried rope, a shovel (behind the tool box in the center of the running board) and a gas can. The spare tires are visible on the right running board. Standing in the car is Jahns; the back-seat passenger appears to be Atwood. (FLP)

With those we wore simple blouses, dusters in warm and dry weather, and for rain, rubber ponchos and hats. Our fair-weather hats were a type of large full cap with stiff visors to shield the eyes in the low western sun, over which crepe de chine veils were draped and came under the chin to be tied in billowing bows.

Flouting Stereotypes

Besides facing the dangers of the road ahead, Ramsey and her female companions were risking public ridicule. Traditionalists censured women who drove autos or who studied to become doctors, lawyers and engineers. On the morning of Ramsey's departure, by coincidence, the *New York Times* reported on a bishop who "bitterly attacked the new woman in her efforts to do man's work, and denounced the woman suffrage campaign as a 'hysterical clamor employed in the pursuit of this chimera.'"[19]

Flouting stereotypes of femininity, women drivers, nevertheless, scored well in the annual Glidden Tours and similar smaller endurance contests and set records against men in over-the-road and track racing. Though there is no evidence she drove, Louise Hitchcock Davis suffered alongside her husband, John, on their difficult, unsuccessful, New York–San Francisco trip of 1899, the first recorded attempt to drive coast to coast. Mrs. Pierre Cohuteau Scott of St. Louis set a speed record by driving from St. Louis to Chicago in an elapsed time of 54 hours during late October 1903.[20]

A year before Ramsey became the first woman to drive across the country, a mother-and-daughter team set out to drive a 2-cylinder, 8-horsepower Waltham from Portland, Maine, to Portland, Oregon. Minerva Miller (Mrs. Edward E.) Teape and her daughter, Vera Teape (Mrs. W.H.) McKelvie, both of Sandpoint, Idaho, were well qualified to make the 4,000-mile crossing, the auto journals noted in 1908. To relieve the "deep depression" into which she fell after the July 3, 1905, drowning of her 12-year-old daughter, Dorothy, Teape in the summer of 1906 drove a 4-horsepower Waltham buckboard from Denver to Chicago and back. Vera McKelvie accompanied her mother on the trip, and recalled the journey in a 1950 interview:

> It required two weeks to go from Denver to Chicago.... I guess we were something of a curiosity, but at the time neither Mother nor I thought about it, we had such wonderful fun. We didn't think it strange or adventurous of us to be traveling alone.
>
> We wondered why folks were often at their fences as we passed until we learned someone telephoned ahead from every town we went through to warn others to be on the lookout for two women in an auto!
>
> Our biggest difficulty was to find fuel. There were no gas stations or garages except in the larger towns. We could usually buy gasoline at a drug store and for repairs we had to go to a blacksmith shop or resort to our own ingenuity. By the time we returned to Denver our little

car was pretty well held together with hairpins and safety pins![21]

In a 1908 *Automobile* interview about her upcoming coast-to-coast attempt, Teape expressed optimism: "I realize the difficulties that two women may encounter, but we have always lived in the West and have plenty of confidence in our ability to overcome every one of the trials and obstacles that may beset us on the long trip. We shall not be bothered with extra equipment or baggage to hamper us, for, as some one has very wisely said, 'the greatest hampers to motorists are the hampers they carry with them.'"[22]

Two hundred people gathered at Nickerson's Garage in Portland, Maine, at 12:30 P.M. on May 12, 1908, to bid bon voyage to the two women. They began their projected two-month trip by driving south to Boston, and across New York state on the route used by Ramsey and many transcontinentalists before and since. They traveled deliberately so Teape could conserve her strength, for "the object of the expedition is to improve Mrs. Teape's health, her physician recommending motoring as the best means of regaining it," according to *Motor Age*.[23]

They arrived in Chicago on June 1, reported the *Chicago Daily News*. "Once or twice when the little rig has been floundering in the mud the men folk have come to the rescue; but it is seldom they have had to appeal to anyone for help of this kind," according to *Motor Age*, which was implicitly predicting their success. "Feats of this sort are of the sane order and their successful completion means that once more the public will be shown that the modern motor car comes up to all requirements." Mother and daughter left Chicago June 2 for Omaha, Nebraska, and from there traveled as far south as Kansas City, where Teape's "severe cold" worsened and sent her to a sanitarium for several weeks, forcing an end to the journey.[24]

Minerva Teape at the wheel and daughter Vera McKelvie set off to drive their Waltham across the country in 1908. (May 14, 1908, *Motor Age*)

Cuneo Feels a Thrill Behind the Wheel

Other female drivers had made a name for themselves. In July and August 1908, Alice Potter of Elgin, Illinois, made headlines by driving her Haynes on a 1,748-mile round trip between Chicago and New York in a reported running time of 17 days. Three female friends rode to New York with Potter and one returned with her. Potter's 75-year-old mother also joined her daughter for the return trip.[25] Joan Newton Cuneo's many achievements included driving in the 1907 and 1908 Glidden Tours; setting one- and five-mile records on the race track at Danbury, Con-

necticut; and finishing second to famous racer Ralph DePalma in a 50-mile race at New Orleans in 1909.[26]

Since 1902, she had owned and driven seven autos a total of 80,000 miles, Cuneo wrote in a 1908 article, "Why There Are So Few Women Automobilists." Women steered clear of driving partly because of the effort required to hand crank an engine and change tires; another reason was "the unpleasant attitude of other drivers," Cuneo said. "Perhaps the principal reason is that they lack confidence in their ability to drive a car." But women tended to be safer drivers than men, she argued: "The spirit of recklessness that often comes when the potential power and speed of a car is

Westgard strikes a dapper pose behind the Maxwell shortly before sending it on its way from the New York City Maxwell agency, 1930 Broadway. (NAHC)

realized is far more a trait of man than of woman." Thus, "I feel that if women could realize the exhilaration that comes from being able to handle a 60-horse-power touring car, the sight of a woman driver would be anything but a novelty…. There is no good reason why thousands of women should sit quietly in the tonneau and let the men have the keenest enjoyment of the greatest sport of to-day."[27]

Behind the wheel in many other motoring events as well as in everyday driving, other women had proved themselves as competent as men. The 10 women, including Cuneo and Ramsey, who drove cars on the two-day, round-trip endurance run between Philadelphia and New York "demonstrated that the driving of an automobile has become a task well within the ability of the average woman," *Automobile* concluded. Many drivers opposed an attempt to ban women drivers from Milwaukee's downtown streets in 1909, *Automobile* elsewhere noted, "reasoning that women make better drivers than men; that they do not take chances, are the least reck-

less, and maintain the speed limits more conscientiously than men. No cases are on record in Milwaukee of accidents to cars operated by women." Ramsey's skills were such that by June 1909 *Motor Age* could call her "one of the best known women motorists in the East."[28]

Leaving Manhattan

On Wednesday, June 9, the four women set off early from their homes in Hackensack for the 15-mile drive into the Maxwell salesroom at 1930 Broadway in New York City. John Ramsey, along with his mother, Maggie's husband, William, and Berry Lewis, the Hackensack Maxwell agent, followed in another Maxwell. Those braving the rain to witness the start included Joan Newton Cuneo and "Senator" W.J. Morgan, the *New York Globe*'s auto editor and a vocal leader of the good-roads movement, according to Ramsey. Westgard, the "pioneer automotive map-maker and Glidden Tour pathfinder," was the official starter.[29]

"They were well prepared for the

Jahns, Powell, Atwood and Ramsey. (NAHC)

storm, all wearing rubber ponchos," the *New York Tribune* said of the four women. In their rain suits and hats, the women posed for photos in and beside the Maxwell, sitting at the curb with its top up and chains on its rear wheels. Despite the weather, "New York motorists were out in large numbers" for Ramsey's departure, *Motor Age* said.[30] Her trip would end July 15 or July 16, various press reports said initially, but later reports said that bad weather would postpone her arrival date to August 1. It was actually a week later than that.

In her trip diary, Ramsey records that she left Manhattan on June 9 as the hour was "approaching" 10 A.M. The *Hackensack Republican* put the departure time at 9 A.M. Few, if any, other newspapers or auto journals give an exact time. Ramsey followed the Albany Post Road northward. It was still raining when she ended her 76-mile day in Poughkeepsie, where she had attended college at Vassar. Next day, Thursday, she drove through Albany to reach Amsterdam — "slightly over a hundred miles." In so doing, "We slipped and slid all through the morning, just missing the side supports of a small bridge," and stopped "many times to attach the dangling ends of rattling chains." The chains resulted in "excessive wear on the rear tires which we changed early in the trip," even before reaching Buffalo, New York, Ramsey recalled.[31] The rain began to let up Thursday afternoon but the roads remained wet.

Menacing Apparitions

On Friday, June 11, Day 3, the roads were muddy to Little Falls, New York, where the weather, and evidently the roads, began improving. The foursome passed Utica and Syracuse to reach Auburn for the night. After a tour of the Auburn State Prison the following morning, Ramsey could not get the Maxwell to start. A local mechanic worked in vain for an hour before Ramsey telephoned back to the Maxwell agent at Syracuse, who sent a mechanic. He installed a new coil and, at 5:30 P.M. Saturday, Ramsey, Atwood, Jahns and Powell started a 138-mile night drive over dry roads to Buffalo, where friends were waiting.

> After dark, objects took on an entirely different aspect in the eerie artificial light. We resumed a fair speed; but Maggie seemed to be suffering from a case of the jitters. Every little thing along the roadside was another spook to her. First the shining eyes of a cat gave her a scare; then a particularly menacing apparition, looking for all the world like a brilliantly illuminated trolley car on the left, turned out to be nothing more than a group of milk cans waiting to be picked up for the creamery. Several rabbits enlivened the evening.... These various ghostlike apparitions increased the tension of the lonely drive.

They reached the Iroquis Hotel in Buffalo at 1:15 A.M. Sunday. On Sunday and Monday, friends showed them around Buffalo and took them to Niagara Falls. On Tuesday, June 15, Day 7, Ramsey drove to Cleveland, where, on Euclid Avenue, she saw her first brick paving. Ramsey's trip from Buffalo to Cleveland set her best one-day distance record—198 miles. By coaxing the Maxwell up to 42 mph on the Cleveland Parkway, Ramsey also hit the car's highest speed since leaving New York City. But she drove even faster on far rougher roads to beat a cloudburst into one Iowa town, Powell would later tell reporters.

The tourists, who spent the night at Cleveland's Hollenden Hotel, left early Wednesday afternoon, June 16, for a 132-mile drive to Toledo, Ohio. After a blow-out west of Lorain, they hit "a bad piece of road before entering Toledo," recalls Ramsey, who "drove up to the Boody house about 8 o'clock last night," reported Thursday's *Toledo Blade*.

> This is the first cross-country run ever attempted by a woman driver, and at every city the tourists have been accorded enthusiastic receptions. On this account, Mrs. Ramsey says, it has been almost impossible to get away from many of the towns.... Mrs. Ramsey left the Central Auto company, local Maxwell agents, this morning and today will drive to South Bend. While en route she will take in the Cobe races, over the Indiana course, and will reach Chicago Saturday night.[32]

Hit-and-Run Driver

The trip to Chicago transpired differently than the *Blade's* prediction, however. According to accounts Ramsey wrote in the August 19, 1909, *Hackensack Republican*, and in her much later book, the women reached Chicago on Friday. Then, on Saturday, they drove to the Cobe Cup races in Crown Point, Indiana, some 50 miles southeast of Chicago. West from Toledo, which the travelers left Thursday in the rain, Murphy rode ahead of Ramsey in a pilot car that guided them to Wauseon, Ohio. From there, Murphy rode in the transcontinental Maxwell to Goshen, Indiana, where he caught a train to Chicago. The women spent Thursday night, June 17, in Goshen, and passed through South Bend Friday, June 18, Day 10, on their 132-mile drive into Chicago. On her three daily runs between Cleveland and Chicago, Ramsey drove 132, 151 and 132 miles.

On Friday, the Maxwell was struck by a hit-and-run driver in a traffic jam near

Chicago. The accident occurred on dusty roads in the "heavy traffic of autos returning from that day's running of the Cobe Cup automobile races," Ramsey said. "One Cadillac, pulling around to pass us on the right[,] struck and dented our hub cap and, in the fray, lost his entirely; but he never stopped." One stretch of Indiana road along Lake Michigan was composed of hillocks built up of blowing lake sand, and, overall, between Cleveland and Chicago "the roads were not so excellent as we had anticipated — very bumpy and rough," Ramsey said.

To reach downtown Chicago, truly a railroad center, the Maxwell on Friday bounced over tracks for mile upon mile, Ramsey recalled. "When the car turned into Michigan Avenue it attracted a great deal of attention," the *Chicago Inter Ocean* reported:

> It was covered with mud from radiator to the trunk rack in the rear and certainly looked as though it had gone some distance. In the car the four women, all wearing gowns exactly alike, which they had made especially for the trip, were a bit dusty, but a happy smile was on each face, for two days of sightseeing are ahead of them here.
>
> The arrival of the car in Chicago was the completion of more than 1,000 miles of the trip, which calls for 4,100 miles to San Francisco, from where, by the way, it may be continued to Seattle or Los Angeles, to be determined on later....
>
> With her desire to see the country and tour across it, she [Ramsey] is also making the run for the purpose of showing to other women who own motor cars that the transcontinental run has not the terrors that some might like to have them believe. She is, in a way, blazing the route for other women who might like but have not so far attempted the trip.[33]

Entering the Real West

Ramsey and her companions stayed not two but three days in Chicago — Saturday, Sunday and Monday — sightseeing, resting and preparing themselves and the car for further travel. Besides attending the auto races, Ramsey bought extra supplies and the travelers planned their route through Illinois. Accompanied by three escorting cars, they left Chicago Tuesday, June 22, Day 14, hoping to cross the state and the Mississippi River to reach Clinton, Iowa, by nightfall. Under their schedule, as given in the *Chicago Daily Tribune*, the Ramsey party would reach Cedar Rapids, Iowa, on Wednesday; Jefferson, Iowa, on Thursday; Omaha on Friday; and Columbus, Nebraska, on Saturday.[34]

Moving into rolling country, the four autos traveled briskly through Geneva and DeKalb, Illinois, over a road with a "fairly good gravel base" and, consequently, no ruts, Ramsey said. East of Rochelle, Illinois, Ramsey stopped to fix a flat tire by removing, patching and reinserting the tube (see photographs, pages 41 and 42). After remounting the tire, however, she allowed her male escorts to operate the hand pump. "I hated to pump a tire," she confessed in her book. "With all those able-bodied men standing around I would hate to waste their strength while I broke my back unnecessarily!"

During an afternoon lunch break in Rochelle, as Ramsey afterward recounted in the *Hackensack Republican*, "a terrific thunderstorm came up, obliging us to stay in that little town for the night. The following day and the five succeeding days similar storms dropped down, each lasting about two hours, so you can begin to imagine the havoc this weather was playing on roads which are nothing to boast about in the best season."[35]

The ditches were full of water as Ramsey's Maxwell and a single pilot car proceeded west from Rochelle on Wednesday,

Left to right: Ramsey, Powell, Atwood (partly obscured) and Jahns as they prepare to leave Chicago. (NAHC)

June 23. Other vehicles, however, had packed down a track for them to follow over the muddy roads, Ramsey said. They passed through Dixon and Fulton to reach the tall, narrow, plank-floored bridge spanning the Mississippi River to Clinton. For Ramsey and her passengers, the bridge marked "our entrance into what we regarded as the Real West." Though they were hoping to reach Cedar Rapids, rain again intervened. A cloudburst stopped them at Mechanicsville, Iowa, where they took rooms at the Page Hotel and left their car overnight in a livery stable, Ramsey said. And thus began a 14-day crawl through Iowa mud.

Red-Faced and Out of Gas

The next day, Thursday, June 24, Day 16, Lattner Brothers of Cedar Rapids, agents for Ford and Maxwell, sent out D.A. Hiner as a guide, Ramsey wrote. He evidently took the train to Mechanicsville and then rode in Ramsey's Maxwell as she ground her way through a quagmire of mud into the city. Preoccupied by two days of tense driving on slick roads, Ramsey had neglected to test the gas level in her under-seat tank, which she normally kept at least half full:

Just as we reached the top of a particularly long slippery hill, our motor choked, sputtered and ceased running. Much to my chagrin, we were out of gas! What a predicament! Was my face red?! Poor Mr. Hiner walked back a mile and a half to the last farmhouse we had passed. He had noticed telephone wires leading in to the house. Thank goodness a few farmers had invested in that newest form of communication! He called Mr. Lattner, who saved the day—and us!— by bringing some gasoline.

As her companions look on, Ramsey begins repairing a flat tire near Rochelle, Illinois. (FLP)

Mentioning nothing about the incident, the *Cedar Rapids Daily Republican* reported that the Ramsey party left Mechanicsville at 5 A.M. Thursday, bound for Cedar Rapids,

> where they breakfasted soon after six, making the run of about twenty-eight miles in a trifle more than one hour. Through the state of Iowa, so far, the roads have been very good, according to Mrs. Ramsey's report, but the rain put them in such a condition that she did not attempt to make the run to this city Wednesday evening on account of conditions and the heavily loaded car.
>
> The tourists are, without a doubt, the most famous who have ever passed through this city, for the reason that it is the first time that four women have ever attempted to cross the continent without at least one man in the party. A number of men, of course, have made the journey, but should Mrs. Ramsey and her three lady companions reach Los Angeles [*sic*] as they expect to do, in about thirty days, it will have opened the way for other women, and have proved what Mrs. Ramsey started out to prove, that the combination of a reliable car and a woman who knows it, can make the trip between the two oceans as well as any man.[36]

The newspaper said the Maxwell tourists left town after breakfast Thursday, bound for Jefferson. In her 1961 book, however, Ramsey contends the women remained

After patching the tube, Ramsey allows her escorts to man the tire pump. (NAHC)

Thursday in Cedar Rapids, spending the night at the Montrose Hotel, and left Friday, June 27, on roads she no longer described glowingly. Friday's journey was, in fact, "a terrible ordeal. Roads were horrible! The accumulated rains of the past several days had already soaked deep enough below the surface of the roads to render them bottomless."

Slithering through a muddy morass in low gear for mile after mile overworked the car's engine and, between towns, the radiator water began boiling away. Though lacking a pail, Powell suggested that she and Atwood use small cut-glass jars from their posh luggage sets to refill the radiator with ditch water. They did this once and then twice more before the car reached the next town, Ramsey said. At a crossroads that day, they met a woman who had driven six miles behind a team of horses to watch the transcontinental car pass. In Iowa, Ramsey overcame any lingering doubts she may have had about her sisters-in-law as traveling companions. They were, in fact, "beginning to get a certain thrill of adventure in our conquest of the Basin of Mud!"

Waylaid by Weasel Creek

While crawling along the approximately 40-mile stretch between Cedar Rapids and Belle Plaine on Friday, Ramsey pulled up short at Weasel Creek, where high water had flooded the approach to the bridge. Wading part way into the water, Ramsey judged it would be unsafe to attempt driving to the bridge until the water receded. As they waited, Jahns walked to a farmhouse to buy bread and water. The water was still too high at nightfall, so they raised the Maxwell's top, unrolled its side curtains and celluloid windshield and slept in the car. As Powell recounted the incident to a *Sioux City Daily Tribune* reporter,

We left Cedar Rapids for Belle P[l]aine and when about 24 miles out we came to a swollen stream. As you can never tell what is under water we decided to get some information before going into it. A farmer at a house nearby advised us not to attempt to cross, so we parked our car along the roadside, got out our camping outfit, cooked supper and made a night of it. We are prepared for such an emergency, but that is the only time we have had to stay out all night. We do not run at nights, but stop at hotels.[37]

They crossed the creek the next morning, Saturday, June 26, and reached Belle Plaine at 8 A.M. After breakfast, Ramsey repaired a short circuit in a spark plug. "Plugs were manufactured then so they could be taken apart, cleaned with fine sandpaper or emery cloth and reassembled, which I did on the spot.... The girls were interested in watching the process, so the time passed rapidly and we were soon on our way again. I could only wipe off the grime with a rag — no chance for a real clean-up until later." Over drying roads, they passed Tama and Marshalltown to reach Boone in central Iowa, about 100 miles for the day, before the rain resumed. As Powell told the Sioux City newspaper:

We have raced with the rain in Iowa until we feel as though we never wished to see another drop of water. Last Saturday morning [June 26] we started to resume our journey and had gone but a little way when we saw the clouds forming behind us and knew that rain was imminent. We started ahead as fast as we could go over the very rough road and for 30 miles we had a race with that rain. It was great sport, but just a little hazardous.

Mrs. Ramsey is one of the best drivers in the country for a woman. At times we were making 45 miles an hour over that rough road. We beat the storm, however, and got into Boone and safely housed

before it broke. And then what a deluge. It was actually a cloudburst, and you can imagine the condition of the roads when we started.[38]

The long-distance touring car pulled into town at 7:20 P.M., according to the *Boone News-Republican*. "While here the party turned in the Maxwell to the Boone Auto company, where it was overhauled and put into condition for the hard western trip. Mrs. Ramsey roasted the Iowa roads, or rather the condition of the weather. She said that it had done nothing but rain since the party struck the west, making the roads 'Out here in Iowa as bad as our garden patches in the east.'"[39]

The women spent the night at the Northwestern Hotel, and learned that the roads were worse ahead on the approximately 150 miles between Boone and the Missouri River at Council Bluffs. While they ignored suggestions to ship the car by rail to Omaha, Ramsey and crew did decide to lighten the load. Consequently the next morning, Sunday, her three passengers, their luggage and two spare springs boarded the train for Omaha. Advance man J.D. Murphy, who would ride the rest of the way across Iowa in the Maxwell, left with Ramsey at 1 P.M., according to Ramsey's book, or "shortly before noon," according to the Boone newspaper. Getting towed from "one awful hole" east of Jefferson, they reached that town, and evidently stayed overnight with the family of a banker who also sold Maxwells.

Conquering Danger Hill

They left the next day, Monday, June 28, Day 20, for Vail, Iowa, with chains on the car's rear wheels.

Leaving Jefferson, we soon encountered Danger Hill. This is a climb dreaded by all, since there is a ninety degree turn at the bottom, preventing any advantage which might be gained by making a run for it. After we made the turn and started up the muddy grade we saw ahead of us, possibly two-thirds of the way up, another automobile. The driver was having a difficult time of it as he tried again and again to go forward. Finally his motor coughed, spit, and stopped. The man and woman got out and looked about them. She mounted the bank beside the road and he got out a shovel and tried to rid the wheels of some of the accumulated mud.

Ramsey was able to ease past the stranded Mitchell auto, pass the man a rope and slowly but surely pull the car over the crest of Danger Hill. But she faced an even greater challenge west of Carroll:

> The road from here to Vail had one section composed of a veritable sea of chuck holes of varying sizes, most of them so filled with water that it was difficult to determine their depths. This experience with mud holes was fast becoming a specialized education. Eventually we learned to estimate the depths of them fairly accurately by the comparative slopes of the edges of the puddles.

Nevertheless, a rear wheel slipped into a hole so deep that the Maxwell's differential caught on a high spot, suspending one rear wheel, which spun uselessly. Compounding the problem, one front wheel settled into a deep hole. To first move the front end to a level surface, Murphy and Ramsey placed the jack on the shovel blade for a firm base, raised the front end and used a rope to pull the car sideways off the jack. The front end dropped free of the hole. With a fence rail, Murphy then pried against the suspended rear wheel as Ramsey accelerated; she thus got enough traction to pull ahead. But bad news awaited them later that Monday morning upon arriving in Vail, which

was in an awful condition. [Wooden] [s]idewalks tipped up on edge, buildings at all angles on their foundations, and debris of all sorts floating through the streets showed evidence of a terrible deluge which they had had there the Saturday night preceding. Natives of Vail told us of the pitiable scenes, and employe[e]s in the store were still busy shoveling the last of the foot deep mud which had soaked into the buildings, and the water-mark could plainly be seen on the windows of the nearby frame houses. We were further advised that the roads from there to Omaha were absolutely impassable.[40]

Set Sights on Sioux City

Leaving the Maxwell in a Vail blacksmith shop, Murphy and Ramsey boarded the train for Omaha to consult with Atwood, Jahns and Powell, staying at the Rome Hotel. For the first and only time during the journey, the local Maxwell agent was "most discourteous and disagreeable and would not give us any help," Ramsey said. But W.S. Hathaway, the automaker's district representative from Kansas City, was in town. He suggested that rather than attempt to head southwest from Vail to Omaha, Ramsey and Murphy should head northwest over higher ground to cross the Missouri River at Sioux City. They could then travel southwest into Nebraska, bypassing Omaha, and resume their original route at Columbus.

Ramsey's three female passengers promptly traveled to Sioux City by train to await the car. "The Ramsay [sic] party is the first party to ever choose the Sioux City route in their transcontinental trips," the *Sioux City Daily Tribune* gleefully noted. "The roads are in good shape and the trip will prove to tourists the wisdom of passing through Sioux City rather than going as far south as Omaha."[41]

Accompanied by Eugene Gnehm, sent as a guide by the Interstate Auto Supply Company (the Sioux City Maxwell agency), Ramsey and Murphy set off into the mud beyond Vail on Wednesday, June 30. On an incline just three miles outside town, the left axle shaft broke "and the wheel quietly rolled off into the long grass," halting the car after its smallest single-day progress of the trip. Maxwell agent H.B. Groves sent a new axle shaft from Sioux City. It should have arrived on Thursday morning's train but an inexperienced handler lost it, which cost the travelers another day, Ramsey recalled.

With a new shaft installed, they set out again on Friday, July 2, Day 24 of the trip. They were towed out of mudholes twice during the day but "shortly after noon" reached Sioux City's West Hotel, where Atwood, Jahns and Powell waited, said the Sioux City newspaper, which put their journey from New York City at "1,600 miles or over."[42]

The next morning, the rains began again. Murphy went by train to Columbus but the women waited three full days for the weather to clear. They spent part of their forced layover having the Maxwell "thoroughly overhauled [to] be certain that it is in good condition before leaving here," Powell said. "You know it has been through an awful experience in Iowa and we don't care to take too many chances."[43]

Thirteen Miles of Mud and Holes

Finally, as Ramsey wrote in the *Hackensack Republican*, she set out on Tuesday, July 6 — the day of their scheduled departure from Evanston, Wyoming, two states to the west. She left Sioux City at 3 P.M. behind Gnehm's pilot car:

> Just across the Missouri river bridge the car which had started out to pilot us

to the first village broke down completely in one of the terrible holes in the road and had to be towed back to town. One of the gentlemen in that car begged us to go back with them and wait until the roads dried up a bit, but we had come a half mile [on] what was known as the worst section of highway in that part of the country and I was not for going back.... They left us there then and we went on to Jackson, Nebraska, where we spent the night, having made only 13 miles that afternoon.[44]

The horses that towed Gnehm's car back to town returned to pull Ramsey's Maxwell through the rest of that cratered section, so she could avoid a similar breakdown, according to her book. After a long, slow drive, the car crawled into Jackson under its own power at 7 P.M. Ramsey drove in second gear most of the next day, Wednesday, July 7, to manage 36 miles over bad roads to Wisner. She got stuck twice within one mile: "The farmer's son caught one of their horses in pasture and pulled us out — for a fee — then walked on to the next hole, repeated his towing but *doubled* his fee!"

As if atoning for the earlier affront, two affable well diggers in a cart later hauled Ramsey's passengers up a steep hill to lighten the Maxwell's load. She also had some repairs to attend to. "I found that the screws in the magneto plate had loosened and one had fallen out and could not be found. It was a mean spot to reach, but I tightened the others as well as I could and they held." And when a small spring broke, she slid under the car to wire the brake pedal in position.

Ramsey reached Leigh, Nebraska, on Thursday, July 8 — which had been scheduled as her first night's stay in Utah — and Columbus by lunchtime Friday, July 9. That afternoon, the Maxwell continued on drier, faster roads toward Grand Island, 65 miles away. A sudden hailstorm ten miles from their destination forced the travelers

Top: Jahns, Ramsey, Powell and Atwood beside a tarp-covered Maxwell pilot car on a muddy city street, quite possibly as they prepare to leave Sioux City. (NAHC). *Bottom:* Another photograph showing a close-up of the same scene. (NAHC)

to take refuge at a farmhouse; it was raining when they reached Grand Island's Koehler Hotel at 6:15 P.M. But in an interview with the *Grand Island Daily Independent*, Ramsey sounded elated after her 100-mile day: "Never had they experienced such bad roads as in Iowa, which were in great contrast to those encountered in Nebraska. 'These,' said Ramsey, 'make riding in a car so enjoyable that it is very easy to forget the bad spots and heavy going over those gumbo roads. From now on, I thin[k] we will be able to make very good time.'"

In speaking of the trip to date, Ramsey said: "It has been simply delightful. Of course bad roads make a tour of this kind unpleasant at times, but there is really so little of this as compared to the good roads. Then too, it is just beautiful to be out in the fresh air all day, driving along through lovely scenery and going as far as you care to each day as we are doing."[45]

In Cheyenne, Brown as Berries

But just four miles west of Grand Island the next morning, the Maxwell broke its right rear axle shaft. The Denver Maxwell agent sent out mechanic H.H. Miller, who traveled more than 400 miles by train Saturday, installed the new shaft Sunday and overhauled the magneto in time for a 4 P.M. Monday departure. Feeling poorly, Powell took the train ahead to Cheyenne, making room for Miller to ride that far in the Maxwell.

On their way to Overton, Nebraska, where they stayed with the family of W.H. Hill, the Maxwell agent, they had to hire a man and horse to pull them out of a hole near Elm Creek. Their next night stop was at Ogallala, where a mounted posse, seeking a killer, halted Ramsey's car for two hours. Earlier, at North Platte, Ramsey stopped for repairs. "Our Maxwell had been so shaken up with its strenuous journey

that numerous bolts had loosened and some minor troubles developed. We adjusted a few important ones and kept on climbing the lower foothills toward the glorious mountains of the Rocky range."

As the car ran through the Nebraska Panhandle into Wyoming, the party had to open and close wire gates between ranches. "No matter how inconvenient it was, no one would think of neglecting this little chore in return for the right to pass. This part of the road was a mere trail from here into Cheyenne as it crossed the ranches and hills. But it was a beautiful ride, with ever-expanding views, as one looked across the rolling land to the distant horizon." Ramsey reached Cheyenne early Wednesday evening, July 14, Day 36, after a 178-mile drive from Ogallala, according to Cheyenne newspapers. Observed the *Cheyenne State Leader*:

> When the four ladies drove into town, dust covered and brown as berries from long exposure, they attracted a deal of attention and when they alighted at the Inter-Ocean Hotel there was a rush to see the travel-stained Maxwell and its four fair occupants, who are in a tour the like of which has never before been attempted by women…. When the ladies left New York many predicted that it would not be long before they were again back to the metropolis.
>
> In fact, members of the Women's Motor[ing] Club of New York, of which Mrs. Ramsey is president, claimed that neither of the occupants of the car could possibly stand the strain. Yet they have, proof of which can be had by an inspection of the outfit, and this too in spite of the fact, that both the car and its fair driver and other occupants have been out in some hard weather, especially back in Iowa and Nebraska, driving … days at a time in rain storms and through mu[d] axle-deep.[46]

In her book, Ramsey rarely mentions

dates. The three Salt Lake City newspapers agree that she arrived there on July 20; Ramsey names just four overnight stops between Cheyenne and Salt Lake City — Rock River, Rawlins, Rock Springs and Opal, Wyoming. Her party thus evidently stayed in Cheyenne on Thursday, July 15, perhaps waiting until Friday for local mechanics to complete their work: "They expect to leave here sometime tonight," Thursday's *Wyoming Tribune* reported, "after the car is repaired."[47] The newspaper did not elaborate on the nature of the repairs.

As Ramsey wrote in her *Hackensack Republican* account, Cheyenne "is probably the most typically western town as we easterners conceive of the west. The streets are full of cowboys and cowgirls, and I dare say there are more people on horseback than in any other place of its size in the states." Still, she found a garage for her horseless carriage. "The machine has been overhauled by the Cheyenne Auto and Supply company while in this city, and is in excellent condition," the *Wyoming Tribune* noted.[48]

Rockies: "Bare and Unbeautiful"

Wyoming's Maxwell agents arranged for pilot cars to accompany Ramsey's auto over most of Wyoming's indistinct trails. As Ramsey described the state for her audience back home:

> From Cheyenne we began our trip over the Rockies, which is neither so scenic a route nor so difficult a climb as I had been led to expect. The country is practically free from trees and the mountains are bare and unbeautiful. In that state, too, we found many of our worst roads, sandy, washed-out and abounding in irrigation ditches which cross the roads at any time and place. Here the

block and tackle which we had with us for this part of the trip came into fine use, and we rejoiced that we had been far-sighted enough to purchase it in time.

> Mr. [Jacob] Murdock, who crossed the continent last year in a Packard, has written a pamphlet on the interesting experiences of his tour, and in speaking of the Wyoming wash-outs says that in places they are twenty to thirty feet deep and about sixty feet across; and I think his measurements in two or three places are just about correct. I admit I scarcely expected to reach the bottom of one of these ditches in really good condition, and my courage rather failed me on the downward journey. It was all I could possibly do to hold back the weight of the car and myself alone in it with the aid of the emergency brake and foot-brake also entirely on.[49]

In her book, evidently describing the same washout, Ramsey calls it 60 feet deep. Loose gravel made it hard to pull out of the ravine, she said. "Each passenger stood ready with rocks or blocks of wood to place under the rear wheels. The method was this: Give her the gas in low and pull ahead a few inches. Block the wheels. Repeat this process again and again. Eventually, with good power, stout and willing helpers, and plenty of time and patience, we reached the crest and were up on the plateau once more."

Ramsey on Saturday, July 17, Day 39, got a permit to cross the North Platte River at Fort Steele on the Union Pacific bridge. She had to travel three-quarters of a mile, including approaches, over mostly unballasted ties. "The ties were just the correct distance apart so they might hold the wheels as in a cradle and prevent moving ahead, unless the auto was kept in motion." The bumping the car received on Saturday took its toll on tires. The axles and other parts survived but Ramsey reported two blowouts in the ensuing two days.

In Wyoming, Ramsey followed both the railroad (far right) and telegraph wires. (FLP)

Between Rawlins and Rock Springs on Sunday, July 18, "the party drove all day across the plains and the Red Desert, making 136 miles in less than seven hours, getting on the way an occasional shot at a coyote, prairie dog and such, but, woman like, missing everything," the *Salt Lake Herald* reported.[50] This unattributed account, repeated in other newspapers, of the four Hackensack women blasting away at animals clashes with Ramsey's own version. She, in fact, tells of often braking to avoid running over prairie dogs and rabbits, insisting that the only shooting she did was with a camera, because the women traveled without guns.

Biting Bedbugs, Motoring Mayors

On the unmarked Wyoming trails, Ramsey said, "Many a time we found our correct route by following poles which carried the greater number of wires. Most of the time we were right, yet there were occasions when we chose the wrong direction and were obliged to retrace our way to the intersection and try again." Throughout the West, hotels and beds were generally "acceptable" but food was "fair — sometimes poor," she said. "Whenever it became too sketchy, we could always get along by eating a slice or two of bread with the addition of butter and sugar for nourishment and energy. Fortunate it was that no member of our crew was a fussy eater."

But the bed that Ramsey and Jahns shared in their hotel at Opal Monday night, July 19, was an unacceptable one. It was teeming with bedbugs, as the pair discovered at 2 A.M. They spent the rest of the night nodding over a table in the hotel office.

In Opal, Tuesday morning, July 20, Ramsey's group met former Salt Lake City mayor Ezra Thompson, returning home with a new Pierce-Arrow from the auto factory at Buffalo, New York. Thompson was accompanied by son Lynn, "who has been attending Yale," and "local automobile agent" Frank Botterill, reported the *Salt Lake (City) Evening Telegram.*[51]

Because the Maxwell's pilot would leave them at midday, "it was wonderful to have someone who was familiar with the area whom we could follow into the Mormon capital," Ramsey wrote of the 177-mile trip from Opal, through Weber and Echo canyons to Salt Lake City. Traveling as many as 250 miles per day, the men in the Pierce-Arrow left Buffalo July 7 and reached home Tuesday a day ahead of schedule, the Wednesday *Telegram* said.

> At Opal, Wyo., Mr. Thompson and party met a party of young women from New York on a tour to San Francisco in a Maxwell car. Mrs. Ramsey of Jersey City [*sic*] has been at the wheel since the car left New York on June 9, and is declared to be one of the most daring drivers in the country. There were four young women in the car. They were escorted to the Knutsford hotel last night and will continue within a day or two on a leisurely trip to the coast.[52]

At its late-afternoon arrival Tuesday, the Maxwell's odometer showed 4,199 miles, according to the *Deseret Evening News.* But Murphy, "who travels ahead and often be-

hind the tourists, says that 1,200 miles should be deducted from this as that distance was covered in touring New Jersey." The women, who had thus traveled some 2,999 miles from New York City, rested Wednesday morning but "this afternoon and evening are enjoying the beauties of the city and the great lake," Wednesday's *Deseret Evening News* reported. "The car is being overhauled today at the Sharman garage but there is really nothing much to do with it. The engine is a bit dirty but otherwise it appears to be in splendid condition."[53]

Ramsey, however, writes that while in Salt Lake City the car received unspecified repairs to its weakened spring bumpers and shock absorbers. She also took "the precaution to have the spring leaves separated and oiled and then wrapped for protection on the desert and mountain roads ahead." Ramsey herself scraped carbon from the cylinder heads "while other things were being done" to the engine, she said without elaborating. The tourists spent Wednesday, Thursday and Friday in Salt Lake City. Two local newspapers erroneously reported that Ramsey would partially retrace her path by heading north around the Great Salt Lake. But at 10 A.M. Saturday, July 24, Day 46, the Maxwell rolled out of Salt Lake City heading south of the lake toward Reno, Nevada.

Breakdown in Utah

"With the American flag proudly fluttering in the breeze, suspended from the dash of the Maxwell car at the head of the line, the run for Callao, 140 miles, was begun," the *Reno Evening Gazette* reported.[54] The Thompson family was among "a number of enthusiastic motorists in cars" who accompanied Ramsey a ways beyond Salt Lake City.

In a 2-cylinder runabout, Sam

A prairie dog hole crippled the Maxwell near Grantsville, Utah. (FLP)

Sharman, Maxwell's Utah representative, would escort the Ramsey party from Salt Lake City to Reno. Also joining the travelers were Joe Richards in a Pierce, accompanied by his teenage nephew, Jack, and a friend, Frank Irving. Drivers of the three cars planned to head southwest as a group through Garfield and Grantsville, and then south and west across the desert into Nevada.

When Ramsey's car struck a prairie dog hole beyond Grantsville Saturday, however, "the bolt came out of the tie rod connecting the wheels," Ramsey recounted. Disconnected, the front wheels splayed and the car pitched forward, breaking a spring seat off the front axle. Ramsey wound wire tightly around the axle and spring to temporarily join the two. The car limped ahead to Orr's Ranch, where Irving used a forge to heat and wrap a steel strip around the broken joint. It was better than wire, but still a temporary fix.

They drove on until 3 A.M. Sunday,

July 25, slept three hours by the roadside east of Fish Springs and then resumed their journey to Fish Springs and Callao, Utah. The tourists missed a rainstorm but had to cross a steep washout resulting from it, measuring 12 feet wide and three or four feet deep, Ramsey said. Irving's repair gave way several times as the Maxwell crossed the ravine. Each time, Irving waded into the water, jacked up the car and replaced the steel strip. The Maxwell finally climbed out of the hole but a deeper one ahead prompted the travelers to unload the wounded auto, leave it there and return for the night to Callao in the other two cars.

Next day, Monday, July 26, Richards and his group headed back to Salt Lake City to order a new Maxwell front axle from San Francisco. Atwood, Jahns and Powell went ahead by stage coach to Ely, Nevada, leaving Sharman and Ramsey in Callao to await the axle. Later Monday, discovering the town had a good blacksmith, the two returned to Ramsey's Max-

Temporary repairs to the car's front axle gave way under the strain of crossing this washout near Callao, Utah. (FLP)

well and spent most of the day removing the axle. The blacksmith spent Tuesday and part of Wednesday repairing the damage. When the new axle failed to arrive on Thursday's 11 A.M. stage, Ramsey and Sharman drove out and installed the repaired axle on the Maxwell. Finishing at 5 P.M., they drove on to Ibapah, Utah, just a few miles from the Nevada border, where they stopped for the night. Of western Utah and the Nevada stretches to follow, Ramsey said: "Mountain after mountain we crossed, and valley after valley we passed through, with probably only a small ranch as a whole day's goal. The climbing we found rather tiresome as there was no relief from the constancy of it and no fine views to reward our tired vision. Here also we enjoyed the extreme pleasure of paying sixty-two and one-half cents per gallon for gasolene, and we used a lot there, too."[55]

Great Big Bows and Arrows

On Friday, July 30, Day 52, when Ramsey and Sharman came to an unmarked fork in the "mere trail" between Ibapah and Ely, they headed left — south toward Ely. Within a few miles, however, it was obvious they were lost. Ramsey suspected that her maps, published by the Clason Map Company of Denver, had inadvertently been shipped ahead with her passengers. But a search uncovered them under the rear seat. "It took a while to find the correct section in the right state, as they were very detailed maps occupying many separate sheets. At last we found it. Yes, *there* was the fork in the road and sure enough is was the *right* one which led up over Schellbourne Pass into the Steptoe Valley to Ely."

As they drove from Ely to Eureka, Atwood spotted a dozen mounted Indians,

Ramsey said in her book. During a 1977 "On the Road" television interview with CBS correspondent Charles Kuralt, she related the details:

> I can only think of one time when we were a little bit scared. We rounded a little hill, and off to the right was a group of Indians riding bareback, with drawn bows and arrows, great big bows and arrows. All of a sudden they wheeled to the left and came right toward us, and then my heart sort of went down in the bottom of the car, I think. Finally, in front of us, across the road, jumped a great big jackrabbit. They were hunting this poor jackrabbit with the bow and arrow, and they nonchalantly crossed the road ahead of us and paid no attention to us at all.[56]

Through Nevada, Ramsey said, "each day was a succession of more climbs, more difficulty getting on the right road, sometimes a blow-out and plenty of rough going." In her book, Ramsey writes of overnight stops west of Eureka at the Pat Walsh ranch near Austin, at Rawhide and finally at Reno. With Sharman still acting as the pilot, the cars reached Reno at nearly midnight on Tuesday, August 3, according to press accounts. Though nowhere as bad as the soggy sojourn through Iowa, "the trip from Salt Lake City to Reno was made very difficult by shifting sand, loose stones and undergrowth," a newspaper reported. As Ramsey later told a San Francisco newspaper, "Instead of following the Union Pacific trail from Ogden to San Francisco, I went by way of Ely and Austin from Salt Lake. I do not advise others to take this route, as it leads away from the railroad and from the main points of communication and the roads are bad."[57]

In Reno, the group lodged next to the Truckee River at the Riverside Hotel. "Here we found representatives of the Maxwell Company's branch ready to escort us to the coast and very enthusiastic over the success of our journey," Ramsey said.[58] The two California Maxwell representatives awaiting Ramsey were William J. Mannix of the Sacramento agency and T.F. Holmes of the San Francisco branch, Reno newspapers revealed.

California, Here We Come

During a one-day 70-mile trip from Reno on Wednesday, August 4, the burgeoning convoy headed south to Carson City, then westerly into the mountains, bound for Lake Tahoe on the Nevada-California border. Despite frequent rest breaks, the Maxwell ran hot as it climbed the steep, sandy stagecoach trail, her book relates. Finally, Ramsey raised the car's center-hinged hood, turned the lower panels under and drove on. "It was a noisy, rattling arrangement but the motor was grateful for the extra circulation of air and rewarded us by pulling all the harder if the grade demanded," she said. According to her *Hackensack Republican* account:

> The trip over the Sierra Nevadas is probably the most beautiful section of the whole distance across the continent, and while the climb is a hard one I enjoyed it fully as it afforded many chances of stopping and looking at beautiful snow-capped mountains and the low valleys beneath them. But the beauty spot of all is Lake Tahoe, the famous California lake resort set high up in the Sierras; the clear blue water reflected from the cloudless sky above it, adding to its own incomparable beauty.[59]

Ramsey and her crew spent the night in a rented cottage at Lakeside Park on the southernmost tip of Lake Tahoe, just west of the California-Nevada border. Combing through 50-year-old journal entries to write her 1961 book, Ramsey evidently erred in asserting that the New Jersey women spent

The transcontinental Maxwell at a cooling-off stop in the Sierra Nevada. "This is a steep grade, in heavy sand and at considerable altitude," Ramsey wrote in a photo album she gave to the Detroit Public Library in 1960. (FLP)

the next night in Placerville, California. Doing so, in addition to their verified stops farther west, would have put them in San Francisco a day later than their August 7 arrival.

Rather, by 6:30 P.M. on Thursday, August 5, Ramsey had pushed through to Folsom, 22 miles east of Sacramento, according to the *Sacramento Union*. In Folsom, she met a welcoming committee that had driven out from the capital city, related Friday's *Sacramento Union*:

> With childish simplicity, the little daughter of W.J. Mannix, the local manager of the Maxwell agency, elbowed her way through the crowd of felicitous admirers to thrust a huge bouquet of California roses and carnations into the hands of the plucky little woman at the wheel of the sturdy stock car which she has driven more than 5000 miles over all sorts of roads.

With a suppressed exclamation of genuine delight, Mrs. Ramsey seized the flowers and pressed them in an ecstasy of happiness to her sensitive nostrils, starved by almost endless Wyoming and Nevada deserts. "They're too lovely," she exclaimed impulsively as the exquisite flowers were handed to her companions. "You take them for a moment before I have all the aroma out of them."

.... [T.F. Holmes] gave the word to start for Sacramento, and with a tooting of horns the escort of six automobiles swung into line behind the honored party.

When Sacramento was reached the party was augmented by a dozen more automobiles, and the main streets of the town were paraded, after which Mrs. Ramsey and her party retired to their hotel....

"The California roads are the best we have driven over since leaving Chicago," said Mrs. Ramsey. "The stretch of road between Folsom and Sacramento just seemed glorious tonight after the hard roads that we have driven over in Wyoming and Nevada. We had but little tire trouble on the trip. Just had two punctures and one pinch, which you might term a puncture, and we also had three blowouts....

"I would like to have seen the Yellowstone park and also Southern California, but I have a little boy 2 years old at home, and I want to see him the most of all. I will leave San Francisco on Monday [August 9] for home....

"Women can handle an automobile just as well as men. You should have seen us get the machine out of an irrigation ditch in Wyoming. We just took our block and tackle which we carried on the rear of the machine, hooked it to a stump at the top of the ditch and although it was hard work, we got the machine out all right."[60]

A Great Outburst of Enthusiasm

"From Sacramento into Frisco is an even 150 miles, some boulevard, some pretty bad roads in process of construction which some day soon will probably be boulevards also," Ramsey wrote in the *Hackensack Republican* upon returning home.[61] On Friday, August 6, Ramsey and her escorts traveled south to Stockton and west as far as Hayward. Darkness fell before her group could reach San Francisco. On Saturday morning, August 7, 1909, 59 days after starting from New York, Ramsey drove the last few miles to Oakland, where she and her passengers waited to board the ferry to San Francisco. The San Francisco newspapers, automobile journals and Ramsey's book all fail to record her exact time of arrival. As one San Francisco newspaper recorded the finish:

When Mrs. Ramsey guided her machine from the ferry building and started up Market street on the last leg of the long journey, and although tired out and dirty and dusty from her tedious journey, she was accorded a reception such as few women receive. Automobilists by the score were on hand to greet the first women to cross the continent, and when the plucky driver and her companions made their appearance it was the signal for a great outburst of enthusiasm and welcome, and the many automobilists tooted their horns and the start up Market street was made to the company of the "honk-honk" of many horns.[62]

The first females to cross the country by auto were actually Anna D. Murdock and her daughters, Florence Lillian, 16, and Alice, 14, in the Jacob M. Murdock touring party of 1908. Ramsey was the first woman to *drive* the distance. Ramsey's car immediately went on display at the local Maxwell outlet, 342–352 Van Ness Avenue in San Francisco. Carl Kelsey, Maxwell's sales manager, "gave her a new Maxwell for her efforts — and sent the used one on exhibition to Maxwell agencies," according to one retrospective account.[63]

Observing her finish on Saturday, automobile reporter R.R. L'Hommedieu — who covered the start and finish of many a transcontinental trek for the *San Francisco Call* — drew some comparisons between male and female motorists, and between Ramsey and other female drivers:

The drive across the continent by Mrs. Ramsey and her sister motor maids is an object lesson that can not be passed over without considering. Heretofore most of such feats have been performed by women who give the impression of a certain amount of masculine composition in their make up, but in the quartette that arrived yesterday the impression was far different.

From the appearance, outside of a beautiful coat of tan, one would imagine that the car had merely been brought up from Del Monte. It was dusty, but clean. It was not caked with mud, battered and scarred, but showed that it had received treatment much more considerate than would have been given by man.

Not only was the exterior of the car pleasing, but when the hood was raised and the engine set in motion it ran as sweetly and more smoothly than the day it left the factory.[64]

False Claims of Mechanical Perfection

On Saturday night, according to the *San Francisco Examiner*, "there was a celebration banquet at the St. James Hotel … on account of the successful completion of the long tour. Many automobile enthusiasts were present."[65] Young and "charming," Ramsey "is perhaps the last person in the world that one would expect to find piloting an automobile across the continent," the *San Francisco Chronicle* said. Hers was

> as remarkable an automobile trip as any ever undertaken in this country…. Just two days less than two months was taken for the journey. The record across the continent[,] of course, is much faster than that, but it has been made by men out for speed. Even at that few have attempted the long and strenuous journey, and the feat of Mrs. Ramsey and her companions, under the circumstances, becomes all the more remarkable.[66]

In a similar vein, the Automobile Manufacturers Association declared in 1960 that Ramsey's 1909 trip "helped mightily to convince the skeptics that automobiles were here to stay — rugged and dependable enough to command any man's respect, gentle enough for the daintiest lady."[67]

Small and large alike, newspapers covering Ramsey's transcontinental trip often based their articles on Maxwell press releases, filling in with local arrival and departure details. Predictably, these factory accounts ignored the Maxwell's breakdowns, including two broken axle shafts. Ramsey apparently did the same in speaking with reporters. At least, a collection of 60 articles in newspapers and auto journals reveals no instance where Ramsey discussed mechanical troubles. A Maxwell press release from Nevada, used in a *San Francisco Chronicle* article at the conclusion, quotes Ramsey as saying "in spite of the shaking the car has had, I have yet to find anything even loosened,"[68] a statement she contradicts in her book. In an ad published a day after Ramsey's arrival, therefore, the automaker had little to fear by falsely claiming that its automobile performed flawlessly:

> In a model DA touring car Mrs. Ramsey drove her Maxwell car from New York to San Francisco over the worst possible roads, over steep grades, and made the trip, one of the most grueling imaginable, without a particle of car trouble. A trip far more difficult than the Glidden or any other tour, and finished yesterday with a perfect score.
>
> No mountains or grades too difficult for the Maxwell. No gumbo too thick, no sand too deep for the Maxwell. The only car for long or short tours. The car for a lady to drive. It is simply perfect and perfectly simple. Get a demonstration in the same model as driven by Mrs. Ramsey.[69]

"Mrs. Ramsey and her companions were the guests at luncheon yesterday of the Maxwell-Briscoe Pacific Company," according to the *Chronicle's* Sunday news columns, "and last evening they were entertained at dinner by E.A. Kelley of the Splitdorf Magneto Company at the St. James Hotel." During the trip, Ramsey had to disassemble and clean a misfiring Splitdorf spark plug. Her Splitdorf magneto first lost a vital screw and later, midway through the trip, had to be rebuilt. Still, the C.F. Splitdorf Pacific Coast branch advertised that Ramsey experienced "not the slightest bit of ignition trouble."[70]

The Ajax-Grieb Rubber Company made the unlikely claim that three of its Ajax tires ran the full distance "with the original New York air in them, and that but one puncture necessitated a change of the fourth, after several thousand miles had been covered."[71] Ramsey mentions replacing at least two tires in New York state and notes various punctures and blowouts along the route, but is silent on the total number of tires used. Retrospective accounts generally put the figure at 11 tires.

Many press accounts said Ramsey traveled 4,200 miles in a running time of 35 days. In her 1961 book and in various articles, however, Ramsey gives the mileage as 3,800; she makes no mention of the car's gas consumption. She actually traveled on 42 of the 60 calendar days that elapsed between June 9 and August 7. The 18 idle days — attributable to rest and sightseeing, breakdowns and rain delays — represent 30 percent of her elapsed time of approximately 59 days. For the 3,800-mile trip, Ramsey averaged about 90.5 miles per day and 3.77 mph for her running time, or 64.4 miles per day and 2.68 mph for her elapsed time.

Though the four women had discussed touring southern California, Ramsey recalls making a one-day visit to Los Angeles before rushing home by train to join her husband and young son. "We discovered hosts of good enthusiastic friends who seemed pleased to welcome us and who proceeded to show us the attractions of their Great West, never realizing that we are most happy when at home in our dear east which we understand and love, probably more than ever for having had all our experiences."[72]

The Achievements of a "Plucky" Woman

Ramsey's trip generated all the splashy headlines the Maxwell company could desire. But its quest for publicity prompted the automaker to sacrifice accuracy and truthfulness — asserting falsely, for instance, that "she will be unaccompanied by men." It depicted the women as less capable and more vulnerable than they were, the Maxwell as more reliable than it was and the route west as wilder than it had become by 1909. Ramsey's 1961 book reveals more than the Maxwell company did in 1909, about breakdowns and about the assistance Ramsey and her companions received from pilot cars mechanics and detailed road maps.

Egged on by the Maxwell company, the press perhaps made too great a fuss over Ramsey's gender. By overlooking the accomplishments other women had made behind the wheel, many reports — most of them based on press releases that Murphy wrote — treated Ramsey's trip as an oddity. Rather, it was a natural progression in the motoring achievements of women. As early as 1905, while he approached Chicago during his second trip across the country that year, Percy Megargel noted, "It is no uncommon sight to see a large touring car, covered with dust, baggage strapped on either running board, driven by a woman and occupied entirely by motorists of the fair sex."[73] Few reporters covering Ramsey's trip bothered to mention how close Vera McKelvie and Minerva Teape came to crossing the country in 1908 — even without factory assistance. Teape's illness canceled a trip that showed every sign of succeeding a full year before the Maxwell company sponsored Ramsey's.

The trip Ramsey records in her 1961 book was easier than the one the Maxwell company misrepresented in 1909. Other automakers, of course, had misrepresented transcontinental trips undertaken by men.

Ramsey at the wheel and Powell beside her, along with back-seat passengers Atwood, left, and Jahns. A pilot car accompanies Ramsey's Maxwell in this unidentified Midwestern scene. (NAHC)

Regardless, Ramsey's accomplishment was legitimate: It *was* the first time a woman had driven an automobile from coast to coast. Such a feat was remarkable in an age when few women worked outside the home, much less drove an auto, and women who engaged in either activity were called "plucky"—the adjective that nearly every newspaper, large or small, along her route applied to Ramsey. Ramsey's journey was also a public affirmation that women were becoming buyers and drivers of autos, and thus represented a new, growing market for automakers to supply.

Ramsey ends *Veil, Duster, and Tire Iron* without revealing the fate of the car that carried her across the country and into the history books. The Maxwell name died 16 years after Ramsey's trip, however. A recession following World War I weakened Maxwell, and a 1922 merger with the Chal-

mers Motor Car Company, makers of the Chalmers auto, did little to improve sales for either make. Engineering weaknesses—particularly its fragile rear axle—further depressed sales of the Maxwell. Hired to save the Maxwell-Chalmers company, Walter P. Chrysler reduced the large supply of unsold flawed Maxwells by recalling them to the factory, replacing the axles and correcting other problems, and redesigning future autos to produce a "Good Maxwell," which improved sales. Chrysler saved the company but phased out the Chalmers when he began selling 6-cylinder cars bearing his own name in January 1924. With alterations, the last Maxwell, 1925, became the new 4-cylinder Chrysler of 1926.[74]

"Now as I think back 53 years," Ramsey wrote in a 1962 article, "I honestly believe the really brave ones were the husband who trusted in my ability, after only a year's experience at the wheel, and the three companions who put themselves in my hands to cross that long and little-known stretch of miles." After her daughter's birth in 1910, "for a decade I left transcontinental driving to others. But I drove my children and some friends across the country in an Overland in 1919 and since then, except during World War II, have made the trip nearly every year," Ramsey said in 1964.[75] She stopped counting after her 30th transcontinental trip.

"I'm probably happiest when I'm holding on to a wheel," she confessed after a 1966 cross-country trip to attend a Vassar College reunion in Poughkeepsie, New York. Shortly after hurting her elbow in a minor fall in 1963, Ramsey drove from California to the Philadelphia area, where an X-ray showed a break. "Transcontinental driving is now so easy that you can even do it with a broken arm!" she quipped.[76]

Ramsey became something of a celebrity in her later years — and she lived to be 96. In 1939, five years after the death of husband John Ramsey, she moved northwest of Hackensack to Ridgewood, New Jersey, and in 1949 moved to Covina, California. Though it virtually ignored her originally, the *New York Times* in 1959 ran a Sunday feature noting the 50th anniversary of Ramsey's historic crossing.[77] The article contained no news about Ramsey; the reporter was clearly unaware that she was still alive. But her daughter in New Jersey, Alice Bruns, wrote a letter to the editor: "I thought it might interest you to know that mother drives east and west every year and has been doing it regularly for the past ten years, and also made many other trips prior to her residing in California."[78] Hermine Jahns and Margaret Atwood were both dead, she wrote, but Powell, 98 (remarried and named Nettie R. Lewis), "is well and lives in her own apartment in Hackensack, N.J." Powell was 101 years old when Ramsey finished her book

in September 1961. Since then, another book has revived the memory of Ramsey's trip. In 1995, Patricia Rusch Hyatt published *Coast to Coast with Alice*, a children's book based on Ramsey's 1961 account of her historic journey. Hyatt's book uses actual trip photos but imaginary journal entries to review the trip as Hermine Jahns, the youngest crew member, might have seen it.[79]

Decades after her 1909 trip, Ramsey received many honors. In 1960, the American Automobile Association heralded Ramsey as "Woman Motorist of the Century." The Automobile Manufacturers Association named her "First Lady of Automotive Travel," and three large antique-auto clubs — the Antique Automobile Club of America, Horseless Carriage Club of America and Veteran Motor Car Club of America — made her an honorary member.[80] Since first taking the wheel in 1908, she had received just one ticket, in 1953, for pulling a U-turn in a business district. "Covina was just being built up then and I didn't think of it as a business district," Ramsey explained in a 1971 *Los Angeles Times* interview.[81]

She continued her driving in America and abroad. "Her last challenge was driving the six passes (completing five of them) through the Alps in Switzerland," according to a short biography. "A snowstorm closed the road one day before her attempt to drive the sixth pass, and her doctor forbade her from trying again because of her pacemaker."[82] Ramsey was on her fourth pacemaker in 1981, she told an interviewer. She died September 10, 1983, in Covina.

In later years, Ramsey freely voiced her opinions about good driving, as Charles Kuralt learned. "These young people — they get a little smarty cat, you know, and they sneak in because they think it'll frighten somebody," she told him as they drove in her car. "Well, that's not my idea of good driving. They may be fast, but sooner or later, they're gonna catch it."[83]

Chapter Three

"The Car, the Girl and the Wide, Wide World"

Blanche Stuart Scott in an Overland, 1910

When Scott and Gertrude Phillips drove the Overland on an exhibition lap at the Indianapolis Motor Speedway, "they made such a hit that they divided interest with the racers."

— *Toledo (Ohio) Daily Blade*

In 1910, the same year she first flew an airplane, Blanche Stuart Scott drove from New York to San Francisco in a white Overland car fitted with a built-in wardrobe trunk and a toilet. She was the first woman to drive cross America, insisted the Willys-Overland Company, blithely ignoring Alice Ramsey's crossing the previous year. But such was the power of advertising: Without a backward glance, many of the same newspapers and auto journals that heralded Ramsey's first crossing by a woman in 1909 gave Scott the same attention during the second "first crossing by a woman," which began in New York City on May 16, 1910.

Growing up in Rochester, New York, Scott worshipped the hometown hero, Percy Megargel, who crossed the country three times by auto in 1905 and 1906. Inspired by Megargel, she gave up other "tomboyish" activities for automobiles, Scott wrote in an unpublished autobiography titled *Not on a Broom*.[1] During her 68-day journey,

Scott meandered from one Overland dealer to another. In fact, the itinerary of the trip has been laid out to pass as many cities and towns as possible, the *New York Times* revealed,[2] making Scott's trip, like Ramsey's, more of a publicity tour than an endurance run.

Scott, for instance, headed sharply southwest from Cleveland to see the auto races at Indianapolis, then backtracked to call on the Willys-Overland factory at Toledo, Ohio. Like Ramsey, however, she generally followed the standard transcontinental route through the heart of America, using road maps and often following pilot cars. One difference, however, was that Scott hobnobbed with the rich and famous en route, from a noted writer in New York state to Barney Oldfield at the Indianapolis Motor Speedway. In California at the end of the run, she reportedly met aviator Glenn Martin, a rising star among early airplane manufacturers.

Scott traveled on muddy roads as far

west as Ohio, as well as in Colorado and eastern Wyoming. On her earlier trip, Ramsey spent two weeks slithering across Iowa on gumbo trails. Luckier, Scott crossed Iowa on dry roads, "the best I have found since leaving New York." In eastern Wyoming, Scott lost her way, driving aimlessly over a trail through the Rocky Mountains late one night. Roads were "packed hard as flint" in western Wyoming, *Automobile* said, and Scott encountered good road conditions from there to the coast.[3] From the road, Scott sent regular telegrams that went to 175 Overland dealers, who showed Scott's daily progress by moving a cardboard car along a special display map in their front windows. The Overland journey badly upset some other automakers: In Omaha, Nebraska, an agent for a competing firm offered Scott $5,000 to abandon her trip.

Despite Overland press releases assuring that "Miss Scott has had absolutely no trouble with her car,"[4] her auto broke a wheel in New York state and two front springs in the Midwest. The "Lady Overland," as the car was dubbed, presumably needed other minor repairs — as did most transcontinental cars — but newspapers and auto journals failed to detail such mishaps. The wheel and spring repairs might also have escaped detection if not for competing automakers, who often sent their agents to travel with Scott in hopes of witnessing just such breakdowns.

The Maxwell-Briscoe Motor Company, which sponsored Ramsey's trip in 1909, undoubtedly alerted Willys-Overland officials to their error in claiming Scott's 1910 crossing as the first by a woman. Yet the automaker persisted in its ruse — with Scott's collaboration. Decades later in her autobiography, Scott insisted upon calling herself "the first woman to drive an auto coast to coast."[5] In making other minor claims, Willys-Overland credited Scott with breakthroughs that unquestionably be-

longed to Ramsey: "Miss Blanche Stuart Scott, of Rochester, N.Y.[,] in an Overland car, was the first person to inaugurate a transcontinental motor trip undertaken for the purpose of interesting women in the value of motor car driving, the wonderful educational possibilities attending such a trip across our continent, and the benefits of long distance touring from a health standpoint."[6]

Harry Tuttle, Overland's traveling press agent, was more modest — and closer to the truth — during a stop in Council Bluffs, Iowa, telling reporters "Miss Scott will be the first person to cross the country since the laying out of the new transcontinental road."[7] But his later press releases nonetheless perpetuated the fiction that Ramsey's trip never occurred.

Great Drum-Beating

In 1909, Ramsey had declared her intention of driving, changing tires and making other routine repairs herself during her trip from New York to San Francisco. She set out in a Maxwell auto "to demonstrate that women are independent of mere men and that they can and dare brave the wilds of various parts of the country, overcome many difficulties and take care of themselves."[8] Some newspaper stories based on Willys-Overland press releases would use this same "mere men" phrase in reporting Scott's trip.

The Willys-Overland Company had a nearly identical purpose in mind for Scott, even down to the wording: "She wants to prove that two girls can go anywhere without the protection of men and she desires to prove that a woman is capable of handling a gasoline car, even to fixing punctures, looking after the engine and putting on tires," said the *Cleveland Plain Dealer*, which received Overland press releases, as did other newspapers on the route. As the

Blanche Stuart Scott in her Overland. (NAHC)

Maxwell-Briscoe company did for Ramsey, Willys-Overland reserved for Scott the option of seeking help from blacksmiths or mechanics for major repairs. She was thus "as independent of garages as a male tourist," the *Des Moines (Iowa) Evening Tribune* concluded.[9] As Scott told the *New York Times* before starting her trip: "It is my belief that touring, especially some distance, has never been indulged in by the different lady motorists largely on account of their extreme modesty or self-depreciation rather than on account of physical unfitness or inability on their part."[10]

Thus, according to *Motor Field*, Scott was "willing to be a sort of Joan of Arc of motoring to lead her sisters into a campaign to demonstrate that woman is not merely an ornament at the wheel of a motor car — that she is not to be confined to the simple child's task of driving a slow electric vehicle."[11]

The automaker's ulterior motive was "to demonstrate to the women of the country the practicability of gasoline cars for the use of women ... and the advantages in general of this kind of car for the use of the great and growing army of automobile tourists," observed the *Omaha Sunday World-Herald* when Scott arrived. Willys-Overland, which claimed to have 2,000 of its autos on the streets of New York City,[12] was hoping the trip to the West Coast would further boost sales in the East. Scott later suggested: "New York City was the key in the Willys-Overland Company's publicity. It was there that they, with great drum-beating and much fanfare, proclaimed that a woman could and *would* drive one of their cars on the long and very rugged coast to coast trip."

"She's a Hummer"

Scott's personal reasons for driving from coast to coast were different from the company's, however. At least two accounts say Scott proposed the trip to improve her health. "Miss Scott is taking the trip partly to recuperate from a nervous condition brought about by her social duties in the Camera City," the *Chicago Inter Ocean* maintained. "She expects to be in perfect health by the time the long tour has culminated" in San Francisco.[13] But as Scott tells it, after graduating from a New England boarding school — she does not say when or where — she moved to New York City. There, "circumstances tossed me into a very knowledgeable and news-making group ... chiefly theatrical personalities whose names were spoken with respect throughout the land. As a great egotist, I thirsted to gain their fame, adulation and importance."

Remembering Megargel's transcontinental exploits (but forgetting Alice Ramsey's), Scott concluded that "no woman had ever driven across the country," she wrote decades later in her autobiography. After comparing the different makes of autos through ads, Scott approached her prospective sponsor when "it was finally decided that Ford's arch rival, Willys-Overland[,] might be the lucky one."

Contradicting Scott, at least one account (in the Ely, Nevada, newspaper) contends that the Overland company approached Scott with the trip idea: "The plan of advertising the Overland automo-

bile and the *Wide World* magazine throughout the country was conceived last spring by Mr. Tuttle and through his efforts Miss Scott was persuaded to drive the machine on the four thousand mile journey."

Another object of Scott's trip, said the *San Francisco Examiner*, was "to make road maps and through assistance of the Automobile Club of America start a campaign for a transcontinental highway." In fact, Scott claimed in post-run interviews that from Salt Lake City to Sacramento "we have laid out a new route for the Blue Book,"[14] a reference to the road guides published by the Automobile Blue Book Publishing Company of New York City.

In the issue of the automaker's house organ, *Overland Scout*, that announced Scott's upcoming trip, the Willys-Overland Company printed a poem titled "The Overland Girl":

> She's a sprinter in the winter,
> Through the spring and fall.
> In the summer, she's a hummer.
> Holds the men in thrall.
> Now love's meeting, pleasure fleeting.
> Life's a merry whirl,
> For the daring, scaring, flashing,
> Dashing Overland Girl.[15]

"If she is successful, Miss Scott will receive $1,000," according to *Automobile*. Actually, her fee was much higher, according to the free-lance writer to whom Scott dictated her adventures decades later. "She made a deal for $5000.00 and expenses with Willys[-]Overland to drive a stock model car coast to coast with dealer stopovers enroute," William J. Adams contended.[16]

According to *Overland Scout* magazine, sales manager Frederic A. Barker organized the coast-to-coast trip as a $1,000 bet with a man he met in Kansas City, Missouri:

It seems that Mr. Barker had, in the course of conversation with H.G. Kirkland, of that place, made the statement that an intelligent woman could drive one of his cars anywhere, and that even a trans-continental trip would be among the easy possibilities.

"All this talk about 'the awful privations of cross-country riders, their perils and the tremendous difficulties encountered' is pure exaggeration," said Mr. Barker, "written merely to advertise the few cars which have been driven from coast to coast. Why, even a woman could drive a car anywhere they went. I have half a mind to start someone off now, to demonstrate it…. I'll wager you a thousand dollars, here and now, that a woman will drive an Overland this summer from New York to 'Frisco, all without the slightest assistance, and with no troubles that she cannot herself surmount."

This proposition was immediately taken up and Miss Scott's daring trip is the result.[17]

Amy and Gertrude

Only her maid would accompany Scott, according to a preview article in the May 5, 1910, *Automobile.* Late in the tour, referring to "her colored maid," an Overland agent's ad in a Salt Lake City newspaper repeated this error, which apparently originated in the automaker's *Overland Scout* magazine. Many other articles left the impression that Scott was making a solo trip. As far west as Nebraska, the newspapers that named Scott's traveling companion called her Miss Amy L. (for Lyman) Phillips, variously reported to be a newspaper correspondent or "well known writer" from Boston, New York City or Rochester. After an all-day drive, "she is kept busy sometimes until the wee small hours in furnishing accounts of the day's doings to the factory and the hundreds of

newspapers and trade publications that are watching the trip with considerable interest," said the *Toledo Daily Blade.*[18]

In a collection of 100 articles on Scott's trip, the first mention of "Gertrude Phillips" appears in the *Toledo Daily Blade*; the last mention of "Amy Phillips" appears in a southeastern Nebraska newspaper. One retrospective article accounts for this name change: "For a few days Blanche's traveling companion was Amy Phillips, but the travel routine was too rugged so her sister Gertrude undertook the task."[19]

Amplifying this, the *Toledo Daily Blade* said Amy Phillips accompanied Scott as far as Toledo, but that her sister Gertrude took her place for the remainder of the trek. In photos, Amy appears to be the older of the sisters. "Miss Amy Phillips is a newspaper free lance in the east and returned home to look after her private affairs, leaving her sister, who joined Miss Scott in Indianapolis, to continue the journey westward."[20] Scott drove first to Indianapolis and then backtracked to Toledo. The *Blade* implies, without explaining how, that all three women rode in the two-person car between Indianapolis and Toledo. Perhaps one of the Phillips sisters actually took the train between the two cities.

In a series of pre-run publicity photos, Scott appears in some scenes with Amy and other scenes with Gertrude Phillips, suggesting that the switch in Toledo was prearranged. According to many accounts, Gertrude was from Colebrook, New Hampshire, and was also a writer. Mentioning only Gertrude Phillips in her own account of the journey, Scott says the "talented newspaperwoman was to accompany me. Her chore was to create a little booklet of the trip highlights which Willys-Overland later used as an advertising handout," published as *5000 Miles Overland.*

Gertrude Phillips, "a buxom blonde of 23 … is a young newspaper writer, who is also familiar to magazine readers," as the

Gertrude Phillips. (NAHC)

Cheyenne (Wyo.) State Leader put it. "Her home is in Boston and having been a chum of Miss Scott at college, she arranged to take the trip also." In an evident reference to Gertrude, the *New York Morning Telegraph* reported that "Miss Phillips ... is an expert at the culinary art, being the editor of a noted cooking magazine." Together, the automaker said in its *Overland Scout* magazine, Scott and the younger Phillips were "just two happy, fearless American girls."[21]

The Willys-Overland Company hired Harry Tuttle of New York City, mentioned in newspapers from the Midwest to the West Coast, as Scott's traveling press agent. "I have a special assignment from the *New York Telegraph*, *Motor Age* and *The Automobile*," Tuttle told the *Council Bluffs Sunday Nonpareil*. "I travel on trains where the schedule makes it possible for me to keep up with Miss Scott, and at other times I use my car." One Nebraska newspaper said Tuttle, "who is making a blue print of the road which will be a guide to all autoists in the future," was also sending special reports to the *Toledo Times*.[22]

Tuttle's "persuasive ways brought amazing returns," as he got articles in most of the big daily newspapers, Scott wrote. His persuasive ways also got other results: Scott in later years recalled that "the press agent who later became my husband proceeded us via train and arranged the welcoming proceedings in each city."

To prepare for the trip, Scott recalls, she spent several weeks in Toledo at the Willys-Overland plant "in a cram course on engine care. There was also detailed instruction on tire changing. The demountable rim hadn't been invented and changing a tire was a major operation requiring the removal of the rim. This should have been labeled 'Obstacle Course' ... it was rugged," she writes. "There was also the daily proving ground driving to improve proficiency," according to one retrospective account.[23]

Even before Scott started her trip, the automaker did all it could to publicize its transcontinental stunt. "During the past week," the *New York Morning Telegraph* wrote a day before her departure, "Miss Scott and her car have been the center of much attention at the Actors' Fund Fair, where she conducted a $100 prize guessing contest for the nearest guess as to the number of miles that will be recorded on her odometer when she reaches the Mayor's office in San Francisco."[24] Later articles never revealed how close the winning guess came to Scott's actual mileage.

Starting a "Pleasure Jaunt"

Scott began her adventure in a slightly modified 1910 Overland Model 38 on Monday, May 16, according to the New York City dailies. Before departing, she received a letter addressed from New York City

Gertrude Phillips, right, hands a spark plug to Scott, who demonstrates her mechanical abilities for an Overland publicity photo. (NAHC)

Mayor William J. Gaynor to San Francisco Mayor Patrick H. McCarthy, along with a bottle of Atlantic Ocean water to pour into the Pacific Ocean at San Francisco. Observed a *New York Herald* reporter: "Apparently as unconcerned as if bent on a run through Central Park, two young women, Miss Blanche S. Scott and Miss Amy L. Phillips, left City Hall in an automobile shortly after noon ... with San Francisco as their objective point.... The tourists were escorted from City Hall to the Claremont, on Riverside Drive, by a number of other Overland owners."[25]

Forty cars escorted the women from City Hall, down Broadway to Times Square, according to the *New York Times*, which differed from most accounts by fixing the official starting point at the Hotel Cumberland. The Overland was "decorated with flowers and flags, making an attractive sight," observed the *New York Morning Telegraph*.[26] "Miss Scott's escort from Times Square, up Fifth avenue, across 57th street and up Broadway to Riverside Drive was big enough to take on the appearance of a parade," reported the *New York Tribune*. Other accounts neglect to estimate the crowd size but "cheering thousands lined Fifth Avenue for many blocks," Gertrude Phillips wrote. As the *Tribune* continued the narrative:

On the way out of the city a luncheon was served at the Claremont, on Riverside Drive, at which sixty covers were laid. This luncheon was given by Mrs. Gertrude Hohlman, a personal friend of Miss Scott, who prompted by enthusiasm came to New York for the purpose. Her guests included sixteen women motor enthusiasts of New York, several men who admired Miss Scott's fight for

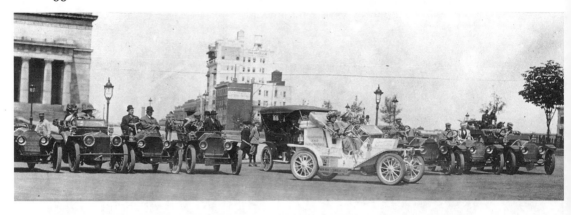

Attended by a line of escorting autos, Scott, left, and Amy Phillips pose in the Lady Overland near Grant's Tomb, far left. (NAHC)

recognition in transcontinental touring, and members of the press.... The car bearing the membership flags of the Automobile Club of America, the American Automobile Association and the newly organized Touring Club of America led the way.

At the luncheon thoroughly informal but abnormally sincere remarks and good wishes were extended by some of the oldest motoring enthusiasts of this country. It was exactly 2:37 o'clock when amid cheers Miss Scott started across the viaduct, with Poughkeepsie her first night's goal.[27]

Other news articles offer conflicting information: Scott left the Claremont at not 2:37 but 2:30 P.M., according to the *New York Herald*. No, Scott made her start from the Claremont "with all the éclat of a social function" at 3 P.M., according to *Automobile*. (To calculate the elapsed time of Scott's trip, her official start is considered to be noon from City Hall.) She posed for photographers in front of Grant's Tomb on Riverside Drive, overlooking the Hudson River at 123rd Street.

"In reply to the good wishes expressed by the guests at luncheon, Miss Scott said: 'It's starting in a pleasure jaunt but we are going through.'" Indeed, the automaker contended that one glance "at the charming

Miss Scott's sturdy figure, her determined little chin and steady blue eyes is sufficient to convince one that it will take more than ordinary difficulties to prevent her going through to 'Frisco in good time."[28]

And what was "good time"? "There is no time limit set for her accomplishment of the trip," *Motor Age* and other reports said at the start. In the Midwest, however, newspapers revealed that Scott "intends to reach the western coast during the first week in August in order to join a party of friends who are going to Japan."[29] Later, newspapers in Salt Lake City reported Scott's desire to reach San Francisco on or before July 25 — a goal she achieved.

Admiring Percy

In her autobiography, Blanche Stuart Scott describes herself as "the only child of moderately well to do parents with all the advantages of a 'proper' upbringing." Her father, John Stuart Scott, was president of the Rochester Chemical Company, reportedly a patent-medicine business. "My parents insisted I think and act for myself." Pursuing "tomboyish" activities as a child, "I determinedly tried to learn trick bicycle riding. It wasn't easy but I made it. I also made it to an ice skating championship...."

Earlier, the coast-to-coast auto appeared outside New York City's Overland agency. (NAHC)

I felt that there was always some interesting new stunt to learn, some new challenge for my wits, skills and interests." And then she crossed paths with hometown hero Percy Megargel, who, with co-drivers, drove in the first transcontinental race (1905) and made the first double transcontinental trip, which was also the first wintertime crossing (1905–6):

> He was a man, to me, whose thinking had scope and imagination. He was not afraid of the first step into adventure.... Percy was the boy-friend of the beautiful young thing next door. I am sure that I, along with the other neighborhood kids, greatly impeded the pace of their romance. With Percy's arrival came all his wide-eyed admiring sycophants, thirsting for every word of his great adventure and probing and prying with endless questions. Exposure to this Machine-Age Paragon infected me with the automobile virus.

Though a young teenager, Scott recalls, she lobbied hard until her parents bought her a 1-cylinder Cadillac, which she

drove around Rochester. One night, on country roads near town, while driving by the feeble glow of the auto's kerosene lamps, Scott saw the light of an oncoming bicycle, she recalled:

> I rang my bell ... but the light came straight towards us without deviating from its course in the middle of the road. "Stay where you are, fellows, I'll go between you!" a voice rang out from behind the light. There was a crash as he hit, fair and square between the two lamps on my car. We dug him out of the radiator, not much the worse for wear, but his bicycle was beyond redemption. The poor man never again mistook automobile lamps for those of bicycles.[30]

When some residents complained about Scott's driving, the city council met to "stop this child from driving a dangerous vehicle," but was powerless to act: Rochester at that time did not require a driver's license.

How old was Scott in 1910 when she became the second woman to drive across America? The few newspapers to give her

Scott, left, and Amy Phillips early in the transcontinental journey. (AAMA)

age said the "Rochester society girl" was 25. "At the age of 20 she took to motoring for the sake of her health, and became proficient in handling all types of cars in a short time," *Motor Age* observed.[31] That was five years earlier, she told the *New York Times* in 1910. So Scott would have been a "child" of 20 — not 13, as she claims in her autobiography — when the Rochester City Council sought to curb her Cadillac.

The book *Women Aloft* puts Scott's birth at "about 1890," though other sources say April 8, 1889, April 8, 1891, and 1892. In later years, Scott told an interviewer that she was born in 1894.[32] According to her obituary in the January 13, 1970, *New York Times*, she died at age 84. If her birthday was truly April 8, Scott was thus born in 1885, meaning she was 25 when she drove across the country.

Automobile, the *Columbus (Ohio) Dispatch*, and other 1910 press accounts report that Scott was a graduate of Vassar College in Poughkeepsie, N.Y. "I stopped at Vassar, where I graduated three years ago," she told the *Des Moines Register and Leader*, while relating a long list of experiences since leaving New York City.[33] Alice Ramsey was a non-graduating member of the same Vassar class of 1907. Scott's birth in 1885 would have made her 22 in 1907, the traditional age for graduating from college. Scott's autobiography mentions "a New England boarding school" but not Vassar, which has no record of her enrollment. More likely, she was "educated at Misses

School for Girls in Rochester, Howard Seminary in Massachusetts and Fort Edward College in New York," as one of her obituaries states.[34]

Across New York state beyond Poughkeepsie, Amy Phillips and Scott traveled through Albany — where they met Governor Charles Evans Hughes — Utica, Syracuse, her hometown of Rochester, and Buffalo, where she arrived on Sunday, May 22, according to *Motor Age*. Scott's mother was among an escort of autos that met the women at Seneca Falls, east of Rochester. At Utica, "they met 'Fighting Bob' Evans, who gave them large autographed photographs of himself." Robley D. Evans was the "popular" retired admiral of the U.S. Navy, according to the Willys-Overland Company.[35]

Heavy rains forced Scott to use tire chains in the swamps near Montezuma, between Syracuse and Rochester, *Automobile* reported. While in Buffalo, Scott traveled a few miles north to visit Niagara Falls, where she attended "a luncheon engagement given by the women motorists of Buffalo, with their escorts." She also took a side trip south to East Aurora, New York, "where a call was made on Elbert Hubbard, the famous writer and editor of the *Philistine*."[36]

Following the Lake Erie shoreline southwest of Buffalo brought the Lady Overland to "a highly crowned piece of road just outside of the little town of Angola, N.Y., [where] we skidded into a ditch and cracked several spokes in one of the rear wheels," as Scott described the widely reported incident to the *Des Moines Register and Leader*. "After getting the car back into the road I found it thoroughly equal to traveling a slow pace and sought the local blacksmith. We spent a most enjoyable night at a little inn, where a dance was

A blacksmith in Angola, New York, fashioned this brace to strengthen the Overland's damaged wheel. (**June 9, 1910,** *Automobile*)

given for us by the sympathetic and interesting townspeople. In the meantime the smithy made a permanent repair,"[37] reinforcing the right rear wheel by clamping a round iron band to the spokes midway between the hub and the rim.

Overland: A Dainty Car

Scott was driving a $1,000 Overland 38, often referred to as a modified roadster or runabout with a large wooden trunk added to the back, containing luggage compartments. Her car was white, most press accounts agree — "gray" to two Salt Lake City newspapers — with nickel-plated "trimmings" or brightwork. The Overland

Scott, left, and Gertrude Phillips demonstrate the trunk's carrying capacity in this publicity pose. (AAMA)

was a "dainty white and gold car," observed the *Toledo Daily Blade*. The automaker described it, variously, as a "white and silver beauty" and "the beautiful white and gold Overland"—silver or gold evidently being the color of the car's ample lettering.[38]

Scott drove a virtual signboard. Photos of the car reveal the words "Overland in an Overland" painted on the hood; the car's nickname, "Lady Overland," near the seat base on both sides; "The Car, the Girl and the Wide, Wide World Between New York and San Francisco" painted on the trunk and both sides; and a "New York to San Francisco" sign hanging below each running board. The radiator carried an American Automobile Association emblem.

In keeping with the car's nickname, some newspapers referred to Scott and her companion as the "Overland girls."

Generating 25 horsepower with $3\frac{3}{4} \times 4\frac{1}{2}$-inch cylinders cast individually rather than in pairs or as a block, the 4-cylinder engine was water cooled but lacked a water pump. For its ignition system, the Overland used a Remy magneto with a coil-and-battery backup. The Lady Overland was one of 15,598 cars that John North Willys produced for 1910 in the former Pope-Toledo auto factory in Toledo. That was triple the 4,907 cars he made for 1909, and dwarfed his 1908 production of 465 cars. Equipped with Goodyear tires and a 2-speed planetary transmission, the transcontinental auto had a 102-inch wheelbase

Scott packs extra inner tubes into a box on the Overland's right side. (NAHC)

and, more important, a generous ground clearance of 10¾ inches at the differential.[39]

If the automaker installed an oversize gas tank, as so many transcontinental cars carried, the press made no mention of it. Except for installing a trunk behind the car and placing an acetylene tank beneath the crank handle in front of the radiator, the factory reportedly gave Scott a stock Overland. Three suitcases fit neatly inside the trunk, photos reveal.

Dipping into their suitcases upon arriving in Salt Lake City, the women "changed their traveling costume, consisting of khaki divided riding skirts, army shirts of olive drab and high-laced boots, to what Miss Scott termed some 'real clothes,'" a local newspaper reported. "The travelers carry besides the suit cases another which is sent from stop to stop with laundry," according to the Toledo newspaper. "They also have thermos bottles, field glasses, rubber cushions, rubber ponch[os] for rainy weather, a camera and an automatic revolver which has a formidable look."[40] The women also equipped the car with "two spare tires ... a tent, water bottles, two five-gallon cans of gas and oil, acetylene gas for the night lamps, a compressed air cylinder for first aid to flats, tools and a block and tackle," Scott recalled.

The silk tents and "dehydrated food-stuffs, aluminum dishes and alcohol lamps, together with other necessities for camping out on the way," actually awaited them at Hastings, Nebraska, reported the *Nebraska State Journal* of nearby Lincoln. According to other reports, either the women or Tuttle in his pilot car also carried an ax and a "medicine chest."[41]

Having "A Bully Time"

The auto reached Cleveland on Thursday, May 26, Day 11 of the trip, Friday's *Cleveland Plain Dealer* reported. "Twenty-two Cleveland motorists met Miss Scott near Painesville yesterday afternoon and accompanied her to The Hollenden." Scott, who arrived at 3:30 P.M., "says she is having a bully time."[42] Added the *Cleveland Leader*:

> Although the roads between New York city (Miss Scott's starting point) and Cleveland are ordinarily fair, during the last week they have been veritable quagmires for many miles. The result has been that Miss Scott has been obliged to make many long detours and in a number of places has found herself in mud up to the axles of the wheels, all of which necessitate slow running and careful driving.
>
> Several times the intrepid young lady has been caught in violent thunder storms so severe that she has been forced to seek refuge in farmhouses and other wayside shelters, but she has pushed forward day by day and is still fully confident and full of enthusiasm as to her ability to finish the trip. Miss Scott is of the opinion that the famous comet has had considerable to do with the weather. Consequently she is rather opposed to comets in general and Halley's comet in particular. However, she says that now

her friend, the comet, has proceeded on its way she hopes for better weather conditions.[43]

Scott's social schedule during the auto trip from New York to San Francisco was at least as rigorous as the driving. "City celebrations usually found us flanked by the Mayor and his retinue of officials, VIP's from the automobile clubs plus VIP's who were just auto enthusiasts. The spontaneous greetings were great but there was always more driving just ahead for me." Work awaited her even after a full day of driving and greeting, she wrote: "Nightly it was my job to send a similarly worded telegram to the one hundred and seventy five Overland agencies[,] giving them a fix on our route. In each Overland dealer's window was a painted map of the United States. The arrival of the wire [telegram] moved a small cardboard cutout of Gertrude and me in the car to the current position. The display of the wire adjacent to the cutout underlined the authenticity of the message."

From Cleveland, Scott headed southwest for Indianapolis, where she hoped to see the Indianapolis Motor Speedway races on Memorial Day. The tourists thus left Cleveland on Friday, May 27, bound for Columbus. At the State Capitol Building in Columbus, Scott met Governor Judson Harmon, "a firm believer in outdoor sports for women," according to one account:

> The Governor was very much interested in her tour and asked her many questions concerning it. When Miss Scott told him that she was making the trip to demonstrate to the automobile world that a woman can drive her car across the country as well as a man, he applauded her vigorously.
>
> "Good work," he cried; "I am glad to see that one woman at least has the courage of her convictions. I wish that I could take just such a trip," he continued,

Ohio Governor Judson Harmon chats with Scott, left, and Amy Phillips in Columbus. (NAHC)

enthusiastically. "After a hard winter's weary round of routine I feel like getting out and communing with nature in just such a way as you are doing. It's the only way. You never could see the world out of a [railroad] car window like you two girls are seeing it in your automobile."[44]

Never mind that Scott and Phillips had scarcely started communing with nature. They fully intended to, Scott told the *Columbus Dispatch*:

I am awfully keen for the camping-out experiences which we anticipate in the Far West. We will take on our camping outfit at Hastings, Neb., thus relieving ourselves of the burden of this additional baggage through the East and middle West; and, after the hotel accommodations, which we will have enjoyed up to that point, I think that cooking our own meals and sleeping out of doors will be a great lark. And then, just think of going through historic Death valley and across the desert! If I do any fast driving on my trip, it is certainly going to be in the East because I am just crazy about the novel experiences which we anticipate in the western states.[45]

Ladies, Start Your Engines!

In the meantime, Amy Phillips and Scott spent the night in Columbus at the

Chittenden Hotel and left at noon Saturday, May 28, for Indianapolis. An Ohio Automobile Company ad heralded the Lady Overland's arrival in Dayton: "A car containing such simple and reliable construction, that a trans-continent trip has no worry for a young woman to attempt, is surely the car you want to drive. Any woman can drive an Overland."[46]

Making history herself, Scott viewed history in the making that Saturday afternoon at Dayton. "At the outskirts of the city we ran into the greatest people jam I've ever seen. Close to ten thousand were witnesses to a real earth shaker. Aviation history was being written as two planes were up over the same field *at the same time*.... The pilots were Wilbur Wright and the Wright Brothers' first pupil, Al Wel[s]h. As we saw history created I sat in our little Overland and said smugly to Gertrude 'Those men are nuts. They gotta be.'"[47]

Phillips and Scott "were royally entertained" at Indianapolis, home to an Overland factory, and visited the Indianapolis Motor Speedway races Monday, according to the *Toledo Daily Blade*. Scott drove the Overland around the brick race track, according to one account. "Here they made such a hit that they divided interest with the racers."[48]

Before 55,000 fans at the race track Monday, Barney Oldfield in a Benz set an American speedway record in the mile (35.6 seconds); Ray Harroun, driving the Marmon "Wasp" in which he won the 200-mile race at Indianapolis two days earlier, set a 50-mile record in his engine class. But later, the Marmon "burst a tire and hurled itself on the cement wall that guards the upper margin of the track," according to one press account. "Sliding along the top of the wall, the car tore a furrow in the cement for fifty feet and then toppled over, flinging Harroun from his seat. He picked himself up unhurt, but his 'Wasp' was a snarl of steel."[49]

Scott had better luck on the track that day, she reported in a broadcast writing style, using ellipses to represent pauses: "Thrill on thrill ... I met the famous racing driver, Barney Oldfield. He allowed me to drive his world famed Green Dragon. On the Speedway track I couldn't get it above eighty miles an hour even though not all the horses were going for me ... speed beyond that was too much for me. I wasn't strong enough to hold the wheel on the oblong track. I felt I was somebody. I sailed all that day on Cloud Nine."[50]

The Wet, Wet World

After Indianapolis, Amy Phillips and Scott backtracked to Toledo, and reached the headquarters of the Willys-Overland Company from Fort Wayne, Indiana, on Thursday, June 2, 1910, Day 18. Indiana's roads were flawless, according to Scott, but a "driving rain" forced the transcontinental car to wallow in mud between Defiance, Ohio, and Toledo. Consequently, reported Friday's *Toledo Daily Blade*:

> When the two young women reached the Secor [Hotel] they were fatigued and besmeared with mud.... A big reception had been planned in their honor by the local agent of the Overland. Fifteen automobiles, containing Toledo auto enthusiasts, were to have met the travelers at Maumee and accompany them to this city, but the weatherman stepped in and the scheme was abandoned....
>
> After they had reached the Secor and gained the shelter of their room their spirits soon revived and at 7 o'clock they appeared in the dining room as well groomed and as cheerful as though they had just come in from the east on the Twentieth Century Limited.
>
> After dinner they held a little informal reception [for] officials of the Overland company and others interested in their journey.... The "Overland Girls" are

attracting as much attention from the women of the country as they are from the men. Ever since they waved farewell to their New York friends and rolled away toward the setting sun in their dainty white and gold car they have been besieged with inquiries from women all along the line as to the contents of their wardrobe boxes.

These women have marveled at the fresh and dainty appearance of the Overland girls when, after a hard day's run like that of yesterday, which would have taxed the strength and endurance of any man, they have appeared apparently guiltless of fatigue and gowned in correct evening dress, adapted to the requirements of the particular city in which they happened to be, or to the smartness of the best hotel.[51]

Between New York City and Toledo, Scott's Overland had twice skidded off muddy roads into ditches, according to the Willys-Overland Company. Scott drove 14 days to reach Toledo and it had rained on 10 of them, noted the automaker, which suggested revising the sign on the Overland to read: "The Car, the Girl and the Wet, Wet World."[52]

The Overland travelers would spend the weekend in Toledo, leaving on Monday, June 6, for South Bend, Indiana, according to the *Blade*. Gertrude Phillips was aboard for the trip to Chicago, replacing sister Amy. Upon arriving on Tuesday, Day 23, in Chicago, where the women stayed at the Blackstone Hotel, Scott "declared that she was certain she could achieve the distinction of being the first woman to make such an automobile trip," reported the *Chicago Inter Ocean*.[53] Memories were short at the *Inter Ocean*, which one year earlier had reported the arrival of the first female transcontinental driver, Alice Ramsey. Scott had traveled on 16 of the 23 calendar days since leaving New York City, 11 of which were rainy, according to *Automobile*. Ramsey traveled about 1,000 miles on her direct route to Chicago; on her meandering route, Scott traveled 1,987 miles, *Automobile* said.

Phillips and Scott spent Wednesday, Thursday and Friday in Chicago. On Saturday, June 11, they drove north to Milwaukee, where they planned to remain on Sunday, according to the *Inter Ocean*. The 90-mile detour to Milwaukee was to "accept the entertainment of a friend," Scott said.[54] Scott and Phillips reached Milwaukee's Pfister Hotel at 6 P.M. Saturday, according to the *Milwaukee Journal*, which put Scott's mileage from New York City at 2,210.

"Instead of trying to gain repute by trying to see how far I can drive and how little I can sleep, I am trying to demonstrate the pleasure that is open to women in the operation of a modern automobile," Scott explained to a *Milwaukee Journal* reporter. "We have been over 800 miles out of our direct route already in the pursuit of especial pleasure and expect to go more before we reach San Francisco."[55] She and Phillips left Milwaukee on Monday, June 13, the newspaper said.

From Milwaukee, Scott would drive to Janesville, Wisconsin, on Monday, the *Inter Ocean* projected, and work her way southwest through northern Illinois to Iowa. But her early arrival in Cedar Rapids, Iowa, some 200 miles from Janesville, at 1:30 P.M. Tuesday, suggests that Scott traveled on Sunday. She crossed the Mississippi River at Clinton, Iowa, stopped nearby to adjust the Overland's transmission, and passed through Mt. Vernon to reach Cedar Rapids:

> In the towns through which she has passed, she has created a furore, the little white car which she is piloting being the center of all eyes. At Mount Vernon, where Cornell college is located, she arrived just as the commencement exercises were being held, and she viewed some of them from a position on the

Occupants of a passing buggy marvel at the novelty of the Lady Overland, while Scott, left, and Gertrude Phillips prepare for roadside repairs near Clinton, Iowa. (NAHC)

campus. The students, especially the co-eds, plied her with questions, and many envious glances were cast after her as she chugged away up the road on her journey to the Pacific coast.[56]

As the *Cedar Rapids Daily Republican* recorded Scott's Tuesday arrival:

Her trip from Clinton was made in a hurry. A large delegation of motor owners met her at Marion and escorted her to this city. She was very grateful for this welcome and expressed herself as being much pleased with Cedar Rapids.... She remained in the city over night, making her headquarters at the Montrose and her white machine, spick and span despite the travel, attracted large crowds.[57]

Likes Iowa's Roads

Scott would leave Cedar Rapids Thursday morning, June 16, bound for Waterloo, Marshalltown, Des Moines and Council Bluffs in her trip across Iowa, the newspaper said. Thursday afternoon, she reached Marshalltown, an overnight stop, having traveled 2,585 miles from New York City, reported the *Marshalltown Evening Times-Republican*. She left Marshalltown Friday at 8 A.M. and at noon reached Des Moines, where she called on the local Overland agency, the Ideal Automobile Company. Her odometer showed 2,660 miles for the trip, according to the *Des Moines Register and Leader*.

The local agency's newspaper ad alerted

Scott selects tools for "adjusting [the] transmission in heavy sand" near Clinton, according to the Overland company. (NAHC)

Des Moines residents to the challenges facing Scott: "Will she carry the trip to a successful finish? Will she demonstrate that a woman with the right car can make the journey, before undertaken only by trained drivers in especially prepared cars? Yes, she will! Why? Because she has determination coupled with the ideal car, — an irresistible combination."[58]

"We really have had a wonderful time. I cannot imagine anything more pleasurable than a trip of this kind for women who are moderately resourceful," Scott told the *Register and Leader*. "During the afternoon Miss Scott and Miss Phillips met Governor [Beryl F.] Carroll at the state house; also W.W. Morrow, treasurer of state, and W.C. Hayward, secretary of state. The state officials were much interested in the car and the trip as associated with the good roads movement."[59]

In Iowa, where Alice Ramsey spent two weeks grinding through mud during her 1909 crossing, state officials were undoubtedly relieved to hear Scott's praise for the Hawkeye State's roads, as reported by the *Des Moines Capital*:

When seen at the Chamberlain hotel upon her arrival in the city this noon, Miss Scott was radiant with enthusiasm over Iowa roads, Iowa people, Iowa towns and Iowa hospitality.... Miss Scott enthusiastically said that she came to the Mississippi river with such apprehension of Iowa roads from the accounts she had read in the eastern papers of the famous Iowa gumbo, that it was indeed a tremendous experience to her to find the Iowa roads superior to anything she has encountered west of New York City, with the exception of the state of Indiana.[60]

Leaving Des Moines Saturday morn-

An auto-borne road drag smoothes the River-to-River Road east of Guthrie Center, Iowa. Observing from the Lady Overland are Scott, driving, and Gertrude Phillips. (NAHC)

ing, June 18, Phillips and Scott traveled to Council Bluffs over Iowa's River-to-River Road, "taking a side trip to accept a luncheon engagement in Audubon," where they arrived at 12:15 P.M. "The road for a distance of some twenty-five miles was dragged to make the detour an easy one," according to one dispatch.[61] Her trek across Iowa was predominantly over a newly designated "transcontinental route," Scott said. Her allusion was to a new association that Iowans formed to promote the state's all-dirt River-to-River Road as an official transcontinental route through Iowa.

Reaching Atlantic at 3 P.M., the travelers met Council Bluffs Overland agent Harry Van Brunt, the *Atlantic Telegraph* observed. Under Van Brunt's escort, the autoists reached the Missouri River port at dusk, "dusty, grimy and tanned, and pre-ceded by a cavalcade of cars driven by Council Bluffs enthusiasts," as Sunday's *Council Bluffs Nonpareil* reported:

It was with a hearty sigh of relief that Miss Scott and her companion slipped from their seats in the car and struggled through the dense crowd, which had gathered to welcome them into the Grand hotel. "Never again," sighed Miss Scott as she wiped away the outer crust of terra firma which obscured her face. She did not explain what this laconic statement indicated.

Miss Phillips, the New York newspaper woman who is accompanying her[,] and L.H. Tuttle, also a member of the journalistic profession, who is keeping up with the party both by train and automobile[,] did the talking…. Miss Phillips, begging that her manner be not accepted as a criterion of her usual state, wearily sank upon a settee in the Grand lobby last evening and prepared to be interviewed.

"First," she said, "I want to state that I regard the River-to-River road in this state the best we have struck since we left New York. And after that I want to say that we have been flooded with hospitality since we entered this state. We have had one continual parade for the past week. At times we had as many as twenty-five cars as an escort from town to town. In the smaller places our advent was a regular riot. Everybody waited for the 'Transcontinental girl,' and in all places some sort of an entertainment was given for us."[62]

A $5,000 Offer

"After a short stop in Council Bluffs, the pair came in to Omaha and spent the night at the Henshaw," according to the *Omaha World-Herald*.[63] Before leaving Omaha on Sunday, however, Scott learned that the agents for some other automakers

were very uptight about our expedition. How uptight didn't really get to me until we arrived in Omaha. There a dealer of a rival auto offered me five thousand dollars to turn back and start the trip all over again in the car he was selling. My unbelief showed immediately. His unvarnished nerve and his assumption that we'd scrabble our sponsor for a bribe left me aghast[.] I stared at him in amazement, "Turn Back! You simply must be kidding. I may be crazy but not that crazy. Try an expedition like this yourself, mister." A quick turn on the heel and he was alone with his proposition.

Some of cars that fell in with the Lady Overland contained well-wishers, according to Scott. Some did not:

One of the prime advertising gimmicks of The Overland Company in their promotion of the cross-country trip by a woman was that she'd be able to make any necessary repairs, except, of course[,] for an accident or major breakdown. If massive troubles did develop, which we fervently prayed wouldn't and didn't, then the unhappy female (me) could walk ten or twenty miles to the nearest garage, if any, or blacksmith's shop for whatever help might be available. That big and ever-present "if" even in retrospect still induces shudders.

Rivals not only hoped but fervently prayed some serious trouble *would* develop then they could have a field day promoting the trouble-free aspects of competitive cars. As we journeyed through the country our rivals would put one of their cars ahead of us as an escort and stay with us for a couple of days. Passengers in the rival's car included two or three reporters who would have gleefully blazoned the details of any troubles we might have. It was a booby-trapped situation. It did, however, have some virtues. The rival car didn't realize how welcome they were to lead the way. The western plains were completely devoid of highway signs....

Phillips and Scott drove to Lincoln on Sunday, June 19, according to two Lincoln newspapers, one of which put the Overland's total mileage from New York at 2,922. According to Lincoln's *Nebraska State Journal*:

They are the object of much amusement to other motorists, said Miss Phillips, on account of their reluctance to run over anything. "Only yesterday," she said, "we held up a party of some thirty cars to allow a hen with a large brood of baby chicks to cross the road. Another time we stopped our car on seeing a gopher until we were able to find out what kind of an animal it was."[64]

An Emergency Repair

Scott showed her "grit and resourceful ingenuity" on Sunday by tackling an obstacle some 20 miles west of Omaha. According to an eyewitness:

> On the outskirts of Waterloo where they were to be met by an escorting party a bridge had been torn down and the escorting tourists were held up there awaiting Miss Scott's arrival intent on advising her of the way round several miles of detour as the only way of getting into the city. The man who was piloting at this point said it was an impossibility to get through there at all but Miss Scott said, "I will probably have something of this kind to do somewhere before I get through the journey and may just as well begin." She asked the men to remove a section of the fence and going into the field and across a deep ditch and on through the creek and up the bank on the town side, picking her own way amid the astonished cheers and hat swinging of the onlookers who thought the feat impossible.[65]

According to the *Lincoln Evening News*, the autoists would leave Monday, June 20, and camp that night near Hastings, where their tents and cooking equipment awaited them. Their 125-mile trip to Hastings would take them through Pleasant Dale, Milford, Seward, Utica, York and Aurora.

Just 10 or 11 miles out of Lincoln, however, on her way to Pleasant Dale, Scott "came suddenly upon a little wooden bridge with one of the planks broken out," *Motor Age* recounted. "A front spring with all but the top leaf broken and that badly bent was the result," forcing her to make emergency repairs:

> Miss Scott says that she has often been asked since she started why the Prest-O-Lite tank [for the acetylene-gas headlamps] was placed between the frame members in front of the radiator. She always had said that it was to economize space, but now she has a brand new reason that is much more practicable. Miss Scott searched up and down the road for a block of wood on which to place the [j]ack but could not find a single piece of wood that was not nailed down excepting the three blocks that she carries and those she needed to block the spring up with after she had raised the frame up to a normal position with the jack.[66]

Consequently, Scott raised the car by placing the jack directly against the bottom of the Prest-O-Lite tank. But she may not have made an emergency repair, as *Motor Age* implied. Jacking up the car was in preparation for removing the spring, according to the *Seward Independent-Democrat*: "Just before reaching Pleasant Dale a spring on Miss Scott's car broke, which delayed the party until another one could be brought out from Lincoln."[67] In her autobiography, however, Scott recalls that "we stuck a piece of two by four between the spring leaves and limped into the next town." Either way, it appears that Scott left this repair to the experts.

Heading Hastily for Hastings

Overland agent Leigh Lincoln of the York Auto Company and six cars, with reporters on board, left York at 10 or 10:30 A.M. to meet Scott some 15 miles east at Utica, according to York newspapers. Learning of her accident at Pleasant Dale, the escorting cars drove on east to Seward, where the greeters had lunch while waiting for Scott. Meantime, followed by a group of Overland owners, Seward Overland agent Paul Herpolsheimer drove to Pleasant Dale, where mechanics were installing a new front spring on the Lady Overland. With a Miss Emily Brown driving one of the escort cars, Herpolsheimer's young son led Scott into

After an accident west of Lincoln, Nebraska, Scott raises the Overland by placing a jack under the Prest-O-Lite tank. According to a factory photo caption, she is preparing to block up the broken right front spring. (NAHC)

Seward: "When she drove in from Milford she was piloted by ten-year old Walter Herpolsheimer who drove a No. 38, 25 h.p. Overland, (the car driven by the Overland lady) which is built especially for the use of girls and boys," contended Seward's *Blue Valley Blade*. Phillips and Scott "wore khaki shirt waist suits with red belts and were bare headed."[68]

To make up for her earlier breakdown, Scott drove fast during the rest of the day, according to newspapers all along her route. Her stay in Seward, just 33 miles into Monday's planned 125-mile trip, was brief, the *York Times* related:

At two o'clock this afternoon the Overland driven by Miss Scott accompa-

nied by a delegation entered the city of Seward and rode around the square where they were met by a large number of people and the members of the York delegation. A stop of a few minutes was made at the northwest corner of the square where the assembly had their pictures taken and preparations for the trip to York were made.

It was a great sight to see the speeding Overlands going down the road with Leigh Lincoln leading the way followed by Miss Scott and the lady reporter who accompanies her, and then the rest of the party. The glitter of brass and nickel shone in the bright sun through the clouds of dust that were raised by the swiftly revolving wheels. Farmers in the corn fields waved their hats at the sight and were answered in return by members of the party.[69]

The 30-mile trip from Seward to York became "a record breaking drive which set the nerves of the novices of the escort in a highly tense condition, the speed at times being so terrific as to defy danger and break the law if not the record," according to the *York Republican* reporter traveling with the cars.[70] Scott stopped for gas at the York agency. Waiting for her there were Arthur Jones and Ernest Brandes, partners in the Jones & Brandes Overland agency of Hastings, and Overland agent John Dahl of Aurora, 20 miles to the west. With this contingent, Scott left York on what an accompanying reporter called "the dizziest automobile riding the writer ever indulged in." Speeds approached 60 miles per hour over the narrow dirt roads, according to the scribe representing Aurora's *Hamilton County Register*:

> The only accident was when we neglected the warning cry of "high culvert" and omitted to take a brace and the top of the editorial cranium came in such contact with the top of the cover as to cause us to thank our lucky stars (and there were a good many of them just then) for a firm substantial neck that does not kink easily and a cushion of hair that alone prevented getting a big dimple in our dome that would have held coffee like a saucer.[71]

At Aurora, Phillips and Scott "stopped for a time at Dahl's garage and rested," observed a worldly *Aurora Sun* reporter. "John Dahl, Geo. L. Burr, many other parties from Aurora, and Overland enthusiasts from Hastings, went to York to meet Miss Scott and escort her to Aurora. That's all very fine, but, inasmuch as the lady is very comely in appearance, we suspect that something besides loyalty to the Overland car beat[s] in the breasts of these noble patriots, her escorts."[72]

A *Hastings Daily Republican* writer joined agent Arthur Jones in a 40-horse-power Overland roadster, driven by R.C. Carter, that headed east from Hastings at 11 A.M. to meet Scott. "Once outside of the city limits Carter opened 'er up and the pace was of such a swift character that farmers at work in the fields and the women folk about the farm homes could not have looked on in more astonishment had Glenn Curtiss suddenly sailed in view in one of his airships.... The return pace was at a much faster clip than the going one." As Scott approached Hastings early Monday evening, later than expected because of her earlier breakdown, "a number of Hastings women drivers"[73] joined her for the trip into the city:

> "Lady Overland" and its fair occupants with guests in accompanying machines arrived at the Bostwick at 7:15, where quite a crowd gathered to see and greet her. Both Miss Scott and Miss Phillips are of strong physique, Miss Phillips being much the taller. They are both of the optimistic, happy temperament and make a jolly pair. Witty, quick at repartee, tactful and seemingly not lacking in courage, self-confidence and the initiative, the Overland people certainly used splendid judgment in selecting these two charming young ladies to make this great automobile dash across the continent.
>   At the Bostwick Misses Scott and Phillips were tendered a pleasant dinner party arranged by Messrs. Jones & Brandes. Here quite a party of representative Hastings ladies, mostly auto enthusiasts, had the pleasure of chatting freely with Miss Scott and her companion who vivaciously detailed their experiences thus far of their trip, especially some of the amusing features.[74]

Their rush to Hastings was in vain, however. The late arrival of their camping outfit meant Phillips and Scott "will pause here several days before resuming their coast to coast tour," according to the *Hastings Daily Tribune*. "To the *Republican* she [Scott] said she was glad of it for she thought Hastings a lovely town and what people she had met were most charming."[75] Her opinion after spending eight days idle in Hastings — from Tuesday, June 21, to Tuesday, June 28 — went unrecorded.

Western Cordiality

Accompanied by pilot Ernest Brandes as far as North Platte, Phillips and Scott finally left Hastings at 5 A.M. Wednesday, June 29, Day 45 of the trip. Scott drove the 55 miles to Kearney that morning. Altogether, she traveled more than 200 miles on Wednesday, through Kearney and North Platte, to reach Ogallala, Nebraska, that night. At the end of her trip she told the *San Francisco Chronicle* that she covered 246 miles between Hastings and Ogallala, making it the best single day's travel. Easterners had expressed their "pessimisms and admonitions" about the hardships of the West, Scott said, according to the Overland press release published in the *Kearney Morning Times*:

Imagine then my surprise at finding the roads in perfect shape, in fact better than anything in the East with the possible exception of Indiana, the country cultivated and beautiful, the people courteous and kind, the hotels homelike and comfortable, and the towns all prosperous and modern. It is all new to me and I wouldn't have missed this trip for anything in the world. Even the widespread stories of Western cordiality and hospitality do not near come up to the realization. I have been wonderfully entertained in every town and have made more friends and acquaintances so far than in all my trip through the Eastern states.[76]

She traveled 3,287 miles from New York City to North Platte, according to the *North Platte Telegraph*, which ran the same press release the Kearney newspaper did. The editor of Thursday's *Keith County News* in Ogallala, however, ignored the automaker's missive, and penned an article titled "Not Much of a Feat":

The two girls that are making the trip from New York to San Francisco arrived here last evening and laid up for the night. The accomplishment of this undertaking don't appeal to us as much of a feat. They have a pilot car with three or four men to look after them and see that their machine is always in condition. The trip that Helen Hoxie and her lady friend made from Denver to Ogallala alone was, in our estimation, more of a feat than this one. Now if these girls had started out from New York alone and made the trip, they would have just claims of doing something out of the ordinary. We believe Helen Hoxie and two or three other girls in Ogallala could accomplish it.[77]

Resuming their journey, Scott and Phillips traveled some 170 miles from Ogallala to reach Cheyenne shortly before 11 P.M. Thursday, June 30, 1910. Recent heavy rains had left the road in poor condition. The car had rolled up 3,450 miles since leaving New York City. As Friday's *Cheyenne State Leader* observed, Westerners were familiar with the

daring deeds of western women ... but an Eastern woman performing a feat calling for an unusual display of courage attracts even the western man and Cheyennese were last night given cause to take notice of a performance on the part of two young Eastern girls who are entitled to rank with the courageous girls of the Golden West....

With a fresh coat of western tan on their faces, which, however, failed to hide their rosy eastern complexions, the girls seemed to be bubbling over with the

Top: Scott dodges a sinkhole on a muddy road between Lodgepole and Kimball, Nebraska. The travelers have attached new equipment to the left side of the seat; strapped to the left front fender is a tent. (NAHC) *Bottom:* Rain turned the road to a river at this small settlement in what appears to be western Nebraska or eastern Wyoming. (NAHC)

The trail between Cheyenne, Wyoming, and Greeley, Colorado. (NAHC)

spirit that is common to the West and were hearty in their praise of a country that to them was "wonderful," despite the fact that they had been forewarned by their friends that they would meet with impossible people and conditions.

The girls encountered washed out bridges, muddy roads and other discouraging conditions yesterday but they had decided that they would reach Cheyenne before stopping and nothing was encountered which they did not by some ingenious plan overcome and although they were well nigh worn out on reaching this city, as well as thoroughly chilled, they insisted on hearing stories of this country from the newspaper men who met them on their arrival and it was with difficulty that the reporters succeeded in persuading the modest girls to tell of their trying experiences. They seem to think that they are doing nothing out of the ordinary in crossing a continent thousands of miles in width.[78]

Lost in the Rockies

Scott and Phillips detoured south from Cheyenne to Denver, where the Lady Overland had been due on Monday, June 27, while still stranded in Hastings. From Denver, Scott and Phillips "availed ourselves of the opportunity of making a side trip to Palmer Lake, one of the most picturesque spots in Colorado," Scott recalled.[79]

Traveling westward across Wyoming after leaving Denver, the women would pass through Laramie, Medicine Bow, Hanna, Fort Steele, Rawlins, Rock Springs and Evanston, then cross the Utah border to reach Salt Lake City. The *Rawlins Republican* was expecting the transcontinental Overland either Sunday, July 3, or Monday, July 4. But the women had reached only Laramie by Monday night, according to the *Deseret Evening News* of Salt Lake City.

The women saw a natural fireworks display between Cheyenne and Laramie near the Ames Monument at Sherman, which marks the highest elevation on the Union Pacific Railroad. "Here they encountered a very severe electrical storm on the evening of July 4," according to the *New York Morning Telegraph*. "The display made by nature far surpassed anything they had ever seen. Hail stones the size of hen's eggs fell and the tumult of the storm was almost deafening. It was indeed a fitting close for the most glorious of all our holidays."[80]

During her 1909 transcontinental trip, Ramsey got her directions partly from the Clason Map Company of Denver; Scott and Phillips used an unidentified road map, at least in Wyoming, but even so got lost trying to follow it. Traveling in the Rocky Mountains north and west from Laramie, "they lost the trail indicated by the map they were following and they were adrift on the prairies for the better part of the night traveling a distance of 129 miles in making the 28 miles between Laramie and Medicine Bow, finally arriving at the latter place at 2 o'clock in the morning," the *Deseret Evening News* said.[81] (The distance between Laramie and Medicine Bow is actually about twice the stated 28 miles.)

According to an Overland press release that evidently describes the same experience, Scott found her way into Rawlins, not Medicine Bow. "Most of this time was spent in bumping over prairie dog holes and sage brush and in trying to find a way of crossing Sherman's Gulch and fording Sheep Creek," said the release, which quotes Scott:

> After laboring through brush and gullies for several miles, going over alkali pits and past the dreaded Soda Lake, and fording a dangerous creek, we lost the trail near a deep gully. The banks were impassable and the bottoms soft from recent rains, so it was impossible to cross

at any point that could be seen through the field-glasses from north to south. We looked the territory over and decided that we could pick up a trail to the south.

> We made our way with difficulty to a wagon trail on a fairly open space, only to find that it led to the junction of two creeks. Crossing either of these was impossible on account of the steep banks. By going north a couple of miles, however, we arrived at a sheep herder's camp and were directed to a point up creek about five miles for a bridge.

> We went twelve miles over the worst roads imaginable, which resulted in a broken front spring, which had to be blocked up with the axe-handles and wired in place. Still no bridge. It was now sundown and we were nearly frantic at the prospect of a night on the prairie. Nothing for directions but a vague southwest and a broken Presto tank. Fortunately, at this point I was able to rush the car across the creek, and taking advantage of the long Western twilight, headed due west in the hope of finding some trail. We finally reached one and followed it, ignorant of its destination, as long as it carried us to civilization. At midnight the trail ended at Rawlins.[82]

A "Toidy" Trick

How she made it that far without compressed acetylene to operate her headlights is a question Scott did not address. In a Nevada newspaper interview, however, she addressed the subject of Wyoming roads: "The worst part of our trip was from Laramie to Green River, Wyoming, and the roads in that state were in horrible shape."[83] Curiously, a number of auto journals contradict Scott, reporting that she found Wyoming's roads in generally good condition.

It was perhaps at the Medicine Bow blacksmith shop that Scott installed a toilet in the car. Because breakdowns were few,

A friendly and creative blacksmith in Medicine Bow, Wyoming, is probably the one who installed a toilet in the Overland at Scott's request. (July 21, 1910, *Automobile*)

according to the writer who helped Scott prepare her autobiography,

the only situation that required remarkable ingenuity and resourcefulness was Blanche's solution to the problem of a "toidy break." The reason for this was simply that car loads of photographers and reporters followed her pilot car from city to city. The clear atmosphere of the western plains enabled the followers to keep them in view—any slowdown or stoppage brought a crowd to assist....

Blanche and Gertrude were strolling out the riding kinks of the day in a small western town when Blanche spied a stomach pump in a drug store window. She purchased it immediately without satisfying the curiosity of either her companion or the inquisitive druggist. Before getting underway next morning Blanche had the local blacksmith drill a hole in the floorboard between the front seat positions and install the stomach pump. The pump was a wide mouthed funnel with a long rubber hose. It provided an instant "toidy."

On one of their jaunts they traveled without stops all day. At their arrival one of the reporters quickly and delicately informed them the location of the ladies['] room. Blanche and Gertrude thanked him but spent over an hour chatting with reporters and notables and taking care of other details. The anxious reporter hovered and waited. He then headed for the bar as Gertrude overhead him say, "Those damn females must have cast iron kidneys and five gallon bladders. I don't know how they did it."[84]

A photo accompanying a July 21, 1910, *Automobile* article on Scott's progress pictures "Our Friend[ly] Blacksmith, Medicine Bow."[85] Neither the auto journals nor local newspapers detail a mechanical break-

"Coming down into Hanna" is the Overland factory's caption on this photograph. (NAHC)

down that would have sent Scott to the Medicine Bow blacksmith, who was thus likely the one who installed the toilet. Some of the men who accompanied the Lady Overland, many newspapers revealed, were driving pilot cars; as did Ramsey, Scott often used such guides to lead the way.

Chugging into Salt Lake

Westward from Medicine Bow, the Lady Overland passed through Hanna on its way to Fort Steele, Wyoming. At Fort Steele, "Miss Scott detoured from her westward course to take advantage of a perfect day and make a trip south, down through the beautiful [North Platte River] canyon to Saratoga and Grand Encampment," *Automobile Topics* related. In 1901, 260 copper mines swelled Grand Encampment's

population to 2,000. But the region's copper industry collapsed just two years before Scott's arrival, when falling prices made it impossible to recover the costs of extracting copper from the Wyoming mines.[86]

On Thursday, July 7, according to the *Salt Lake (City) Evening Telegram*, Scott headed west from Fort Steele. There, a washed-out wagon bridge forced Ramsey in 1909 and other transcontinentalists before her to cross the North Platte River on a railroad trestle. Press accounts do not reveal how Scott crossed the river. West of Cheyenne, the roads in Wyoming "were packed hard as flint under a thin cushion of dust," *Automobile* said. "Reports from the tourists show that the roads throughout Wyoming were an agreeable surprise as to condition."[87]

The Red Desert of south-central

Scott with her improvised mask. According to the caption on this Overland publicity photo, "Crossing the plains[,] looks should not be considered." (NAHC)

Wyoming "is either desolate or beautiful, according to the way tourists look at it," Scott observed. "Crossing 'Red Desert' was a novel experience to me. The terrific heat was allayed to some extent by the onward rush of the car. We were well protected from the arid climate and alkali dust by our large straw hats and improvised masks."[88]

Salt Lake City's Overland agent, the Consolidated Wagon & Machine Company, used a large ad to play up Scott's imminent arrival:

> Miss Scott's trans-continental trek with the "thirty-eight" stock Overland has well been termed "the most remarkable demonstration of simplicity and reliability ever shown by an automobile."
> Over all kinds of roads and in all sorts of weather Miss Scott has ... driven the sturdy little car from the Atlantic now

within a few miles of the Great Dead Sea of America, Salt Lake. A comparatively few more chugs from that enduring little engine will bring the young woman within the hale and hospitality of our own city....

> A most cordial invitation is extended to all interested to visit us, meet Miss Scott and examine her gallant little "gasoline horse" as she terms it.[89]

From Evanston in extreme southwestern Wyoming, Scott made the 97-mile drive into Salt Lake City on Monday, July 11, Day 57, having traveled 4,321 miles from City Hall in New York. Two representatives of the Consolidated Wagon & Machine Company drove an auto east to meet Phillips and Scott at Devils Slide, Utah. They actually met the Lady Overland near "P.J. Moran's cement plant in Weber canyon," observed the *Salt Lake Tribune*.[90] Reporters accompanied sales manager S.B. Young, Jr., and W.W. Calder of the agency, apparently in a pilot car driven by Dick Richardson. Tuttle went along, carrying three passengers in his own car, according to a composite picture that emerges from lengthy stories in the four Salt Lake City dailies.

"A Room with a Bath"

Observed the next day's *Deseret Evening News*:

The convoy car with Harry Tuttle of New York in command, carried four men and everything from a camera to an ax, a block and tackle to a medicine chest. Briefly the outfit and car weighed 4,450 pounds and whenever a stiff grade or some sand were encountered there were some very strenuous scenes accompanied by remarks not necessary for publication but as an indication of earnestness of purpose.

Everybody was glad to meet because the car, which left Salt Lake and had made the trip into the canyon in 1 hour and 15 minutes running time under the devil-may-care, get-there exertions of Dick Richardson at the helm, was there for the purpose of piloting the party along the foothills to the short cut to Salt Lake. The invited guests with the party, too, were somewhat fatigued with their exertions incident to an endeavor to remain within the tonneau during transit....

The west-bound machines carried an appalling amount of dunnage in addition to two sunburned, begrimed women in the first auto and four men in the convoy machine. One and all were more than sunburned....

The party eventually reached Salt Lake at 7:15 P.M. being received at the city limits by the fire department which had thoughtfully stretched several lines of hose across the road necessitating a detour which took all into the bog lands,

woke up an attacking mosquito fleet and terminated in one grand jump-off of three feet which was taken with due studied carelessness by the intrepid little woman at the wheel.

Naturally the women autoists by this time have acquired a blasé mien incident to auto thrills engendered by flood and field, desert and canyon. They shrink, however, from undue brass band features and when brought triumphantly down Main street to the accompanying toots of the horn of the leading machine, they slackened up and declined to join the parade....

On the arrival of the party at the Semloh hotel there were frantic appeals for "a room with a bath," and within an hour all reappeared in "real clothes" as Miss Scott put it.

From then on with Seymour B. Young[,] Jr., as master of ceremonies an informal reception was held in the hotel parlors and many and divers questions were put and answered....

The pilot car which met the party in Weber canyon carried W.W. Calder, who will accompany the two machines west tomorrow, and some local newspaper men. Richard Reimer who came in with the party met them at Rawlins, Wyo., and escorted them into Salt Lake.[91]

Scott was "perfectly happy and looking none the worse for her experience," said the *Salt Lake Evening Telegram*. "If you want excitement," Scott told a *Salt Lake Tribune* reporter, "just go through the Rocky mountains in an automobile after dark"— an apparent reference to her nighttime drive while lost southeast of Medicine Bow.[92] Though she may drive across the country again some day, she would end her current trip in San Francisco and then take the train back to New York, Scott revealed.

An hour or less before Scott arrived, another female autoist reached the Utah capital. Arriving from the west, Harriet White Fisher was heading east on the last leg of her round-the-world auto tour, "the first woman to accomplish such a feat," contended the *New York Times*. She was a passenger in a slightly modified 40-horse-power Locomobile. "Two Women Auto Enthusiasts Meet Unawares in Salt Lake City," the *Salt Lake Tribune* trumpeted, though failed to specify whether Fisher and Scott personally met.[93] Perhaps "Meet Unawares" is the key phrase: In Fisher's account of her stay in Salt Lake City, she does not even mention Scott, and Scott's autobiography makes no mention of Fisher. Nevertheless, the *Salt Lake Herald-Republican* says the women "exchanged salutations and consoled each other on the 'perfectly horrid' roads they had encountered."[94]

During a rest day Tuesday, Phillips and Scott women heard an organ recital at the Mormon Tabernacle, visited a lakeside resort, Saltair, and took in other Salt Lake City sights. Left behind inside the local Overland agency, however, their car "created all kinds of excitement among the spark and plug experts of this city and today the throng around the window ... has attested that interest is at fever heat."[95]

In announcing her trip, the Overland company projected that Scott would travel north around the Great Salt Lake and enter northeastern Nevada at the small town of Tecoma, Nevada. In fact, she traveled south of the lake through Grantsville, Utah, as Ramsey did a year earlier, following the route of the future Lincoln Highway.

An Enormous Wildcat

Accompanied by an escort car from Salt Lake City, she reached Fish Springs, Utah, near the Nevada border, on Saturday, July 16, according to the *Ely (Nev.) Weekly Mining Expositor*. Escorted by "C.H. Crosson and R. Reimers in an Overland machine," Scott on Sunday, July 17, drove from Fish Springs over the Nevada border

to Tippett. The previous year, Alice Ramsey reached Ely using Schellbourne Pass — nearly on a straight line west from Tippett to the town of Cherry Creek. Scott, however, avoided the Schell Creek Range altogether and reached Cherry Creek by looping far to the north, by way of Goshute Lake (a dry lakebed) and the town of Goshute. From Cherry Creek south to Ely, she followed a road along the west side of the Steptoe Valley. Tuttle was also in the retinue, according to the Ely newspaper.

"I certainly made a mistake in not coming through Schellbourne pass," Scott told the *Ely Weekly Mining Expositor*. "The pilot took us by way of Tippett and Goshute over a road that had not been traveled for years. The party is well supplied with camping outfits and provisions, but we have never had occasion to use them. We have been fortunate to find first class hotels at every stopping place except two since we began our trip. We intend to arrive in San Francisco in four days if some unavoidable accident does not interfere."[96]

The Scott party left Ely on Monday, July 18, the morning after its arrival, hoping to reach the Hot Springs Ranch Monday night and Carson City Tuesday night, the Ely newspaper reported.

Southwest of Carson City, the Overland stalled while trying to mount the Kingsbury Grade on the eastern slope of the Sierra Nevada — a difficulty Scott blamed on the car's planetary transmission. "Try as we might we couldn't get over the grade," Scott recalled. She had Phillips walk to the top of one particularly steep hill and drive a stake in the ground so they could winch the car to the top using their block and tackle. Phillips soon reappeared, pale and shaking. "There's an enormous wildcat up there," exclaimed Phillips, who refused to return to the top.

"Don't be silly," Scott replied. "Your imagination is working overtime." Yet Scott grabbed a .32-caliber Colt handgun from the car before trudging up the hill to discover — an enormous wildcat. She dashed back to the car and "without preamble I jumped in, hauled the block and tackle into a jumble in the trunk, leapfrogged into the driver's seat and yelled to Gertrude as I started the motor and poured on the petrol, 'This damn thing just has to go over that grade come Hell or Christmas.' Amazingly *it did*."

"A Thundering Welcome"

Their route through California took them through Placerville, Sacramento, Stockton and San Leandro, where they arrived on Friday, July 22. Tuttle's telegram instructed them to remain overnight in San Leandro, according to Scott:

The arrangements were for us to arrive in the Bay City by ferry from Oakland on Saturday morning, thus the thundering welcome would create the banner headlines [i]n the Sunday morning newspapers nationwide. Good timing has always been the essence of shrewd publicity....

The official party and a large group of the curious were on hand when the ferry docked at San Francisco [on Saturday, July 23]. But something new had been added — the Army Division stationed at the Presidio turned out military band and all! The massive street parade terminated at the famous Cliff House Restaurant.

By ending her trip at the Cliff House, Scott was — perhaps unintentionally — paying homage to the transcontinental drivers who preceded her: The San Francisco landmark was the official starting point for two of the first three transcontinental treks, all made in 1903.

W.H.B. Fowler, the *San Francisco Chronicle's* automobile reporter, was on hand to record the arrival of Phillips and Scott:

At San Leandro the first contingent of escorting Overland and other cars picked them up and conducted them with all due ceremony and honor into Oakland. The trip to San Francisco was made on the 10 o'clock creek boat. At the ferry a score of other Overland cars had gathered, and the procession wended its way up Market street to Golden Gate avenue, and then out to the Park and beach. At the very brink of the ocean the trip came to an official end, and Miss Scott poured the contents of a bottle filled at the Atlantic into the sister Pacific.

It isn't really any kind of a feat for a girl to drive clear across the continent, according to Miss Scott. Indeed, if one might give full credit to her words, the stories that have been told of previous trips have perhaps dwelt too heavily on the terrible rainstorms, the awful gumbo of Iowa, the many streams to be forded in Wyoming and the mountain roads that are almost impassable.

Miss Scott is a charming and refined young woman, and her belittling of the trip is due not a little to her innate modesty. She must be a disappointment to a press agent, for she is strong for telling the exact truth. But that she had many hard days, she admits, and some of the roads and grades that she drove over are known to local motorists in no favorable light. They are difficult for a man, and that a girl should negotiate them readily and belittle the feat afterward is merely an indication of the character of the girl....

"What kind of a trip did we have? Dandy!" said Miss Scott enthusiastically.... "We were very much afraid of the Western roads. We had read some pamphlets dealing with previous trips and learned from these that the conditions were awful, and we especially dreaded the Bitter Creek district in Wyoming. But we found that conditions were not nearly as bad as they had been painted, and that an injustice had been done to the West. In fact, I think that on average the Western roads are better than the Eastern, although we came over the latter when they were not at their best and the comparison is perhaps not a fair one."[97]

"I Supply the Prop"

Though Scott may have been generally strong on telling the truth, she experienced a moment of weakness in San Francisco. Before leaving New York City, Mayor William J. Gaynor had given the travelers "a small bottle of Atlantic Ocean water which I was to empty into the Pacific Ocean," Scott recalled decades later in her autobiography. "This bottle and its contents had been widely publicized." Unfortunately, it was missing, as was Tuttle, whom Scott was counting on to solve the problem. Instead, she wrote in an ellipses-filled account:

> I called a bus boy. For a generous bribe he supplied a small bottle. I filled it with hotel tap water ... and with the impressed officials and a cheering crowd watching every move, I solemnly poured the water into the Pacific. Inwardly I was almost convulsed as I speculated on what they ... and New York's Mayor Gaynor would say as I perpetuated the phoniest merger of all time.
>
> I've always rationalized this bit of chicanery as essential. The public, the press, the officials and others had gathered for another act in a newsmaking tableau. One of the props was missing. Voilà. I supply the prop; the scene is saved.

Scott left Oakland on the 10 A.M. ferry, according to the *Chronicle*, and presumably arrived in San Francisco at about 10:30 A.M. Thus her transcontinental crossing time was 68 days, 1 hour, 30 minutes, or nine days longer than Alice Ramsey's 1909 time. Scott's running time was nearly that of Ramsey's 42 days. Scott traveled on 41 of the 68 days, according to the *San Francisco*

Chronicle. The automaker's *Overland Scout* magazine and the *New York Morning Telegraph*, however, gave Scott's running time as 42 days.

"When my speedometer broke about a week ago," Scott told the *San Francisco Chronicle*, "we had covered 4751 miles, and we figure that altogether we have made about 5400 miles. Every mile of that distance I have driven myself, not another person touching the wheel of the car."[98] Willys-Overland advertising cited a 5,000-mile figure, while many press citations gravitated around 5,200 miles, a reasonable compromise. Thus in covering 5,200 miles in an elapsed time of slightly more than 68 days, Scott averaged 76 miles per day at an average speed of 3.18 mph.

In San Francisco, Scott reported that her best day's mileage was 246 between Hastings and Ogallala, Nebraska. "On one occasion," she added, "we drove further, but forty-seven miles of the distance was off the right road."[99] Decades later, she wrote in her autobiography that her best day's run — evidently including the 47 unnecessary miles — was 260 miles and the worst was 14. She neglected to explain the circumstances of either performance.

Scott had two punctures in north-central New York's Montezuma Swamp, according to *Horseless Age*, and many auto journals reported that Scott repaired several punctures during the trek. Yet "for the whole trip I had one puncture at exactly three thousand three hundred and thirty-three miles," she maintained.

A Fabulous Flight Fiction

Southern California's Overland dealers "raised a massive bleat because our trip had not included their territory," according to Scott. Thus, after three days in San Francisco, she and Phillips began the drive to Los Angeles over dirt roads covered with up to three inches of dust. "It was our misfortune to meet countless farm wagons pulled by eight giant horses and loaded with wheat. Their size made it imperative we pull off the road and let them by. We ate dust, our noses and eyes filled with it, we gritted it between our teeth and grayed our hair with it." The motorists were treated royally, however, Scott recalled: "School children in town[s] and villages along the way were given a holiday to share the welcoming celebrations. Farm families lined the roadsides as we drove by. We learned that a telephone grapevine from farm to farm reported our progress and insured us an audience as we moved along the country lanes."

At Santa Ana, she met Overland distributor and pioneer aviator Glenn Martin. Scott and Phillips "chuckled long and loudly at the idea of anyone being crazy enough to fly," said Scott, who two years later would be flying with Martin.

Evidently at the Overland company's direction, Scott's post-run publicity tour continued south from Los Angeles through San Diego to Tijuana, Mexico. A young Associated Press reporter who appeared at Scott's San Diego hotel made the "fabulous suggestion" that Scott fly as a passenger in a Tijuana aviator's two-seated Farman airplane. "The correspondent contended that since I was the first woman driver to make it across the continent, it would give him a great feature story, and give me another conspicuous first to be the number one female airplane passenger," Scott wrote, once again overlooking Alice Ramsey's 1909 transcontinental trip.

When Scott arrived at the Tijuana airfield late in the afternoon on what was possibly Saturday, June 30 — Scott never gives the exact date — she discovered the Farman had been wrecked. Her airplane ride was off. But the enterprising AP writer — intent on getting his exclusive story in the Sunday newspapers on the East Coast, where

it was three hours later — had already filed an account of Scott's historic flight. "If it was leaked that the flight never occur[r]ed his job was out the window," according to Scott. She therefore kept her silence.[100]

Driving back into the United States, Phillips and Scott declined the automaker's offer of a two-week California vacation, and boarded a train for the East. "Our memories were too impregnated with the scratch and taste of alkali dust and various other small annoyances that cropped up or inhabited the country there." The transcontinental travelers made a "brief stopover" in Toledo on August 12, to be entertained by Willys-Overland officials, before continuing to New York City by train, according to Scott.

Aviation, Her Final Frontier

On or about September 2, 1910, by most accounts, Scott became the first woman to fly an airplane in the United States. Instructor Glenn Curtiss gave her lessons at his Hammondsport, New York, air field. The opportunity to fly came about because of her Overland trip, according to the September 12, 1955, *U.S. Flying News*:

> Glenn Curtiss was in France at the time, but his press agent read about the daring Miss Scott and contacted her with an offer. How would she like to have Mr. Curtiss teach her to fly? She would — so a contract was signed and when Curtiss returned, Blanche Stuart Scott began her flying career. She soloed in the Curtiss "June Bug" after four days of roaring up and down the field, "cutting grass." A governor on the 35 hp engine kept the ship from gaining enough power to takeoff.[101]

Aviation historians disagree about whether Scott flew that day by accident or design. According to *Women Aloft*, one

Scott at the controls of an early biplane. (NASM No. 72-4803A)

volume in Time-Life's Epic of Flight series, "either a fortuitous wind gust or the connivance of a friendly mechanic gave a boost to the impatient student pilot. 'Something happened to the throttle block,' she recalled later with a little smile." Scott never got a pilot's license, optional at the time, so Harriet Quimby and Matilde Moisant became "America's first two licensed women pilots."[102]

Scott could justifiably claim to be "the first American woman to make a solo flight," according to *Women Aloft*, which adds this caution: "Because it was never established whether her first brief flight was accidental or intentional, the official honor of being America's first female aviator went not to Blanche Scott but to a remarkable flier named Bessica Raiche." A Smithsonian publication, *United States Women in Aviation through World War I*, voices more hesitation: "Opinion is divided as to who, Blanche Stuart Scott or Bessica Faith Raiche, was America's first aviatrix."[103]

Scott appeared at air shows briefly in late 1910, quit flying to marry Tuttle but soon divorced him. Known as the Tomboy of the Air, Scott "joined the small group of barnstormers on the daredevil circuit, expressing the hope that her stunts, which included 3,000-foot 'death dives,' would stimulate more opportunities for women."

While performing low-altitude stunts during a May 31, 1913, air show at Madison, Wisconsin, "a wing cable snapped, the aircraft crashed, and Blanche suffered an injured shoulder," according to the Smithsonian book. "If the plane had not fallen into a swamp, her injuries might have been worse."[104]

Though Scott resumed stunt flying in 1914, she quit "suddenly" in 1916, said *Women Aloft*, quoting her: "In aviation, there seems to be no place for the woman engineer, mechanic or flier. Too often, people paid money to see me risk my neck, more as a freak — a woman freak pilot — than as a skilled flier. No more!"[105]

During her flying career, she actually crashed twice and broke 41 bones, Scott said at a 1960 ceremony honoring the 50th anniversary of her flight. "None of them hurts me now." Two of her three marriages "ended with friendly partings," according to *The People's Almanac #2*. "The successful marriage lasted 10 years; she and her husband operated a motion picture production studio on Long Island, where Blanche wrote and appeared in a few early silents. At her husband's death, she settled into a 14-year career as a writer in Hollywood."[106]

Returning to Rochester, Scott "became a radio commentator, an assistant manager of a radio station and then a special consultant for the Air Force for its museum at the Wright Patterson Base, a position she held until 1956," the *New York Times* said. As she said she would some day, Scott began another transcontinental trip in October 1954, sweeping east to west to collect historical items for the museum. A year later, in September 1955, she reached Chicago. A budget cut eliminated her job in 1956 after she had collected aviation artifacts worth $1.25 million, she told an interviewer. "I'm one of the world's best chiselers."[107]

New Fields for Feminine Motorists

Scott's trip, a publicity windfall for the Overland company, also proved the value of a good press agent. For by relentlessly asserting that Blanche Stuart Scott — never mind Alice Ramsey — was the first woman to drive across the country, Harry Tuttle encouraged a fair number of newspapers and auto journals to swallow the lie. Scott was an accomplice in the deception. Such fictions often take on a life of their own. Thus 55 years later, even after Ramsey published a book about her 1909 trip, the Veteran Motor Car Club of America's *Bulb Horn* magazine claimed that Scott "was the first woman in history to drive an automobile from coast to coast."[108]

In 1908, Jacob M. Murdock had proven that a man could drive his family across the continent safely and relatively comfortably. The combined effect of Alice Ramsey's first automobile crossing by a woman in 1909 and Scott's second "first crossing" in 1910 was to throw open the door for women motorists. Scott's trip "has opened up new fields for the feminine motorists, who now have conclusive proof that long distance touring is as easy for them as it is for men," the *Toledo Daily Blade* asserted.[109]

By her example more than her words, Scott demonstrated that Ramsey's trip was not the fluke it had perhaps seemed to some observers at the time. Scott also broke new ground by afterward declaring that the trip was easier than she had expected it to be, a comment heard time and again from the 40 participants in a transcontinental caravan that involved 12 Premier vehicles in 1911. Women and children participated in both the Premier caravan and a four-car Garford "motor train" that crossed the country later in 1911.

Thus by the close of the year following Scott's trip, two women, numerous families and a host of ordinary citizens —

those not employed by an automaker — had driven across the country. Sea-to-sea motoring trips were becoming faster and safer than ever before. An estimated 150 cars crossed the entire continent or a large portion of it in 1913. By 1923, that number had mushroomed to 25,000 cars annually.[110] Despite the increasing number of Americans traveling long distances by auto, it was not until 1915 that the first solo coast-to-coast trip occurred. The driver was a well-known movie actress, Anita King.

Chapter Four

King Kruises "Koast to Koast in a KisselKar"

Anita King in a KisselKar, 1915

Just why a great corporation would send a little innocent girl like this out into the wilds of Nevada is not known, but she has the sympathy of the community....

White Pine News *of Ely, Nevada, ridiculing stories that King nearly perished in the desert*

With her studio's publicity department in tow, silent-film star Anita King in 1915 single-handedly drove a KisselKar from San Francisco to New York in 48 days, stopping at more than 100 Paramount theaters along her 5,231-mile route. She took the trip in part to assuage her grief over the death of a sister, according to one account. In becoming the first woman on record to drive across the country alone, however, King not only promoted her studio, but won for herself a new automobile, a new nickname and a lead role in a Paramount movie. She reprised some of her experiences by playing the female lead in a 1916 silent film about — what else? — a transcontinental auto race.

Curiously, the story of her 1915 crossing reads like a movie script. The colorful, convoluted and often contradictory reports of King's misadventures suggest that fact merged with fiction to an alarming degree. Newspaper editors along her route evidently had a decision to make: play along with the movie studio's palpitatingly dra-matic press releases, or try to find out for themselves what really happened. They nearly all played along.

Perhaps King shot a vicious timber wolf — though possibly it was only a coyote or a dog. *Perhaps* she slept outside while crossing the desert, where three prospectors revived her from a swoon. *Perhaps* she also fought off a menacing hobo and a lovelorn Wyoming rancher; pulled a gun on a man who questioned her honor; dissuaded a star-struck young girl from running off to Holly-wood; and tumbled off a farmer's hayrack.

A week before starting her transcon-tinental publicity tour, King — who claimed she began racing automobiles as early as 1909 — used the same slightly modified KisselKar to set a women's Los Angeles–San Francisco speed record. Coinciden-tally, it was in 1909 that Alice Ramsey with three female companions became the first woman to drive across the country, doing so in 59 days. In cutting 11 days from Ram-sey's time, King thus set a women's coast-to-coast speed record.

King Races to San Francisco

At 5:50 P.M. Wednesday, August 25, 1915, King who appeared in films produced by the Jesse L. Lasky Feature Play Company and distributed through Paramount Pictures, left Los Angeles. She drove north along the coast, hoping to reach San Francisco within 17 hours, according to the *Examiner* and *Times* of Los Angeles. *Motor West* narrated: "Manager O.B. Henderson of the Pacific KisselKar branch gave Miss King a splendid send-off in the shape of a fleet of KisselKars driven by their owners who accompanied the fair driver as far as Camarillo." Her route "is conceded by racing experts to be the most difficult for fast time between Los Angeles and this city," claimed the *San Francisco Examiner*. After an all-night drive, King arrived in San Francisco at 11:45 A.M. Thursday in an elapsed time of 17 hours, 55 minutes, which "sets a new mark for women motor enthusiasts," the *Examiner* said:[1]

Anita King, posing in a gown she wore in a 1915 silent film, *Snobs*. (WCF)

Miss King held her car to the roads over the mountains ... as steady as a man and maintained a high average of speed on all of the straight stretches. She had one or two narrow escapes, such as sending her car into a hole in the road with such force as to break the mud guard and fender, but even with this she did not let up on the throttle and set a clip for the entire distance that would make any racing driver prove his skill to equal.

"I ran into a terrible bank of fog in the mountains," said Miss King, "and I also lost my route book, but for these happenings I could have made much faster time. I had no trouble with my car, in fact, I could not let it out as fast as it would go. I wanted to prove that a woman could drive long distance races as well as men and in making this trip I am satisfied that this has been demonstrated."

Miss King admitted that such a long distance record drive was a severe test on her endurance, but the fact that she accomplished the trip without trouble and on schedule time made the effort worth while. She intends to drive the same car from here to New York, starting next week.[2]

The fog forced King to throttle down to 15 mph for two hours. While lost, she "consumed much time in waking up farmers along the route to be directed back to the unmarked highway," reported the *San Francisco Chronicle*. Consequently, "she

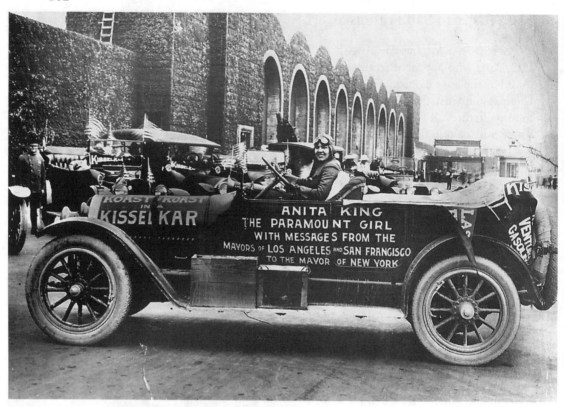

Anita King reaches San Francisco in her KisselKar, painted to resemble a mobile billboard. (HHAM)

promises to return from New York and undertake the Coast run again with the understanding that she will better her former time considerably." At San Jose, near the end of her city-to-city dash, "Miss King was met by another delegation of KisselKars from San Francisco, under the direction of President W.L. Hughson, and her entry into the [Panama-Pacific International] Exposition city was a sort of triumphal march. At San Francisco, she will rest for a few days while the car is put into perfect tune for the long drive."[3]

Hughson, president of the Pacific KisselKar Branch (with salesrooms in Los Angeles, Oakland and San Francisco), helped plan King's transcontinental trip. At the exposition grounds, "she was accorded a reception in the Tower of Jewels and another in the Kissel-Kar exhibit in the

Palace of Transportation," one report said.[4] A photo taken at the exposition grounds shows that Hughson marshaled at least a half-dozen KisselKars, which were flying American flags and KisselKar pennants.

King averaged nearly 27.2 mph in sprinting the 486 miles to San Francisco. None of the press reports revealed that her time was 5¾ hours off the record pace for the intercity run. Over the years, various drivers had gradually lowered the record, which in late 1906 stood at 18 hours 13 minutes over a 512-mile route. In June 1915, four men in a Cadillac V-8 traveled 491 miles between the two cities to lower the record to 12 hours 10 minutes, *Automobile* reported. On May 18, 1916, a Cadillac V-8, traveling the "valley route," would lower the mark to 9 hours, 37 minutes.[5]

Gear Includes Searchlight, Shotgun

King drove a 1915 Kissel Model 6-42, named in part for its 6-cylinder, block-cast engine. With a bore and stroke of $3\frac{5}{8} \times 5\frac{1}{2}$ inches, the L-head engine produced 31.37 horsepower under the formula attributed to the Society of Automotive Engineers. The 3-speed transmission was mounted amidships instead of bolted to the engine. The car, on a 126-inch wheelbase, came equipped with wood-spoked wheels, tires of $35 \times 4\frac{1}{2}$ inches, a Stromberg carburetor and Firestone tires.[6]

Modified slightly, "Miss King's big touring car is stripped of all seats excepting that of the driver's and so arranged that she can camp out over night without getting out of the car," according to the *Wyoming Tribune* of Cheyenne.[7] Photos clearly show the back seat still in place — at least while she posed with her car before the start. A piece of canvas covered the area behind the front seat, evidently to repel rain and dust. She carried a Sparton-brand siren on the car, and a variety of equipment: "In addition to the extra tires, waterbags, gasoline and oil, Miss King carries enough food to last her four days, a sawed-off shotgun, a revolver and a huge searchlight." In short, there was "nothing missing that would add to her comfort in her long drive," gushed a Nebraska newspaper.[8] These items included a tent, blankets and cooking utensils.

Under King's procedure, as *Motor West* described it, "She will have no chauffeur or mechanician; will not even take a dog, but will go it alone, make her own repairs, sleep out on the desert when occasion requires, or camp in pleasanter places when opportunity offers." The *Los Angeles Times* added: "Her only companions will be a rifle and six-shooter."[9] Like many other transcontinentalists, King actually had local mechanics maintain and repair her Kissel-

Kar, as newspapers along her route revealed.

Local newspapers, including the *Nevada State Journal* of Reno, generally reported that King arrived in town traveling alone: "There is no one with Miss King, nor is there a car following her or an advance man ahead. She is making the trip alone, the first time it has ever been attempted by a woman." She was actually far from lonely, however, as she was "attended by all the publicity that trained ingenuity could devise," as Charles K. Field wrote a year later in *Sunset: The Pacific Monthly*. Asserts automotive historian M.M. Musselman: "Paramount's press agents followed Miss King at a respectful distance, and also preceded her, through the unadvertised courtesy of the Kissel Motor Car Company."[10]

Contract Dubs King "The Paramount Girl"

King and Jesse L. Lasky had a contract specifying her obligations and rewards for completing a solo transcontinental trip, the actress hinted, although without providing the exact details. Press accounts supplied some of the answers, saying that in exchange for stopping at Paramount theaters from California to New York, her studio would dub her "The Paramount Girl," let her star in a feature-length film and give her a new KisselKar. Some other contract obligations are uncertain. For instance, King told a hobo who sought a lift to Reno that her contract forbade it, yet in Wyoming she gave a ride to a sheep herder.

King left San Francisco September 1 "on a schedule that would enable her to reach New York city in twenty-six days," said the *Omaha (Neb.) Daily News*. Obviously printing a Paramount press release, the *Los Angeles Examiner, San Francisco Chronicle* and other papers had predicted three weeks. Just before King's start, however, the *Chronicle* conceded it might be a "very little over that." The *Examiner* also hedged—"perhaps one day over that period"—because the San Francisco Kissel agent had announced that King would follow an 18-day, 2,457-mile itinerary to Chicago.[11] From there, it would certainly take King several days to drive to the East Coast. But even this schedule would have smashed the 59-day women's coast-to-coast speed record that Alice Ramsey set in 1909. No such schedule existed, however, King told another Omaha newspaper in outlining her reasons for the trip:

> Jesse L. Lasky told me when I started from San Francisco that if I had pluck enough to make the trip through to New York I could be known hereafter as "the Paramount girl," and that I could have a picture all my own. What more inducement could a girl want? I do so hope my picture will please my friends throughout the country. I am not trying to break any records, or make the trip within a specified time, but I am trying to make friends for the Paramount service.[12]

King's grief over the loss of a sister inspired the trip, according to Field's *Sunset* article:

> She had sent east for an invalid sister, hoping that California might mean health, but her care was in vain. The death of this sister served to take all the life and sparkle out of the movie girl. She struggled against a depression that seemed to be crushing her down. Then, in a moment of inspiration born of a desperate desire to get her mind off her loss, she decided to drive her automobile alone across the continent. That ought to keep her busy! Business enterprise seconded the movement of her inspiration, and Anita King started eastward, as the Paramount Girl.[13]

King's less personal objectives were "to set a new economy record for long distance touring as well as to demonstrate that women drivers can travel alone through the country," the *San Francisco Examiner* declared.[14]

Actress Starts for East Coast

The Kissel Motor Car Company of Hartford, Wisconsin, joined Lasky and Paramount in promoting King's coast-to-coast adventure, launched on Wednesday, September 1, 1915, from the San Francisco exposition grounds. Press accounts fail to state her exact time of departure. Kissel agents in Omaha and elsewhere drove out to welcome King. According to Kissel publicity manager H.S. Daniels, who became a virtual color commentator for the *Press* and *Times* of Hartford, "The Kissel company has arranged to have a car meet her on arrival at the principal points and escort her part of the way East from each of these stops so, though she drives alone and makes her own repairs, if any are necessary, she will not be entirely lonesome after all."[15] The Paramount company, however, furnished her car, according to King, who told the *Los Angeles Examiner* of her brand loyalty: "The first car I ever had was a KisselKar, when I learned to drive seven years ago. Since that time I have driven many cars, but I am loyal to the Kissel, for it has always served me well. For that reason I have chosen it for this trip."[16]

As the *Hartford Press* revealed, King's transcontinental auto had been owned by Adolph P. Kissel, a Hartford real-estate baron and brother of Kissel Motor Car Company founders George A. and Will Kissel: "An additional local interest is given to the trip, as the car which Miss King will drive as far as Chicago is one that formerly belonged to A.P. Kissel of this city, which was left by him in California on his return this spring."[17]

Geraldine Farrar, standing, bids farewell to Anita King. The car has a coil of heavy rope lashed to the running board and a water bag hanging from the windshield post. (HHAM)

Dozens of press accounts described King's KisselKar without giving the year of the car. But because Adolph P. Kissel was driving it in the spring of 1915, it was evidently a 1915 and not a new 1916 model, and Kissel company records confirm it.[18] Though it implied that King would switch cars in Chicago, the *Press* neglected to provide details. No other reports indicated that King switched cars. As part of her prize for reaching New York City, one Nebraska newspaper said, "she will ... receive the best KisselKar that can be made." King "is not doing this 'stunt' for glory alone," added the *Hartford Press* in confirming the Nebraska newspaper account. "If she succeeds in completing the trip, she will receive the finest KisselKar

the factory can build from her manager, Jesse Lasky."[19]

There to see her off at the start was Geraldine Farrar, a leading attraction at New York's Metropolitan Opera from 1906 to 1922 and "the best-known American opera singer of her time." In 1915, Jesse L. Lasky "scored a tremendous public relations coup in signing Farrar," according to *The Motion Picture Guide*. Farrar appeared with King in two 1915 silent films—*Carmen* and *Temptation*, both directed by Cecil B. DeMille.[20]

Surviving photos show that, besides the "Paramount Girl" nickname painted on the left and right sides of King's open touring car, both sides of the hood bore the words "Koast to Koast in a KisselKar." A sign on the car's right side read: "Jesse L.

Lasky Studio Hollywood Cal./Executive Office New York." Painted on the lower part of the windshield was the assurance that "Paramount Pictures Please." Lettering on the car's collapsible top likewise advertised "Paramount Pictures." According to a sign painted on the car's left side, King was carrying "Messages from the Mayors of Los Angeles and San Francisco to the Mayor of New York."

The contents of the mayoral message from James Rolph, Jr., of San Francisco to John P. Mitchel of New York City were undisclosed. Colorful "Sunny Jim" Rolph, who would serve as mayor from 1912 to 1930, had a propensity for long-distance communications, however. In 1914, the same year he played a bit part in the silent film *Rip Van Winkle*, Rolph sent Mitchel a letter via the first ship to carry California products to New York City via the newly opened Panama Canal. Early in 1915, Rolph "amazed" a group of newspaper publishers meeting in New York City by delivering a 15-minute speech over the technological marvel of the age — the long-distance telephone. Afterward, Rolph in San Francisco chatted with Mitchel in New York as the publishers listened in on telephone earpieces.[21]

Other signs or pennants on the Kissel-Kar promoted Lasky films, and indicated King was using Ventura gasoline and Firestone tires. To an inspired *Los Angeles Times* caption writer, King thus became "the Paramount Girl, the Firestone Queen, the Kissel Doll Baby and the Ventura Venus." What's more, "her car carries a large Paramount Banner and she will be easily recognized," a Reno newspaper advised.[22]

King's send-off from San Francisco was as eye-catching as her automobile. The night before her departure, she drove her Kissel-Kar onto the stage of the city's Imperial Theater, where "Mayor Rolph intrusted to her a letter to be delivered to the Mayor of New York on her arrival there."[23]

"Early Attracted to the Stage"

Born and educated in Chicago, King was "a protegee [*sic*] of Lillian Russell and early attracted to the stage," according to the publicity department at the Jesse L. Lasky Feature Play Company.[24] Some accounts say she appeared on the New York stage with Russell, the well-known early star of burlesque and vaudeville theater.

King's early film producer, Jesse L. Lasky, in 1914 became one of three principals (including W.W. Hodkinson and Adolph Zukor) who formed Paramount Pictures — originally set up solely as a distribution company.[25] Films in which Anita King appeared from 1914 to 1916 are listed in one film encyclopedia as, variously, either Lasky or Lasky-Paramount productions.

When King's mother died, Field wrote, she left her daughter some property in Mexico, where Anita moved and lived with her "nurse" — probably meaning a nanny. Field's "nurse" was quite possibly the "maid" that Grace Kingsley mentioned in her August 1916 *Photoplay Magazine* article, "All-Around Anita," which, for drama, reads much like a movie script. "Carey King, her husband, now dead," related to Kingsley an incident that Kingsley resurrected for *Photoplay*:

> A few years ago, at the beginning of the strife in Mexico, she [Anita King] was living on the outskirts of Mexico City. Some Mexican soldiers stopped at her house one day and asked for a drink of water. Her Mexican maid served them. One of them recognized the girl as a friend of the rival faction, and started to seize her.
>
> Miss King heard the girl's screams, and rushed to help her. There were no men of the family on the place — and Anita King got a bullet through her arm. The soldiers finally seized and shot the Mexican girl, but not until Miss King had

made a valiant battle and risked her own life! Some spark of manhood must have remained in the Mexican leader, for he called his men away, and left the brave girl alone. She managed to bind up the wounded arm, but fainted before the family came home.[26]

Field refers to the forced resignation of 30-year Mexican dictator Porfirio Díaz, who was deposed in the spring of 1911, during the early years of that country's 1910–1920 revolution. While Díaz fled to Europe, King boarded a train for the coast, but "the train was held up by rebels and Miss King and her companions were forced to spend the day in a filthy Mexican jail before being released," according to Boswell McGaffey, the Lasky studio historian.[27]

Young Daredevil Crashes Race Car

"Automobile racing was just then becoming popular, so she secured a position as demonstrator with a Los Angeles automobile firm and then took up racing and had the distinction of being the first woman automobile racing driver," McGaffey wrote. According to his account, King started racing in 1911, although she would claim 1909. Regardless, a great many female racers had preceded King into the sport, including Joan Newton Cuneo of Richmond Hill, Long Island, New York. Cuneo was "the first eminent woman race driver," contends Virginia Scharff in *Taking the Wheel: Women and the Coming of the Motor Age.*[28]

Speaking at Cheyenne's Lyric Theater during her 1915 coast-to-coast trip, King revealed that she had been driving at least six years:

I have driven a great deal and have participated in races, one a regularly sanctioned 150-mile race for women, held at the Phoenix, Ariz., fair in 1909.

They have a matinee of races there at the conclusion of the big annual Los Angeles–Phoenix race. I was in a fair way to win the first day when something snapped and I smashed into a fence. When they picked me up, I was counting the stars in the Arizona sky, but I got out the next day and drove in another race. I am happy to say that I did not lose my nerve, which is so often the case when a driver has one bad spill.

I toured Mexico in a machine five years ago; I also drove the first race on the Los Angeles Motordrome course; and made the drive to Phoenix in a racing car, tho [*sic*] not in a race at the time. So you see, I have had some automobile experience.[29]

Press reports fail to confirm King's participation in races at Phoenix and Los Angeles, however. According to the *Arizona Republican* and *Phoenix Gazette*, none of the four races held on November 11, 1909 — part of "Automobile Day" at the Arizona Territorial Fair — featured or even included any female drivers. The longest race of the day was a 50-miler; the fair's first 150-mile race occurred in 1915.[30]

The *New York Times'* wire reports on the first week of racing at the new Los Angeles board track make no mention of Anita King or any female racers. But mechanic Carey King — evidently Anita's husband — who was riding in Harris Hanshue's Apperson automobile, was injured on April 10, 1910, when their car lost a tire and rolled.[31]

King and studio historian McGaffey diverge widely in describing injuries the actress-driver may have suffered at Phoenix. King says she was back in the driver's seat a day after crashing. According to McGaffey: "Miss King entered a number of events and won several and finally, in Phoenix, at a race meet, she was hurled through the fence while driving at top speed and nearly lost her life. After leaving the hospital, Miss King sought the quieter life of motion-picture acting."[32]

Anita King's Silent Films	Date	King's Role
The Man from Home	1914	Helene, Countess de Champigney
The Virginian	1914	Mrs. Ogden
Carmen	1915	a Gypsy girl
Chimmie Fadden	1915	Fanny Van Cortlandt
The Girl of the Golden West	1915	Wowkle
Snobs	1915	Ethel Hamilton
Temptation	1915	
Anton the Terrible	1916	Vera Stanovitch
The Heir to the Horrah	1916	
Maria Rosa	1916	Ana
The Race	1916	Grace Van Dyke
The Golden Fetter	1917	
The Squaw Man's Son	1917	Indian maiden
The Girl Angle	1917 or 1918	
Petticoats and Politics	1918	
Whatever the Cost	1918	
Mistaken Identity	1919	
One Against Many	1919	
Stripped for a Million	1919	

* * * * * * * *

Sources: Seven encyclopedias of film: *The American Film Institute Catalog*; *Filmarama: The Formidable Years, 1893–1919*; *Halliwell's Filmgoer's Companion*; *The Motion Picture Guide*; *Twenty Years of Silents, 1908–1928*; *Who Was Who on Screen*; and *Who's Who in Hollywood*.

Anita King's filmography.

Her first well-known silent film was *The Virginian* in 1914, directed by Cecil B. DeMille. King's lifestyle change was a minor one, says Field, whose *Sunset* article includes a photo of an airborne car "showing our heroine driving an automobile at high speed off a bridge and landing miraculously right-side-up while the camera man ground busily at a safe distance." The "beautiful transcontinental motorist," as Field described her (a 1917 studio directory said King stood 5 feet 4 inches, weighed 130 pounds and had auburn hair and hazel eyes) needed no stunt double.[33]

King's Stunts "The Sincere Stuff"

"If you see Miss King in a photoplay, racing an automobile, or nursing a wounded soldier ... or sailing a boat, or cooking a meal, or fighting a timber wolf, or running an airship, or teaching school, there will be nothing 'phoney' or faked about it," Kingsley claimed in her *Photoplay* piece. "It will be the 'sincere stuff,' as the newspaper men say. Miss King not only can but has done all these things 'off-stage.'"[34]

Kingsley's *Photoplay* article, published a month before Field's *Sunset* piece, shows a publicity still of Anita King — head lolling,

According to *Sunset* magazine, this photo shows Anita King jumping a car for a movie stunt. (September 1916 *Sunset*)

apparently unconscious — in the car she used during filming of a 1916 silent film, *The Race*. The car, with several shattered rear-wheel spokes, rests on a tangled pile of driftwood alongside a river; this is perhaps the aftermath of the bridge-jumping photo from Field's *Sunset* article. Reads the *Photoplay* caption: "The fraction of a second after making a 72-foot leap — not hurt, just stunned."

King starred as Grace Van Dyke, opposite Victor Moore as Jimmy Grayson, Jr., in *The Race*, in which King duplicated her actual 1915 transcontinental auto trip. This was apparently the "picture all my own" that King was promised for completing her 1915 stunt. [35] The *American Film Institute Catalog* describes the comedy-drama:

Fed up with his son's wild life style, James Grayson Sr. disinherits Jimmy and then throws him out of the house. Through Grace Van Dyke, a chauffeur, Jimmy gets a job in a garage, and then he and Grace's father Andrew invent a revolutionary automobile engine. It will take months to get the patent, however, and Jimmy must pay back a $10,000 debt almost immediately.

To get the money, he enters a transcontinental car race which has a large cash prize, and which Grace also has entered. Just as Jimmy is about to

win, however, he learns that Andrew is also deeply in debt. As a result, he lets Grace pass him and finish first, so she can get the money for her father. At the finish line, Jimmy is arrested for not paying his debts, but then, far ahead of schedule, the patent rights arrive for the engine, as well as a royalty check that more than covers what Jimmy owes.[36]

Robert Connelly, author of *The Motion Picture Guide*, drubs the film: "There are enough directorial errors in this uninspired effort to make up a blooper reel.... Among the picture's other shortcomings is the unfortunate miscasting of the gifted Moore." Connelly did not single out King for either praise or criticism.[37]

Repels Tramp, Reaches Reno

On her actual transcontinental trip King would travel what *Motor West* called "the Blue Book Route," better known as the Lincoln Highway. The journal listed her scheduled overnight stops as far as Omaha: Sacramento and Lake Tahoe, California; Fallon, Austin and Ely, Nevada; Fish Springs and Salt Lake City, Utah; Green River, Rawlins, Laramie and Cheyenne, Wyoming; and Kimball, North Platte, Grand Island and Omaha, Nebraska. East of Omaha, "the greater part of the drive will be along the same highway, but there will be a number of cities visited

A movie poster for *The Race*. (AMP)

that are off the route, north and south."[38] Beyond Omaha, the Lincoln Highway passed through Iowa, Illinois, Indiana, Ohio, West Virginia, Pennsylvania, New Jersey and New York.

On Thursday, September 2, the second day of King's trip, she drove eastward into the Sierra Nevada, intending to reach

Opposite, top: A publicity still from *The Race* purports to show a stunned Anita King an instant after she jumped her "Ocean to Ocean" car 72 feet off a bridge into a pile of driftwood. (AMP) *Bottom:* As a coast-to-coast driver in *The Race*, King elicits the sympathy and concern of everyone she meets. (AMP)

King dressed for utility, not glamour, as the gauntlet-length gloves, tall boots and military-style outfit attest. (September 1916 *Sunset*)

Lake Tahoe. As the *Omaha Daily News* later related the incident:

> While crossing the mountains … she was stopped late at night by a tramp, who demanded that she give him something to eat and then drive him to Reno. "I was scared to death," said Miss King, "but I told him that I had nothing to eat

myself and that the only thing I could give him was a drink, and that I couldn't drive him to Reno because of my contract which says that no one can ride with me. I gave him the little flask [of whiskey] which I carry for emergencies, and he took a small drink. I asked him to try to get to Reno as I would be there for the next day. The next day while I was speaking at the theater he sent me a little bouquet. There's some good in everybody, even in the down-and-outer."[39]

In its nearly identical account, the *Omaha Daily Bee* said the tramp accosted King in one of the wooden snowsheds that the railroads built to protect their tracks through the mountains. The snowsheds had openings or gates where the Lincoln Highway intersected the railroad tracks. At Reno, the hobo presented her with "a wilted bouquet of flowers," King told the *Daily Bee*.[40]

King reached Reno on Friday, September 3, as the *Reno Evening Gazette* related:

> Anita King, the Paramount girl who is driving an automobile alone across the continent, arrived in Reno shortly after noon today, a little behind the schedule she expected to keep. The reason for it was tire trouble. But she got out of the machine and repaired it, all alone.
>
> Miss King was met at the state line by a number of automobile owners and Paramount enthusiasts. When she reached the corporate line of the city Mayor Byington met her and presented her with a key to the city. The key is about the same size as is Miss King, and she was so pleased with it that she is going to carry it all the way to New York with her on her car.
>
> In view of this the mayor is having the key decorated and Reno will have unusual publicity because of the position Miss King will give it on her machine. The car was placed in the Mack Garage,

where some minor repairs will be made, and the motion picture actress will start again tomorrow morning.

This afternoon and this evening Miss King will explain to the audiences at the Majestic how Paramount pictures are made.[41]

She would resume her eastward journey at 6 A.M. Saturday, September 4, according to the *Nevada State Journal* of Reno.[42] Photos taken when King reached New York City show the large key, apparently wooden, resting on the cowl of the KisselKar, just in front of the windshield. At nearly every stop on her route, someone gave her a souvenir to display on her Kissel, observed one Midwestern newspaper, which added: "On the back of the car was a printed announcement that the gasoline tank had been filled at Los Angeles and below it were the names of every person who had filled the tank along the route."[43]

King Kills Kanine?

Several accounts maintain that King shot either a coyote, a "timber-wolf" or her own dog (some press accounts claim she had one) while traveling through the "Great American Desert"—a vague reference to her route through Nevada and Utah. Because her KisselKar was equipped with a "huge searchlight," one newspaper contended, "most of the desert travel was made at night." During her three days and nights in the desert, King told the *Omaha Daily News*, "I'd drive until I was dead tired and then I'd shut the engine off and sleep right where I was. While I was on the desert I shot a coyote. Gee, he looked big as a house when I first saw him, but I got him all right."[44] She gave no reason for shooting a coyote, rarely a threat to humans.

In its terse summary of King's adventure, *MoTor* matter-of-factly endorses the coyote-shooting incident: "While the trip was eventful, it was not dangerous by any means. At one time she went four days and three nights without having an opportunity to change clothing and one night she slept in the desert. She killed a coyote, and once lost her way." *Photoplay* improved the tale, however, in writing about King "single-handed[ly] destroying a timber-wolf which attacked her on the edge of the big American desert."[45] The *Omaha World-Herald*, undoubtedly with help from Paramount's publicity department, countered with a version that reads much like a movie drama:

> Coming across the great American desert, Miss King's water supply, both for her car and for herself, ran exceedingly low. The dust and sun parched her own throat until it felt raw, and her little pet dog—the lone companion to start the trip with her—looked pleadingly up as he begged for a drink. His tongue was so dry that he could not bark.
>
> And to conserve her scant supply of drinking water, Miss King took her revolver and shot her pet. But she buried him in the sand, and marked the spot, she says.[46]

Because King was not traveling with a dog, as photos show and *Motor West* stated, the *World-Herald's* tale revealed its creator for what he was: a wag.

Rescued from Desert Death

At some unspecified point in Utah's "Great Salt Desert," King wilted in the heat, as automobile historian M.M. Musselman recounts in a playfully skeptical tone:

> Halfway across she found herself lost on its salt-encrusted expanse. With all the water boiled out of her radiator and her last drop of drinking water gone, it looked as though Miss King was a goner.

She stumbled out onto the hot desert sands and fell fainting beside her faithful KisselKar.

She knew not how long she lay thus in the broiling sun, but when she came to she was in the shade of a Joshua tree, strong arms were holding her, and cool water was trickling down her throat. She had been rescued by three desert prospectors. They filled her radiator and sent her on her way, followed closely by her press representative and two photographers, who had been recording this thrilling life drama from behind a nearby giant cactus plant.[47]

Gadzooks! This was a riveting tale. But there's more: On Monday, September 6, King reached Elko, Nevada, and sent a telegram to the American Theatre in Salt Lake City. The *Salt Lake Herald-Republican* published the telegram. In it, King claimed her death-defying nightmare occurred not in Utah (as Musselman suggests) but between Reno and Fallon:

Have been lost. Stuck in mud trying to cross to Fallon. Worked for eleven hours, but could not get out. Fell exhausted. Was found at 2 A.M. by three men that were prospectors and had heard me shooting my gun for help. Was taken to Lovelock, started out next day and have been on the desert for two days and nights. Just found this town [Elko]. Will try and get to Salt Lake Wednesday, with the help of God.[48]

King's telegram is confusing. If the prospectors found her early Sunday morning and she left from Lovelock "the next day," does that mean King left on Sunday or Monday? If she left Monday, how did she drive the 200 miles to Elko in a day? Given her Saturday departure from Reno, why doesn't she say in her Monday telegram that she has been three days in the desert?

In a letter King reportedly sent from Salt Lake City to the Kissel Motor Car Company, King gives a more complete accounting of her movements:

Was lost and in distress from Saturday morning until Monday night when I arrived in Elko, Nevada. In leaving Fallon en route to Austin, via the Lincoln Highway, I lost the road, undoubtedly through lack of being properly posted with guiding signs. Got on the Wadsworth road, and many miles out of town my car became mired in the mud of the Salt beds.

Worked ten hours trying to extricate myself. Had no food and finally fell exhausted. Was picked up at 2 o'clock next morning (Sunday) by three prospectors, and leaving my car, I was taken to Lovelocks [*sic*]. I got no sleep but was revived with food and shelter.

Several hours later I returned to the car and succeeded in getting it out unaided. Drove steadily all Sunday, that night and all day Monday. Did not find a place to sleep or stop until I reached Elko. Arrived here at 1:30 this afternoon.

From Lovelands [Lovelock] to Winnemucca, Elko and Ogden [Utah], the roads have been terrible. Drove almost three days and two nights without a stop. Motor took terrible grades, sand and ruts fine. Will stay at Salt Lake City until Friday and follow Lincoln Highway from here on. If all does not turn out well, I shall at least not be a coward. You can say that I held out until the last breath.[49]

Nervous Breakdown Looms

King's letter indicates she drove north around the Great Salt Lake, passing through Ogden on her way to Salt Lake City. This agrees with long accounts in the four daily newspapers published in Salt Lake City, where King arrived at 1 P.M. Wednesday, September 8. Harry A. Sims, manager of

Salt Lake's American Theatre, and J.L. Gilmer, the local Kissel agent, began worrying about King when she failed to appear Sunday in Ely, Nevada. On Tuesday, they drove north from Salt Lake City with a search party. The newspapers did not indicate what prompted the searchers to head north through Ogden instead of west along the Lincoln Highway. Regardless, they found King late Tuesday night or early Wednesday morning — reports differ — "lost on a road several miles from Tremonton,"[50] a small Utah city 75 miles north of Salt Lake City. Upon finding her, Sims grabbed a telephone and called the *Salt Lake Tribune*:

> Miss King seems on the verge of a nervous breakdown from the terrible two days and nights she was lost on the desert, compelling her to change her route altogether. We have asked her to delay her appearance at the American, or to postpone it altogether, but she insists that she will tell her friends and admirers in Salt Lake of her experience and that she will not delay, since her Nevada experiences already have put her a day behind her schedule.[51]

Musselman intimated that a camera crew filmed King's struggles, perhaps for her 1916 movie, *The Race*. None of the Salt Lake City newspapers mention it. Thursday's *Salt Lake Tribune* gave this accounting of Anita's desert drama:

> Moonlight on the desert. Only a girl and a coyote in sight. Girl shoots at coyote. Coyote is undismayed.
>
> Thus would a scenario writer approach the climax of the wild night on the Nevada desert experienced by Miss Anita King, movie star — mercy, no, photoplay artiste, for she detests "movies" — who arrived in Salt Lake yesterday by automobile....
>
> But to return to the scenario. Here's a cutback: A little flivver car inhabited by three quaint natives of the desert,

An ad announces Anita King's appearance at the American Theatre in Salt Lake City. (September 8, 1915, *Deseret Evening News*)

> prospecting in the moonlight, singing songs — the men, not the car — inspired by refreshments from Fallon, Nev. Their tiny car stops. Business of listening. Explanation on the film that they hear shots. Each draws his pistol. Wild dash of natives in flivver for girl marooned in the moonlight. Clatter of flivver scares coyote. Girl is rescued by brave natives. (Another five-reel installment next week.)
>
> .... Without serious mishap Miss King reached Wadsworth, Nev. Bright and early last Saturday [September 4] she started for Fallon. At 9 o'clock in the forenoon she ran into a mud hole and got stuck. She shoveled until her shovel broke, then used her hands. Twelve hours later she extricated the car and, laughing and crying with joy, started to back the car back to Wadsworth, or at least until she could find a place to turn around. She had gone fifty feet when she

went into a mud hole worse than the first.

There she was when the coyote arrived and there the scenario writer begins one of his climaxes of the exploits of Anita. It is only necessary to state that the coyote ran back to his family in the desert; that the three young men in the little car pulled Miss King's car out of the mire and piloted her to Elko, whence she made a new start, safe and sound.[52]

"The Gamest Looking Girl"

"Miss King said that she has no very clear idea yet as to how she missed the road and got into the mud," according to the *Deseret Evening News*. But she had figured it out by Chicago: "I blame this nerve wracking experience to the lack of proper sign posting on the Lincoln Highway." Lectured the *Hartford Press*: "Miss King's experience adds weight to the allegations of other transcontinental motorists who believe that some definite action should be taken to see that the Lincoln Highway is adequately marked across the state of Nevada."[53]

King's appearance — not her misadventures — dominated some Salt Lake City newspaper accounts. Upon arriving at the Hotel Utah, the actress changed "from her dust-coated knickerbockers ... to a light, filmy gown, in which she looked more like a high school graduate than an experienced motion picture actress," the *Salt Lake Herald-Republican* observed.[54] And Wednesday evening's *Salt Lake Evening Telegram* gushed:

Anita King, she who charms you in the movies, dainty, bright and always so neat and faultlessly attired — you should have seen her when she "landed" in Salt Lake this afternoon, completing the first leg of her transcontinental automobile journey — ALONE!

Not that pretty Miss King wasn't pretty under an inch or two of desert dust, that had recently been mud, but — well, imagine those pretty eyes weighted down with fatigue.... And those gloves — they were used to actually dig mud from under her stranded machine when her shovel broke, fifty miles from nowhere, out on the desert.

And then imagine the gamest looking girl you ever saw, one who drove all night and all day for days in order to keep her schedule after she had lost her way — and there you have an inadequate picture of the pretty movie favorite who arrived here this afternoon from Tremonton, where she rested last night, the first night's rest she had for several days.[55]

"An Alarming Story"

Imagine *not*, sniffed the editor of Ely's *White Pine News*, who recalled with sarcasm that King had planned to stop in Ely the day after leaving Reno:

It is perhaps well that she did not because according to the story in the *Tribune* [of Salt Lake City] she experienced so much difficulty in pulling out of and backing into every mudhole along the route from 'Frisco to Salt Lake, it is hardly to be expected that she could have possibly missed the big pit at Copper Flat [a copper mine near Ely], and certainly a picture of the fragments that remained of her gigantic touring car being unloaded on one of the dump cars in the pit, while search was being made in an effort to find enough of the star to warrant the holding of a funeral, would not be an attraction upon the screen.

According to the *Tribune*, it appears that Anita broke into Salt Lake in the greatest state of excitement imaginable and told an alarming story about having encountered a coyote away out on the desert in Nevada, and after the animal's eyebrows had been shot off one by one, either by Anita or a band of cowboys who happened to be herding sheep only about thirty miles distant and were attracted to her rescue by the frantic screams of the star — of course the real details have not yet been told — well, anyway, while Anita is only incidentally advertising Paramount pictures, if she ever succeeds in placing in the hand of Mayor Mitchell [*sic*] in New York the message she bears to him from Mayor Rolph of San Francisco, some thrilling stories will be told upon the screen of her perilous trip across the deserts of the West — YOU BET YOU.

Perhaps if Anita had followed the Lincoln Highway instead of striking off on some sort of exploring trip into the sagebrush ... she would not have had all these either real or imaginary accidents and hair-raising or hair-splitting experiences, but it is all a part of the important duty of delivering that very important message to one mayor from another — to say nothing of advertising.

The harrowing experiences of Anita are more or less pathetic, when it is learned that she became so greatly alarmed at the sound of a distant coyote — particularly when it is a known fact that a coyote is a natural-born coward and will run away from anything half its size twice as rapidly as any other known animal.

Just why a great corporation would send a little innocent girl like this out into the wilds of Nevada is not known, but she has the sympathy of the community and all the people regret that she should have seen fit to leave Ely off her calling list and take some other route instead of the Lincoln Highway, and they are deeply grateful to the "prospectors" (who were in an automobile), for having rescued her.[56]

Water Up to Her Neck

Meanwhile, back in Hartford, Wisconsin, the editors of the *Press* and *Times* — trusting souls — continued to print without question the Kissel factory's press releases. "It is hardly possible that a better combination could have been secured than that of Anita King and the KisselKar," one release asserted, in stark contrast to the Ely editor's assessment. "She has already encountered enough hardships on the trip to unnerve many a strong man," declared the *Hartford Times*, referring to her Nevada experiences. "Then to keep on over all kinds of bad roads and dangerous hills, night and day, has won for her the admiration of the entire automobile world."[57] That is, with the exception of a certain critic in Ely, Nevada, and perhaps others elsewhere.

Under *Motor West's* itinerary, King would reach Omaha on Tuesday, September 14, but mid–September found her in Wyoming. As reported in the *Laramie (Wyo.) Republican* of Thursday, September 16, Day 16, King

reached the city from the west in her large touring car last night, and a few minutes later appeared on the stage of the Empress theater, the "Paramount theater" of this section, to greet a crowded house and to tell something of her trip alone, in her automobile, on her way from one ocean to another.

She said she had been outfitted by Mr. Lasky of the Paramount company when she suggested that she dared make the trip, and that, while she had encountered much bad weather and "water up to her neck sometimes," she had met a delightful lot of people and had received every courtesy. The trip had been full of interest, she said, with not an untoward act in the whole time.[58]

"Miss King spent the early part of the day here," reported Thursday's Laramie newspaper, "waiting for a large coat she left at Rawlins yesterday. Her car stood at the Third street entrance to the Connor and was the object of interest to a large number of people."[59] Having recovered her coat, a "tanned and weather beaten" Anita

King drove on to Cheyenne, where she arrived at 1:30 P.M. Thursday, according to the following day's *Cheyenne State Leader*:

> Last night, Miss King spoke before a large crowd at the Lyric and interestingly related brief experiences she has had and encountered as a motion picture actress and some of the hardships she has coped with during her journey across the continent.
>
> "I realize that it is no usual thing for a girl to attempt a trip such as I have, without company, and thus far it has been no snap," said Miss King last night. "I was lost two days on the Nevada desert, had especially hard traveling at several points in Utah and encountered some heavy roads west of Rawlins. I do not intend to try to make any record from coast to coast and will content myself with a leisurely mileage every day."[60]

Somewhere in Wyoming, "Miss King also received a proposal on her trip," the *Omaha Daily Bee* later reported. "In Wyoming she gave a lift to a sheep herder who was carrying a wounded lamb to town. He said he admired her courage in making the trip alone and after detailing all his earthly possessions asked, 'Wouldn't you like to make this trip our honeymoon trip?'"[61] Elsewhere in Wyoming, "she was delayed for several days due to a terrific downpour of rain," which King described in the *Hartford Press*: "It was a genuine mud lark. Car skidded all over [the] road in places and was almost mired a dozen times. I looked like I'd seen service in the trenches for a month. I started to hunt for the [tire] chains I lost now and then, but discovered I was taking the Lincoln Highway east with me in carload shipments."[62]

Big Thrill, Big Spill

Another Wyoming experience changed the course of King's life, according to Field, who wrote his *Sunset* article after interviewing King "on the flower-hung porch of her microscopic bungalow in a tight little bouquet of white bungalows at Hollywood." The "real big lasting thrill" of her trip came when King met a 16-year-old Wyoming girl who begged King to take her to Hollywood.[63] King advised the girl to prepare for a life in the movies by finishing high school and, privately, told the girl's mother how to handle her star-struck daughter.

"You think I'm so much more fortunate than you because I'm in the pictures," King tells the girl in a farewell that Field reconstructed for *Sunset*. "But I haven't any mother and my sister died only the other day and I'm so lonely. I'd give the world for what you have right there in that house. Don't let go of that! And someday you'll have all the rest."[64]

King reached North Platte, Nebraska, Friday evening, September 17. The next day, while traveling eastward on the Lincoln Highway near Kearney, "she met with a slight accident to the car which delayed her several hours," according to the *North Platte Semi-Weekly Tribune*. An Omaha newspaper mentioned the same "road accident" but, like the North Platte paper, provided no details.[65]

The "accident" occurred a few miles west of Kearney at Elm Creek, according to the *Daily Hub* in Kearney, where King spent Saturday night, September 18: "She had been caught in a mudhole near Elmcreek [*sic*] and appealed to local garage men for assistance.... She is making the trip alone and up to the time she struck the bad hole at Elmcreek [*sic*] she had a most enjoyable time." Meeting the day after King's departure, the Kearney Commercial Club declared that "the condition of the Lincoln Highway, both east and west of the city, was a deplorable one," the *Daily Hub* reported.[66]

While east of Kearney heading toward Grand Island on Sunday, September 19, King

King greets her fans at a typical stop, location unknown. Note the siren mounted near the car's right-side windshield post. (UMSC)

got stuck in the mud again, according to the *Omaha Daily Bee*. "A farmer came along with a load of hay and hoisting the pretty movie actress atop the load of hay with him, he offered to send another team to pull her car out of the mud. They drove along a little way when the hay cart struck a rut, upsetting the hay, movie actress and farmer all in a heap."[67]

King Voices Dubious Claim

Monday's *Daily Independent* reported King's Sunday arrival in Grand Island:

Heralded by loud calls of the siren on her car, Miss Anita King arrived in this city yesterday about noon, being on the trip, unaccompanied[,] from the Pacific coast…. The young lady is one of the leading lights in the moving photo plays, and stated that she was a little behind time due to a breakdown experienced near Kearney. The car she is driving is a powerful one, however, and she expects to make up for lost time later on her journey.[68]

King drove on from Grand Island to Columbus. At this overnight stop, she "appeared at the North theatre Sunday evening, where Paramount pictures are shown, and made a brief talk to the movie fans," according to the *Columbus Telegram*. "She told of her contract with the Paramount Film Co. and how she undertook to make her trip by herself," added the *Columbus Journal*, which quoted King: "I am traveling absolutely alone in a Kissel car which has been furnished me by the Paramount Film company, and if I succeed in making this trip I will be the only person that has ever made the trip across the continent alone. I have encountered a number of bad roads on the trip on account of the recent heavy rains, but am making fairly good time."[69]

Some observers echoed King's dubious claim that no one — male or female — had accomplished a solo transcontinental trip. Others contended that she would become the first woman to accomplish the feat. Even this more modest claim is questionable, as the Lincoln Highway in 1915 was becoming relatively crowded with coast-to-coast traffic. Back in the summer of 1910, "probably an average of one party a week crossed the continent by automobile," according to *American Motorist*, which predicted the number would double in 1911. The American Automobile Association estimated that 500 autos — carrying an average of four persons apiece — would cross the country over a single transcontinental route, the Trail to Sunset, in 1912.[70]

The international expositions that San Diego and San Francisco opened in 1915 lured many Eastern autoists to California. How many? Between June and November 1915, the Reo Motor Car Company predicted, "More than one thousand Reos will make the transcontinental [trip] if we are to judge by the letters we receive from owners of Reo cars, telling us of their plans and asking for suggestions as to the proposed trip." The AAA's touring bureau "estimates that no fewer than 6,000 motor cars this year traveled from points east of the Mississippi river to the Pacific coast or vice versa," according to a December 1915 *MoTor* article. Between 1915 and 1917, transcontinental motorists formed a virtual "moving chain," observed *Sunset* maga-

zine: "In big automobiles and small they came; solitary drivers, either man or woman, parties and whole families...."[71] Chances are at least fair that one of these "solitary drivers, either man or woman," quietly traveled across the United States long before King conceived her trip.

Tearful Motorist Reaches Omaha

On Monday, September 20, King — averaging about 100 miles per day, according to Omaha newspapers — drove through North Bend and Fremont en route to Omaha. A caravan of autos from Omaha met the actress in Fremont. The caravan carried Omaha's mayor, "armed with a big bouquet of flowers"; local representatives for KisselKar, Paramount and Firestone tires; reporters; photographers; and Lionel Tobias, a friend of King's. "She is a blonde, with big sparkling blue eyes, and a pair of saucy lips," observed the *Omaha Daily News* reporter who made the trip to Fremont. "Miss King was so surprised and pleased to see Lionel Tobias, an old companion in the movie game in California, that she gave him a big kiss and hug right in front of the crowd. Many were envious of the honored Tobias."[72]

King was similarly pleased to at last reach Omaha at 5:15 P.M. Sunday, according to a melodramatic account in the following day's *Omaha World-Herald*. The newspaper lopped several inches from her 5-foot-4 stature, making her appear more vulnerable than ever:

> Tears crept into her voice as well as her eyes when Miss Anita King, star of the Paramount moving picture service, checked in last evening at the Henshaw hotel. Her hand trembled so that it was difficult for her to write her name on the register. And then she smiled.

"You've no idea what a relief it is to reach a city like Omaha," she said. "I have had so much trouble, and I am so tired. But you have been very good to me — awfully good."

This little actress — she's only a few inches more than four and a half feet in height — is touring from San Francisco to New York — absolutely alone....

"It is so nice to know that I will have comparatively easy touring for the balance of my trip," said Miss King last night. "I have endured so much hardship that the sight of friendly faces in a friendly city makes my heart jump right up into my throat, and I just can't keep the tears away."

The first thing Miss King did, upon reaching her room, was to telephone for a hairdresser and a manicurist. "Gracious," said the little actress, "I do hope my clothes are not ruined. I haven't been 'dressed up' for so long, though, that I suppose I won't know how to act."[73]

Her driving clothes were as business-like as her city outfits were fancy. "She wore a gray suit, with short knee skirt and big lace-top boots when she reached Omaha," according to the *Omaha Daily News*. Added the *Omaha Daily Bee*: "Although jauntily attired in a rose-colored suit and large black hat while in the city, Miss King wears none such fripperies en route. She wears a costume designed especially for her of heavy, rainproof material. She wears the trousers, over which she slips a skirt of the same material when she approaches the city, and high boots and a tight-fitting cap."[74]

King Holds Up Putdown Artists

King, who in her *Omaha Daily News* interview described shooting a coyote, added:

There was only one other time that I used the gun, and that was when a man

called me a liar and said that I wasn't traveling alone. I made him apologize and take back what he said. There was another man and his wife who stopped a few moments to talk to me while I was resting. He became very insulting and called me a liar. Well, I beat them into the next town and when they arrived I had him arrested. I felt so sorry for his wife that I had the authorities let him go. I haven't had much of this kind of trouble.[75]

On the day she started, *Motor West* projected that King would reach Omaha September 14, but muddy roads and bad weather had put her six days behind schedule. Nevertheless, from San Francisco to Omaha she had traveled every day, including Sundays, according to *Motor Age*. One day off the road in Omaha would be her only rest day between the coast and Chicago, the journal added.

While saying that transcontinental motoring was more difficult than she had expected, King pledged to continue to New York City, according to the *Omaha World-Herald*: "'Do you dread the remainder of your trip?' the mere reporter asked the movie star. 'Do I?' she answered. 'I should say I do. I really hate to leave Omaha, to start with, and I dread climbing back into my car to go. But business is business, and I'm going to finish the trip if it takes all winter.'" She had no plans to repeat the trek, King told the *Daily Bee*. "You can just bet when I get to New York, I'm going to travel back to 'Frisco like a lady, on the best overland road" — that is, by rail.[76]

King, who planned to leave Omaha at 7 A.M. Wednesday, September 22, traveled to nearby Council Bluffs, Iowa, Tuesday night, to speak at the Majestic Theater, according to one news report:

Then she returned to the Hipp theater [in Omaha] and spoke to another audience. Still later she was entertained at an informal dinner at the Fontenelle [Hotel], where a few invited guests did her honor.

Miss King's big KisselKar has been thoroughly overhauled during her stay here, and the Firestone agency has inspected the tires and added a number of inner tubes and casings and the like. The machine will be able to finish the trip to New York city without any further overhauling, the mechanics say.[77]

Even as she crossed the Midwest, the *Hartford Times* reported, "every day's drive of Miss King is being recorded on a big board at the Panama Exposition, where there is a tremendous interest in her daring adventure."[78] Across Iowa, her route took her through Ames, Des Moines, Marshalltown, Cedar Rapids and Clinton, plus many smaller towns. She arrived in one of them, Boone, an overnight stop, at 8 P.M. Wednesday, September 22. Rather than retire to her hotel room, she immediately went out on the town. According to the *Boone News-Republican*,

Two carloads of movie enthusiasts went to Scranton and met the plucky little girl and escor[t]ed her to this city. She was attired in regulation auto traveling garb and as soon as she reached the Lyric [Theatre] was escorted down the aisle and, occupying the place of honor on the top of a chair, told the big audience something of herself, her trip, of the photoplay work, etc.

Then the party repaired to the cafeteria where some rich steaks were enjoyed. Miss King then returned to the Lyric and gave the [second] big audience a talk. After this, she expressed a desire to attend a dance and enjoyed a few numbers at Conn's hall and delighted those she met there.[79]

On Thursday morning, September 23, King detoured south off the Lincoln Highway to visit the state capital, Des Moines,

where a sardonic *Register and Leader* reporter caught the irony of King's purported solo trip across the continent:

Miss King is traveling from San Francisco to New York in her machine, alone. Except for a convoy of four other automobiles loaded to the guards with newspaper reporters, motion picture magnates and magnates' wives and daughters, representatives and employe[e]s of tire manufacturing companies, sales agents for automobiles and press agents for motion pictures, she made the trip from Ames to Des Moines alone.[80]

After an overnight stay, King left Des Moines Friday for Marshalltown and points east. In hopes of meeting her on the Lincoln Highway, a "cavalcade of KisselKars" containing reporters, Kissel representatives and movie fans started westward from Cedar Rapids. After passing through the small town of Chelsea without stopping early Friday afternoon, as an accompanying *Cedar Rapids Evening Gazette* reporter recounted, the autoists decided to revisit Chelsea to

ascertain if Miss King has been heard from. She had. The whole town had heard from her because she had reached the town and had gone into the leading grocery store to buy crackers, while the crowd remained on the outside and looked in....

She was munching a cracker just like any other hungry woman would do, and she was enjoying it. She was dirt from head to foot, and she was making no effort to clean it off. In fact the little woman appeared to be proud that her garments contained mud and dust from almost a third of the states of the union....

Cedar Rapids was reached at 7 o'clock, and the cavalcade of nine automobiles made enough noise to wake the dead. Everybody and his sister were on the front porch to welcome the little woman

King's arrival in Chicago. (September 30, 1915, *Motor Age*)

and nearly everybody was down town to give her the glad hand in front of the Isis [Theater].[81]

Chicago: Next on Perilous Path

King reached Chicago, her birthplace, on Sunday afternoon, September 26, Day 26, "having encountered almost as many adventures as Kathlyn and escaped about the same number of perils as Pauline in the serial films," *Motor Age* commented. King, who in Chicago "appeared on the stage at Orchestra hall and spoke a few words about her trip and the company she represented," planned to resume her eastward journey on Tuesday, according to the *Chicago Daily Tribune*.[82] In fact, she delayed her departure until Wednesday morning, the *Hartford Press* related:

Miss King was royally treated while in Chicago. At the big society and charity event of the year [—] the Motor Pageant at Midway Gardens — she was an honored guest, Monday night. She was received there by a personal representation of Mayor [William Hale] Thompson....

On Tuesday she went to the City Hall where a crowd of approximately 7,000 people crowded around and cheered her. She visited the Mayor and Chief of Police [Charles C. Healy], from each of whom she received a letter.... Chief Healy's letter was addressed to all Mayors, Chiefs and Police Officers recommending Miss King to their courtesy and protection....

Before her arrival in Chicago, Miss King was met at Aurora, Ill., by a delegation of fifty people, representing the Film manufacturers, the Reel Fellows' club (an organization of movie actors), Orchestra Hall and the KisselKar. The KisselKar factory was represented by H.S. Daniels [publicity manager].

About 1000 feet of moving pictures were taken showing the departure from Chicago of the [welcoming] committee in Sunday morning's drenching rain, the reception at Aurora, Miss King and escort leaving Aurora, meeting between Miss King and her two sisters at Forest Park, arrival at the KisselKar building, trip down Michigan avenue, arrival at Orchestra Hall, arrival at Blackstone Hotel, leaving Hotel for City Hall, arrival at City Hall, Chief Healy handing Miss King a letter, and her departure.[83]

Stopped for "Fast Driving"

As in Chicago, mayors in Salt Lake City, Omaha, Des Moines, Cedar Rapids and other cities had entrusted King with letters to deliver to New York Mayor John P. Mitchel, according to the *Hartford Press*. In fact, King received messages "from the Mayors of nearly every city" on her route, as the newspaper later amended it.[84] "But the letter which Miss King prizes most, because of its decidedly unusual character, was handed to her by Superintendent of Police Healey [*sic*]," the *Press* related:

> To Mayors, Chiefs of Police, Sheriffs, Marshals and Police Officers: — Gentlemen:
>
> The bearer of this communication is Anita King, "The Paramount Girl" who is traveling alone by automobile from California to New York City.
>
> The wonderful courage of Miss King in undertaking the trip is worthy of the greatest admiration, and you will find her a charming, amiable young lady, whom it is a pleasure to meet. I commend her to your kind consideration and bespeak for her every courtesy which you can possibly show her.
>
> I thank you in anticipation of your kindness to her, and assure you that I will be under many obligations to you for the same.
>
> Respectfully,
> C.C. Healy, Genl. Supt.[85]

Healy evidently belonged to King's fan club. The actress used his letter twice when motorcycle cops stopped her for "fast driving" at undisclosed locations. "In both cases she was promptly released," the *Hartford Press* reported.[86]

Her car's mechanical troubles as far as Chicago included two broken fan belts and a broken spring. "There is Los Angeles air in the front tires of her car and she has changed only four rear casings, three of which blew out in crossing the desert because the driver did not take the precaution of reducing the air pressure in traveling across the sand," *Motor Age* said.[87]

The *Hartford Press* reported that King's trip east from Chicago would take her through the Indiana cities of Valparaiso, South Bend, Elkhart and Fort Wayne. King's trip nearly ended in Indiana, the *Hartford Press* recalled after the actress arrived safe and sound in New York City:

> Although the pretty "shadow actress" finished her task triumphantly, the latter part of the journey was accomplished solely on nerve and after it was nearly over, woman-like at last, she burst into tears and collapsed. This happened at South Bend, Indiana, and her condition was such that her friends begged her to abandon the effort. But, after a day's rest she was again "pounding the road" to Gotham.[88]

Entering Ohio's northwestern corner, King reportedly traveled south to Dayton and then traveled east across central Ohio through Columbus — a route well south of the Lincoln Highway. She closely followed the Lincoln Highway through Pennsylvania, from Pittsburgh in the west to Philadelphia in the east. She would travel through Camden, Trenton and Elizabeth, New Jersey, on her 100-mile drive from Philadelphia to New York City, press accounts indicated.

Anita King arrives in New York City in her faithful KisselKar, which is covered with stickers and decorations affixed by her fans. (November 1, 1915, *Horseless Age*)

Luncheon Caps Long Journey

The *Hartford Press* jumped the gun by announcing in its October 8 edition that King arrived in New York City "today." A headline in the same day's *Hartford Times*, however, alerted readers that "Anita King Will Reach New York October 18." Someone at the *Press*— which was obviously holding a canned press release from Paramount or the Kissel factory — evidently misread October 18 as "October 8," and thus the story slipped into print prematurely.

The Paramount Girl and her Kissel-Kar actually reached City Hall in New York on Tuesday, October 19, 1915, nearly 55 days after leaving Los Angeles and 48 days after leaving San Francisco. King arrived "tired but happy," as she put it.[89] Newspapers failed to report her exact arrival time. The two Hartford newspapers said King arrived Tuesday morning and met with Mayor John P. Mitchel at noon. But King actually reached City Hall on Tuesday afternoon, reported Wednesday's *New York Herald*, which added:

Miss King was the guest yesterday at a luncheon given for her at the Knicker-bocker Hotel by Paul V. Clodio and Russell A. Engs, agents here for the car in which she made the trip. By successfully completing the long tour Miss King wins the right to be known as the Paramount Girl. She will remain here a week before returning to Hollywood, Cal., to appear in Lasky pictures.[90]

Since leaving the West Coast, the newspaper added, "she has rested but three days."[91] According to the *Hartford Press*:

Miss King's reception in the metropolis was a splendid tribute to the plucky little woman. She was met at Hoboken, N.J., by a large delegation, and preceded by a tallyho and about one hundred cars was escorted down Broadway and Fifth avenue to the city hall where she was promptly received by Mayor Mitchel.

Her visit to the Mayor was made the occasion for the presentation of a big silver loving cup, the gift of the Kissel Motor Car company. The inscription on the cup recognizes Miss King as "the first woman to cross the American continent in a motor car, alone."

After receiving the congratulations of the Mayor and other officials, a luncheon was given Miss King at the Knickerbocker

A jubilant Anita King in New York City. The key to the city of "Reno Nevada" is visible at the base of the windshield. (November 1, 1915, *Horseless Age*)

Hotel by Clodio and Engs, the New York KisselKar representatives. At either side of the guest of honor sat President [W.W.] Hodkinson of the Paramount Picture[s] Corporation, and other officials of the Paramount and Lasky companies.[92]

Covered with Autographs, Cards

King covered 5,231 miles on her meandering west-to-east route, "stopping at 102 moving picture theaters on the way across," *MoTor* said. "Tire trouble consisted only of one blowout and four punctures," according to *MoTor*, which conflicts with the *Motor Age* report that King had installed four new tires between California and Chicago. For her elapsed time of 48 days, King averaged 4.54 mph and covered 109 miles per day. Her KisselKar averaged 14 miles per gallon "and never once show[ed] the slightest engine trouble," according to the *Hartford Press*. According to a Kissel ad, she experienced "the worst imaginable roads and weather" for 27 of the 48 days.[93] There were no reports on the total cost of the trip or the fate of the car King used.

"We will not dwell upon Miss King's trip any more than to say it was of the most trying and grilling kind," asserted the *Hartford Times*, evidently printing a Kissel press release. "Sunshine and rain, deserts and cities, mountains and plains, mud and sand, were encountered and passed through, testing the mettle of the driver and the staunchness of the car. Both came through the ordeal like veterans, and the only reverses that will be made is that Miss King will never again make the trip, while her big car is in fit shape to take her right back."[94]

King's car, however, was a curiosity, the *Hartford Press* noted: "The white lettering on the car is covered with autographs of persons whom she met on the tour and the canvas covering over the back seat carries fully a thousand signatures. She also collected many hundreds of cards and other mementos of her journey."[95]

Newspapers from California to New York had mentioned the KisselKar in hundreds of articles about King's thrilling adventures. The Kissel factory played up the trip for all it was worth. In its regular *Hartford Press* column, "News from the KisselKar Factory," the automaker on October 29, 1915, claimed:

On her entry to New York City last week, Miss Anita King was heralded by the screeches of fifty siren horns. It was

What This Paramount Girl Did with a Stock KisselKar

All motordom is wondering at the performance of a stock KisselKar 42-Six driven from San Francisco to New York—alone by Anita King, the Paramount Girl. Miss King made this grilling trip without motor trouble of any kind whatever—carburetor and ignition perfect. Although encountering the worst imaginable roads and weather for 27 days, no mechanical trouble of any consequence was experienced.

KisselKar

EVERY INCH A CAR.

What Miss King accomplished is a great tribute to one woman's pluck and daring—it is likewise a great tribute to the power, sturdiness and simplicity of the KisselKar.

Write for literature describing the new KisselKars—Touring Cars, $1050 to $1750—Roadsters, $1150 to $1650—ALL-YEAR Cars, $1450 to $2100 F. O. B. Factory. Unparalleled values.

The ALL-YEAR *Car*

The KisselKar was the first and, up to now, is the only successful ALL-YEAR car. Offered either with a Coupe or a Sedan top —the changes easily made by anyone.

Pacific KisselKar Branch

SAN FRANCISCO   LOS ANGELES   OAKLAND

A Kissel agent's ad in the November 15, 1915, *Motor West*.

an exultant and enthusiastic greeting to the dauntless little "Paramount Girl" upon completion of her great coast to coast drive.

Then the first woman who ever drove a motor car across the continent alone, and who had braved every peril like a real stoic, burst into tears and had "a good cry"....

During the balance of the week Miss King appeared at several New York theatres and gave a brief account of her experiences, according a large measure of praise to the car which she drove. When asked why she selected a KisselKar, Miss

A publicity boon for both Paramount Pictures and KisselKar, King's trek made headlines from coast to coast.

King promptly replied: —"Because my life depended on the car."[96]

"Pals with my Car"

One account said King would take the train to Chicago to spend time with her family. On Tuesday afternoon, October 26 — exactly one week after reaching New York City, King paid a visit to Hartford. Interrupting her tour of the KisselKar factory, the actress sat down in the office of George A. Kissel, company president, to speak with a *Hartford Press* reporter:

> She arrived in Hartford about half past three, from Milwaukee, in company with H.S. Daniels, the advertising manager of the factory, and R.T. Fisher, of the Indianapolis agency, and G.V. Martin of the Milwaukee agency.
>
> Attired in [a] pretty velvet, fur trimmed suit, with a big black velvet hat covered with a big veil, she sat in the office and told us enthusiastically about some of her experiences on her trip.
>
> "What did you enjoy most about your trip?" we asked her. "The daily companionship with my motor," she replied. "You cannot realize how close we seemed. There were many, many times in my long and tiresome trip, when had my motor failed me I would surely have perished, as I was miles beyond help, and as I realized how perfectly to be depended upon my KisselKar was, I grew more and more pals with my car....
>
> "You see I am called the Paramount Girl but I call myself the 'KisselKar Girl' and I am, ain't I?" she asked turning to President Kissel who smilingly assured her that she had certainly earned the title.[97]

King returned to Milwaukee Tuesday evening, escorted by two KisselKars containing many Kissel officers, including the company attorney and the manager of the repairs department, according to the *Hartford Press*. On Wednesday, King again boarded the train to continue her trip to California.

"To me, the most impressive thing about the trip was the fact that it proved the possibility that a woman, unattended, can cross this great continent unmolested," she told the *Hartford Times* while visiting Hartford. "I was well armed and expected to have to defend myself, but the occasion never arose. I met people of all sorts, including many tramps, but was invariably treated with the greatest kindness and consideration."[98] Forgotten, it appears, were the tramp who accosted her in the Sierra Nevada snowsheds and the two men who insisted she was lying about traveling alone.

As she told the *Hartford Times*: "I am on my way to Los Angeles, where I will immediately begin rehearsals for the new picture, *The Paramount Girl*, which will be based upon the incidents of my tour." The various silent-film encyclopedias do not list such a title; King was presumably referring to the film released in 1916 and titled *The Race.*

In Later Years

King had vowed that upon returning to California she would make an attempt to lower her San Francisco–Los Angeles time. She evidently did not do so. For driving coast to coast, King received a new KisselKar. When she went car-shopping in the spring of 1916, therefore, she bought not a KisselKar but a King V-8, made in Detroit. "While it is powerful the extreme flexibility of the motor instantly appeals to the woman driver," a King Motor Car Company press release quoted the actress as saying. "Many of my friends drive eight cylinder Kings and their praise of it generally is sufficient to make me feel proud to be numbered among its drivers."[99]

In autumn 1916, Anita King was writing the story of her transcontinental trip, according to Field's *Sunset* article, though it was unclear if she was writing it as a book, article, play, movie, or perhaps in some other form. A search of the *Cumulative Book Index* into the 1920s contains no reference to a book by Anita King.

Thereafter, King set a goal of "the protection of girls who have dreams of becoming motion picture actresses," Kingsley wrote in *Photoplay*.[100] Hypnotized by the silver screen, many frenzied young women flocked to Hollywood, as moths to a bright light, according to Field. When "a faint odor of singed wings came to the official nostrils" of Los Angeles authorities, "they went to a young woman who was famous for dare-devil movie stunts, who photographed beautifully, whose portrait was in demand among screen-struck girls, and they figuratively and actually pinned upon her up-to-the-minute gown the badge of Deputy City Mother of Los Angeles." King formed her plan for protecting these young moths "in consultation with Judge Thomas White, of the Women's Court, in Los Angeles, and Police Chief Snively, and in furtherance of the plan Miss King has been appointed a City Mother, and each motion picture plant will also have its woman officer, who will look into the qualifications, the lives and actions of all girls applying for work."[101]

"Soon she was talking to them, en masse. In high schools, in department stores, she found eager audiences. Under cover of a talk about 'life in the pictures' she preached the gospel that had come to her when she faced the problem of the Wyoming farmhouse. And presently she had a very considerable correspondence, not only from screen-struck girls but from the parents thereof who acknowledged with thanks improved conditions at home. No crusader ever had more encouragement; the work grew and the love of the work grew with it."[102]

King had remarried, to Timothy M. McKenna, "steelman and cousin of steel magnate Andrew Carnegie," but McKenna died in the mid–1940s, according to press accounts. When McKenna was diagnosed with an incurable illness, King took up horse racing "to keep him interested with some sort of hobby," she said in a 1952 *Los Angeles Times* interview. Instead, it turned into her own hobby. King's stable won the 1951 Santa Anita Handicap with her most famous horse, Moonrush, who earned $438,000 in his career and retired as "the only horse ever to take the Bay Meadows Handicap three times,"[103] according to King's obituaries. Childless, King willed her stables and ranch in nearby Temple City, California, to her horse trainer of 24 years, and divided her estate among some 25 relatives.

During its own lifespan (1906–30), the Kissel Motor Car Company — which would eventually produce hearses, trucks and taxicabs — sold higher-priced autos and offered many body styles, notes Kissel historian Val V. Quandt. "This certainly gave the buying public a large choice, though at the cost of the slow and very tedious process of custom building all these bodies with their wooden frames." When production dwindled to 899 cars and trucks in 1929, a receivership followed in 1930. A new company that emerged from the receivership in 1932, Kissel Industries, made a variety of products — most notably outboard motors. West Bend Aluminum bought Kissel Industries in 1944 and in the 1960s sold to the marine division of Chrysler Corporation, which has since sold its holdings, according to Quandt.[104]

To Believe, or Not to Believe?

When King, 74, who reportedly had a heart condition, died of a heart attack at her Los Angeles home on June 10, 1963, the

New York Times ran a four-paragraph Associated Press story in which one paragraph details her cross-country adventure of nearly 50 years earlier. The article, however, mistakenly identified her as "the first woman to drive a car across the country," rather than as the first woman to do so on a solo trip.[105]

Ultimately, even the claim that King was the first woman to make a solo trip is debatable. For one thing, King acknowledged giving a ride to at least two people, including a sheep herder in Wyoming. This, technically, would invalidate her "solo" record, though the average observer would forgive her minor infractions. The herder was trying to get help for an injured lamb, after all.

More troubling is the question: What really happened when the film star dropped out of sight in the Nevada desert? As the Ely, Nevada, editor saw it, King "broke into Salt Lake [City] in the greatest state of excitement imaginable and told an alarming story"—and one hard to swallow: Lost in the desert, stalked by a coyote, King collapses from fatigue and would have perished ... except that three auto-borne prospectors happen by in the middle of the night, discover her seemingly lifeless body, revive her and whisk her to safety. Or was she still conscious and firing her gun as a signal for help, as she claims in another account?

Questions abound: Why doesn't the account of her auto-racing experience at Phoenix and Los Angeles check out? On her 1915 trek, did she actually shoot a wolf, a coyote or possibly a dog? Draw a gun on a man who questioned her honor? Escape from a threatening hobo who, repentant, appeared later to present her with a bouquet of "wilted" flowers? Nobody knows. Was a camera crew out on the desert, as M.M. Musselman suggests, grinding away to capture the true-life drama that overwhelmed the poor, defenseless Paramount Girl? Did anyone ride with Anita or take the wheel of her KisselKar during this time?

The newspapers and auto journals, which eagerly gulped when given some hard-to-swallow stories, printed breathless accounts of King's adventures. The press did not press for details, and for that earns a performance rating of PG: "Pretty Gullible." Largely, what appeared in the newspapers and auto journals were press releases—verbatim reports that appeared days and weeks apart all across the country. These accounts evidently came from two sources: King's movie studio and (given the amount of gratuitous praise for her trusty steed) the Kissel company. Now movie studios and automakers *have* been known to shade the truth....

King undoubtedly inspired a great many girls and women by her daring exploits, both on and off the screen. Clara Bow, another silent-film star, was nicknamed the "It" Girl. Anita King perhaps deserves this slight variant of Bow's nickname: the "If" Girl. For *if* King's story held together, we could accept without reservation her claim of being the first woman to drive alone across America. As it is, we must cry: "Lights! Camera! Document your actions!" Questions about the reel truth of King's 1915 adventures, and speculation that she was acting in a comedy rather than a drama, have earned the movie star an RD rating—Reasonable Doubt.

"Of course the real details have not yet been told," fumed the editor from Ely. And perhaps they never will.

Chapter Five

"Just a Matter of Good Driving, Coolness and Nerve"

Amanda Preuss in an Oldsmobile, 1916

I hit it with a crash, bowling it over, and, before it had a chance to recover, rolled upon it with the front wheels of my car. There I hung, with the neighing, kicking horse beneath me.

— Amanda Preuss

What took Alice Ramsey 53 days in 1909 and Anita King 48 days in 1915 took Amanda Preuss just 11 days in 1916. Despite her arrest for hitting a horse in Wyoming, Preuss, 25, set a women's transcontinental speed record in driving an Oldsmobile V-8 roadster along the Lincoln Highway.

Sponsored by the YWCA and Olds Motor Works and supported by the Lincoln Highway Association, Preuss started from Oakland, California, on August 8, 1916. Driving alone, she covered 3,520 miles in 11 days, 5 hours, 45 minutes. That beat by 90 minutes the one-driver speed record that Erwin G. "Cannon Ball" Baker set 15 months earlier on a southern route but had since lowered.

Preuss — who broke her arm while practicing for the trip — had most of her journey's bad experiences in Wyoming, where rain and repairs slowed her progress. Driving from Cheyenne toward western Nebraska, she strayed from the Lincoln Highway and wound up in Colorado. Once she found her way, she hit a horse that was running loose in the road. Her radiator, damaged in the accident, sprang a leak in Illinois, where a sympathetic fellow Oldsmobile owner gave Preuss his own radiator. The rest of the trip to New York City was so "easy and monotonous," as she describes it, that her greatest fear was of falling asleep at the wheel.

"I Can Beat That"

Summarizing her coast-to-coast trip in a 24-page pocket-size booklet, *A Girl — A Record and an Oldsmobile*, Preuss describes herself as a law-office stenographer and YWCA member in Sacramento, California.[1] "Aside from being an expert automobile driver she is a crack rifle and pistol shot, having won several tournaments with the latter firearm," the *Salt Lake (City) Tribune* added.[2] As Preuss told the *San Francisco Chronicle*: "I spent a good part of my earnings on a car. I've driven one for about eight years. I love to drive and I love to work over the internals when something goes wrong. There were no boys in our family, so I thought I'd show people a girl could do as many things and do them just as well as a boy could."[3]

The transcontinental trip "was nothing more nor less than the outcome of a vacation idea," as Preuss tells it:

Amanda Preuss behind the Oldsmobile's steering wheel, which she taped to improve her grip. (October 19, 1916, *Automobile*)

> I had always been an out-of-doors girl, very fond of motoring. In Chicago, my former home, I had driven a machine owned by my parents for years. What [could be] more natural then, as I planned my vacation last winter, than to imagine an automobile trip for myself— a trip filled with wonderful, strange, novel experience[s].
>
> I had read of Miss Anita King, a moving-picture star, making a trip across the continent the summer previous in 43 days [*sic*], which was considered a remarkable performance. "Gracious," I said, "I can beat that and never half try."
>
> .... I soon made up my mind my only hope lay with some enterprising automobile manufacturer who would let me have a car for such a trip as I had in mind to demonstrate the worth and merit of his product. And indeed, I told myself, a car would have to be mechanically perfect to stand what I proposed to put it through. For, once having entered into the spirit of the thing, I made up my mind to drive as fast and as far as I could, every day—to set a record.[4]

King's trip actually spanned not 43 but 48 days. Preuss was hoping to drive

between coasts in less than 12 days, according to the *San Francisco Call*. "When asked if she did not think that two weeks for the distance was a little severe, she answered that any healthy woman should be able to do it and that she never felt better in her life, so there you are."[5]

Preuss Trains by Driving, Dancing

Because she admired Oldsmobiles, Preuss sent her first query letter to Olds Motor Works. In reply,

> I received a letter on Oldsmobile stationery, asking me to forward further particulars concerning myself, also photographs. I complied with the request.
>
> Then ensued a period of waiting, the most anxious moments of my life, during which, I am told, the Olds Motor Works investigated every fact in my career. I am glad to say that I came through with a perfect score, and was finally adjudged fit and able to carry out my plans. A new Oldsmobile eight-cylinder Model 44 roadster, painted a special gray, was

sent me, and I was instructed to get into immediate training for my trip.

In the meantime, however, Preuss had begun practicing for the long trip in "an old machine of another make," she relates in her booklet. While she was crank-starting this car for a June 1916 outing, the engine kicked back and broke her right arm just above the wrist; doctors set the break twice before it would heal properly. When Preuss asked Oldsmobile officials in Lansing to postpone the trip until fall, the factory replied "with a cordial, cheerful note, expressing admiration for my grit, and leaving it to me to fix my own time of departure." But word of the change did not immediately reach Oldsmobile officials in California, according to Preuss:

> About this time, I received my first visit from a representative of the Olds Motor Works, Mr. Owen Bird, of the Oldsmobile Co. of California, Pacific Coast Oldsmobile distributors. Mr. Bird, it seems[,] had not been informed of my accident, and when he sighted me, with my arm in a sling, his jaw nearly sagged a foot. It took a couple of hours to convince him that I was going through with my trip, and even when he left, I could see he was not very enthusiastic.
>
> My arm healed rapidly. In two weeks, I was again at the wheel, this time in my own Oldsmobile, a self-starter, believe me. However, I nursed my sore arm very carefully while driving.
>
> I now entered upon an extended and arduous course of training, driving many miles both morning and night, both to familiarize myself with the machine, and to get in condition. By the time six weeks had elapsed I was as hard as nails.
>
> To complete my training, I spent four days in San Francisco under the instruction of Mr. Owen Bird, the same gentleman who had previously visited me in Sacramento. This time I found Mr. Bird more cheerful, a mood which grew on him as he watched me drive.

> During my entire stay in San Francisco, when I wasn't driving, I was dancing. Next to automobiling, dancing is the finest exercise I know.

During her training, Preuss drove "hundreds of miles" and "covered all kinds of roads in her 'Olds' Eight without the slightest difficulty," newspapers said. She thus arrived at the starting line "trained to the minute, and thoroughly hardened through outdoor life," as the *Salt Lake Tribune* put it.[6]

An "Absolutely Stock" Olds

Oldsmobile supplied Preuss with one of its 1916 V-8 roadsters. With a bore and stroke of $2\frac{7}{8} \times 4\frac{3}{4}$, the car's Northway engine developed 26.45 horsepower as calculated by the SAE formula. The auto was "absolutely stock, with the exception of a spot light and a coat of battleship gray paint," according to the *San Francisco Call*. Mounted on a 120-inch wheelbase, the Model 44 used 33×4 Goodyear tires and wood-spoked wheels.[7]

Having secured Oldsmobile's backing, "I went to my branch of the Y.W.C.A. and told them to keep their eye on me — I was going to prove that a capable, self-respecting, well-behaved young woman could go alone from one end of this country to another without molestation or trouble of any sort — for I do hate girls who are always whining about the persecutions of men and the dangers of solitary adventurings," Preuss told the *San Francisco Chronicle*. Thus while Oldsmobile financed her adventure, Preuss would make the journey under the "auspices" of the Sacramento Y.W.C.A., newspapers reported. Further, upon arriving in New York she would speak to East Coast women about "the great out-of-doors as a means of physical and mental regeneration for the members of her sex."[8]

Preuss and her Oldsmobile V-8 roadster. Here, she fills the gas tank for one of several publicity poses that Olds Motor Works distributed to the press. (SAMCC)

The Y.W.C.A. wrote a short article about Preuss in its October 1916 *Association Monthly*. But exactly how — and why — the Y.W.C.A. backed Preuss is an open question. "The transcontinental trip of Amanda Preuss is non-typical of Y.W.C.A. activities," according to Elizabeth D. Norris, historian of the Y.W.C.A. of the U.S.A. "Most Y.W.C.A. programs for this period had clear-cut moral or religious motivations. Outside of the 'physical and mental regeneration' of her sex purpose, the Association would be on shaky ground to justify the expenditure, which is assumed in a sponsorship." Another question arises, according to Norris: "Why did she stay at hotels when there were

more than 255 Y.W.C.A. residences across the country?" More typical of the Y.W.C.A.'s attitude toward automobiles was a 1919 poster referring to the 22,250 American Y.W.C.A. members who owned them: "The purchase price of these cars would put a modern, fully equipped ... Y.W.C.A. in every town in the United States."[9]

The Lincoln Highway Association eagerly lent its support and Preuss met with its representatives en route. "It was a sort of official Lincoln Highway trip," she told the *New York Herald*[10]; her car even carried the Lincoln Highway "L" logo on its doors. With the highway association and Oldsmobile backing her, Preuss' announced

Preuss changes a tire in another publicity photo. (SAMCC)

purpose for taking the trip evolved somewhat. The *San Francisco Call*, publishing what sounds like a reworked Oldsmobile press release, noted that Preuss would begin her journey during National Touring Week, August 6 through 12:

> The powers that be of the Oldsmobile factory and of the Western Oldsmobile Company hope that this trip on the part of Miss Preuss will definitely prove to all that there are no longer terrors to be encountered via the transcontinental route. The United States has never been properly exploited by automobile touring, and this is just another way of developing the idea of "See America First." ... For a woman to drive to New York from San Francisco should ... also show that the day of mechanical imperfection is

past. The "Olds" is a standard car, and for this reason is expected to make the trip without any adjustments and very likely without any tire trouble.[11]

Preuss Packs Puttees

Other press releases, picked up by newspapers across the country, carried the fiction that Preuss "expects to make the journey in leisurely fashion, enjoying herself every inch of the way."[12] Quite the opposite was true: East of Cheyenne, after she fell behind her self-imposed schedule of more than 300 miles a day, a frantic Preuss began driving day and night.

Like some other newspapers covering the trip, the *Call* in one article implies that

Preuss slung a water bag over the top bows of her car, here stopped at an undisclosed location en route to New York. (OHC)

Preuss would be the first woman to drive across the country. In fact, Alice Ramsey in 1909, Blanche Stuart Scott in 1910 and Anita King in 1915 had proven that women drivers could do it. Ramsey and Scott — very possibly King, as well — traveled with local pilot cars (as did many male transcontinentalists) to avoid getting lost. Similarly, Preuss, though purportedly making a solo trip — that is, she had nobody else in her car — nonetheless also traveled at times with other autos. Preuss is "making the trip alone, except for the Oldsmobile agents who pilot her through their districts," commented the *Rock Springs (Wyo.) Rocket*, oblivious to the irony.[13]

Packed for self-sufficiency, Preuss carried "a complete camp equipment, consisting of a little canvas tent, a portable stove, a frying pan, one or two kettles and pans, knife and fork, two or three spoons, a cup and saucer, coffee pot and a Thermos bottle — all of aluminum. In addition she will carry a full fishing outfit, as this is a sport of which she is very fond and may find opportunity to enjoy en route."[14]

She would sleep in hotels and garages instead of her tent, however. In her own account, Preuss reveals that she carried water — photos show a canvas water bag hanging from the roadster's left side — and at least some food, but she makes no mention of fishing. Though an expert pistol shot, Preuss "is carrying no weapons on her tour, considering them to be unnecessary," said the *Salt Lake (City) Telegram*.[15] She carried two spare tires strapped to the back of her roadster, photos show. The *Tribune* of Salt Lake City made special note of the clothes Preuss selected for her trip:

Her touring costume, which she designed herself, is rather novel, consisting of khaki riding breeches, a Norfolk khaki coat, heavy tan walking shoes with puttees, and a leather cap and goggles.

The riding breeches are necessitated by the fact that Miss Preuss may have to do some tire changing in the middle of the desert, in which event the conventional skirt would not permit a sufficient freedom of movement....

Her wardrobe, aside from her touring

H.D. Ryus "of the Oldsmobile Co. of California" greets Preuss before her departure. (*A Girl* booklet/OHC)

costume, includes a number of dainty evening gowns for use in the hotels in which she will stop, as she is very fond of music and dancing.[16]

The 1916 *Complete Official Road Guide of the Lincoln Highway* recommended the packing of puttees — strap-on leather leggings — as well as a variety of other "personal equipment," including gauntlet-style driving gloves, khaki riding trousers and a "Teamster's Canvas Coat."[17]

Starting Point: Oakland Hotel

On Monday afternoon, August 7, the day before departing, Preuss would meet with San Francisco Mayor James Rolph, Jr., "on the high steps of the City Hall, with Joseph Caine, Lincoln Highway consul for California, members of the Board of Supervisors and some of the judges," according to the *San Francisco Call*. As "consul" or state director, Caine, of Oakland, was responsible for promoting and improving the Lincoln Highway in California. "The mayor will deliver a letter to Miss Preuss for Mayor [John P.] Mitchel of New York, and then will deliver a short address upon her laudable efforts to create interest in transcontinental travel." Another newspaper said Rolph's message is one "endorsing the mission on which she is engaged and inviting a still closer co-operation between the two great termini of the Lincoln highway in an endeavor to link the east and west closer together."[18]

Who started Preuss on her way east? According to Frank Herman, reporting in the *San Francisco Call* of August 8, "At 6 o'clock this morning the start was made with the Lincoln highway consul and the writer acting as the official checkers." *Automobile*, however, writes that Preuss "was checked out of San Francisco on Tuesday,

A pre-run publicity shot shows Preuss on the Yolo Causeway near Sacramento. (SAMCC)

Aug. 8, by Major Hilton of the U.S. artillery,"[19] who is not even mentioned in the *Call's* story or Preuss' account of the start. The *Call* also fails to specify the exact starting point. Preuss names only Herman, whom she says "checked me out, in front of the Oakland Hotel, in Oakland, Cal., across the bay from San Francisco, at 6 A.M. Tuesday." Thus her trip — widely billed as between San Francisco and New York City — was actually between Oakland and New York City. According to Preuss:

> Up until now, the real nature of my tour had been kept a secret, the trip having been announced as a mere vacation prank, the attempt of a California girl to drive every foot of the way across the American continent herself. I had looked upon the enterprise as a glorious lark.
>
> As I rolled away from the starting line that morning of August 8th, however, the seriousness of the thing suddenly came upon me. I realized for the first time what I was really about — that I was facing a venture, success in which meant achievement, approval, honor; and that failure meant disappointment and obliv-

ion. Not only my own, but the name of the Olds Motor Works was at stake, a name worth every effort to sustain. An intense gravity seized me, and from that moment I fought a battle — to win.

In his article, Herman adds: "The run will be official in every respect, as ... at every important city en route the documents will be officially signed, so that a complete check will be had on the Oldsmobile from coast to coast."[20] Preuss writes of using her diary to record officials' signatures.

Hills, Sand and Desolation

Over marshy ground west of Sacramento, Preuss would cross a new $395,000, three-mile concrete causeway — the world's longest, according to *MoTor*. Alternately called the Yolo Bypass or Yolo Causeway, the 21-foot-wide elevated road "is one of the greatest engineering features to be found on the entire route of the Lincoln Highway," the Lincoln Highway Association

An earlier publicity pose shows Preuss crossing the American River at Folsom, California, northeast of Sacramento (SAMCC).

said shortly before the causeway's scheduled May 1916 opening. "Its completion means that the route ... between Sacramento and San Francisco will be shortened some 30 or 35 miles."[21]

The trip was uneventful, Preuss wrote, "the beautiful, hard, macadamized roads of California carrying me into Sacramento with ease and dispatch." In her hometown, "members of the State Motor Vehicle Department and a committee of city councilmen will greet her at the state capitol building," the *Call* foretold.[22] But "a host of my old friends" were in the crowd, as well, said Preuss, in an account that sounded much like an Oldsmobile testimonial. Accordingly,

> It was 1:30 P.M. before I could tear myself away to set sail for Reno, with the Sierra Nevadas ahead. Then my work commenced.

As I approached the foothills of the mountains the road became steep and tortuous, twining ever upward and upward, from precipice to precipice. Around one curve after another I flew, giving the car more gas every time I glimpsed a little straight stretch ahead. I took some awful chances. However, I had absolute confidence in my car, and so did not hesitate to run any risk.

Passing over the Sierras, I negotiated three snow-sheds, the last one at the summit, over 7,000 feet above the sea. Coming out of this shed, the road drops 1,800 feet in less than a mile, curving wickedly toward Donner Lake, in the heart of the mountains. Thanks to the car, I negotiated it safely.

From then on it was easy sailing into Reno, where I arrived at 8:15 P.M. I had covered 270 miles the first day, including a mountain range 7,000 feet high, which I thought not at all bad.

The next morning I started for Ely, Nev., passing through the Fallon Sink. It was plough, plough, plough, through heavy sand all the way. At one place, despite the magnificent pulling power of my eight-cylinder motor, which had carried me over the Sierras in high gear, I had to travel fourteen miles in first and second speed.

And my, but that desert was a lonesome place!

After passing through Salt Wells, which is merely a gasoline station, the only living thing I saw for miles was a coyote…. Much of this part of my trip was rather tiresome. The country all around looked as though it had been painted with a giant whitewash brush. One alkali bed after another — and not a living thing to break the monotony.

Five hours of travel in this alkali land brought me to "Frenchman's Camp," consisting of one house and a well. The well bears a sign, "If you don't want to pay for this water, let it alone." This, however, is not as inhospitable as it seems, as the water had to be hauled a great distance.

I myself did not drink the water, as I carried a supply of my own, to avoid stomach trouble. I bought some, however, for the car, paying five cents for it. I needed less than a pint to fill the radiator, though I had traveled 150 miles through heat and deep sand.

About three o'clock in the afternoon I came to a little oasis in the desert where one lone farmer lived with a few cattle. Gratefully, I stopped in the shade of the trees and ate the first and only lunch that I carried on the entire tour.

At seven in the evening I reached Austin. I had made so little progress that I decided to press on, after buying some gas and oil.

I made Eureka, the next stop, at about midnight, arriving with a suddenness that was surprising. The town lies deep down in a pocket of the mountains, and the descent into it is so steep that I didn't see it until I was already in its midst. It felt as though I had dropped off a mountain into town.

When I arrived the entire place was asleep, with the exception of a few men who were playing cards in the hotel lobby, which was also the bar. I registered over the bar, and then told the proprietor and bar-keep that I was hungry. Very obligingly he went out into the kitchen and fetched me a couple of hunks of bread — hunks is the word, as they were two inches thick — and some sliced cold beef. This I ate before an interested group of spectators, and then stumbled up the staircase to my room, where I slept soundly until morning.[23]

"I Couldn't Eat Enough"

On Thursday, August 10, Day 3, Preuss met Gael S. Hoag in Ely, the next town of any size east of Eureka. Hoag, Nevada consul of the Lincoln Highway, "who is working very hard to place the roads out west in better condition," undoubtedly shared some personal experiences in briefing Preuss on the latest road conditions, for he had traveled the route often enough. The 1924 *Complete Official Road Guide of the Lincoln Highway* pictures Hoag — by then the association's field secretary — and his Packard "after a season's run of 15,000 miles on the Lincoln Way."[24]

"I did not stay long in Ely, however, merely eating lunch, and then starting for the great Salt Lake desert," Preuss writes. Some 70 miles northeast of Ely at Tippett Ranch, Nevada, Preuss paid 55 cents a gallon for gasoline — several times higher than Sacramento gas prices. She traveled another 25 miles to reach Ibapah, Utah, before nightfall, "and decided to call it a day's work, as I was pretty well tuckered out from my strenuous grind the night before. I slept like a log." Preuss had traveled 205 miles for the day.

On Friday, August 11,

City	Date	Distance[1]	City	Date	Distance[1]
California			**Nebraska** (*continued*)		
Oakland	Aug. 8		Cozad	Aug. 14	
Sacramento	Aug. 8		Omaha	Aug. 15	
Folsom	Aug. 8		**Iowa**		
Nevada			Council Bluffs	Aug. 15	580/2,022
Reno	Aug. 8	285/285[2]	Ames	Aug. 15	185/2,207
Salt Wells	Aug. 8		Cedar Rapids	Aug. 16	
Frenchman's			Clinton	Aug. 16	
Camp[3]	Aug. 9		**Illinois**		
Austin	Aug. 9		Fulton	Aug. 16	
Eureka	Aug. 9	258/543	Dixon	Aug. 16	
Ely	Aug. 10		**Indiana**		
Tippett Ranch	Aug. 10		South Bend	Aug. 16	480/2,687
Utah			Fort Wayne	Aug. 17	
Ibapah	Aug. 10	205/748	**Ohio**		
Thomas	Aug. 11		Lima	Aug. 17	
Salt Lake City	Aug. 11		Canton	Aug. 17	328/3,015
Wyoming			**Pennsylvania**		
Evanston	Aug. 12	276/1,024	Pittsburgh	Aug. 18	
Rock Springs	Aug. 12		Gettysburg	Aug. 18	284/3,299
Rawlins	Aug. 12	233/1,257	Philadelphia	Aug. 19	
Cheyenne	Aug. 13	185/1,442	**New Jersey**		
Colorado[4]			Trenton	Aug. 19	
Wyoming			Newark	Aug. 19	
Pine Bluffs	Aug. 14		Weehawken	Aug. 19	
Nebraska			**New York**		
Kimball	Aug. 14		New York City	Aug. 19	221[5]/3,520
Big Springs	Aug. 14				

* * * * * * * *

1 — Distances are from "Woman Drives Across Country in Eleven Days," *Motorist*, September 1916, p. 45:1.

2 — Preuss puts the distance at 270 miles but the *Motorist's* mileage table says 285.

3 — Actually "Frenchman," according to Nevada highway maps dated 1935 and 1962.

4 — Preuss recalls losing the road between Cheyenne and Pine Bluffs, Wyo., and straying some dozen miles south into Colorado at some unspecified location.

5 — Preuss (212 miles) and the *Motorist* (221 miles) differ on the length of the last day's run. But the *Motorist's* account still adds to 3,520 miles, which Preuss agrees is the total.

Note: Though there were many other cities along the Lincoln Highway, these are the only ones mentioned in more than two dozen articles, and in Preuss' own account.

Sources: Auto journals, local and national newspapers and the Preuss booklet, *A Girl — A Record and an Oldsmobile.*

Amanda Preuss' City-by-City Itinerary, 1916

I was on the road again bright and early, and stopped at Thomas' cabin for breakfast. I had developed a wonderful appetite by this time, and it seemed as though I couldn't eat enough. I had sliced pineapples, sliced peaches, four eggs, bread and butter, sliced ham, and two cups of coffee, all in but a few minutes more than it took to fill my car with gasoline. Asking Mr. Thomas for my bill, I nearly shouted with joy when he said, "fifty cents," but my enthusiasm died a moment later when he continued, "But the gasoline is 60 cents a gallon." It seems that the precious fluid has to be hauled seventy-five miles by motor truck, which accounts for its high price.

Beyond her breakfast stopping point, Preuss said, the Lincoln Highway, skirting the south edge of the Great Salt Lake Desert, became unusually dusty. "I got off on the wrong trail at one time, and had to cut across an immense valley with nothing but a tiny ribbon of road on a mountain side in the far distance to aim for, in order to get back again. If I hadn't had confidence in my car I would have become very nervous on this occasion."

"Twist, Turn and Bump"

Stopping briefly in Salt Lake City on Friday afternoon, Preuss had her photograph "snapped in front of the Randall-Dodd Auto company's salesrooms, where Oldsmobiles are sold," according to the *Salt Lake Telegram*.[25] Heading east, she climbed into the Rocky Mountains to reach Evanston, Wyoming, late that night and complete her 276-mile drive from Ibapah. "Due to my late arrival, I found the hotels all crowded and was unable to get a room. A wealthy sheep raiser, learning of my predicament, offered me his suite of rooms over a local bank, and went out to spend the night with a friend. I was glad to take

advantage of his kindness, and soon went to sleep, serenaded by a bunch of cattle and sheep men who stood guard all night over my car."

On Saturday, August 12, Day 5, Preuss headed east from Evanston toward Rock Springs, Rawlins and Cheyenne, where Denver Oldsmobile agent Ross C. Brown was waiting for her, according to the *Cheyenne State Leader*.[26] She did not reach Cheyenne on Saturday, however:

I plunged into the heart of the Rockies — and then it rained. All day I fought not only the grades, which were rough and steep, but the rain as well. It was drive, slip, slide, bounce, twist, turn and bump. I look back on it now and wonder how the car held together.

One particularly severe bump did fracture a minor element of the braking mechanism; however, the injury was not serious, and so I continued, though a little more carefully.

Finally, after an all-day battle, and pretty well discouraged, as I was losing time, I arrived in Rawlins, Wyo., where I went to bed as quickly as possible, to get a much needed rest.

The next day was horrible. It was raining again, and the roads were as slippery as grease. I passed over an abandoned railroad grade, out of which the ties had been lifted, leaving the road like a section of washboard. The result was that my car did a series of acrobatics which made my teeth chatter. I only made Cheyenne.

One cheering thing marked my arrival in Cheyenne. This was that I found an Oldsmobile service station in which I could have my brake mechanism repaired.

Coming into Cheyenne, I had made some rapid mental calculations. According to my diary, in which I kept every detail of my trip, duly verified by residents en route, I had averaged less than 250 miles a day, when I had originally figured on doing more than 300. Something had to be done!

Then and there I made up my mind that from Cheyenne on I would take the wheel and hang onto it until I dropped, sleep a little and drive until I had to quit again.

Arrested for Hitting Horse

As Preuss reported in her booklet afterward, she suffered her only tire trouble of the trip coming into Cheyenne, "where I hit a sharp rock with terrific force. The tire was done for, and I had to buy a new one in Cheyenne. I carried two spares all the way, one of which I never used." Preuss left Cheyenne "bright and early" on Monday, August 14, Day 7,

> and so eager was I to get along that I lost my way. Not having seen any Lincoln highway signs for quite a while I finally stopped a stranger and asked, "Where am I?"
>
> "Lady," he replied, "you're in Colorado!"
>
> "This is no place for me," I said. "I ought to be in Wyoming. How do I get out of here?"
>
> A few brief directions and I was on my way again, rejoining the Lincoln highway somewhere west of Pine Bluff[s], Wyo.

Just 4½ miles west of Pine Bluffs, near the Nebraska border, Preuss had her one and only serious accident of the trip, according to the *Motorist*, an auto journal published in Omaha, Nebraska. As Preuss writes in her own account:

> Running along at about 45 miles an hour I saw standing loose in the road ahead of me a beautiful bay horse. Immediately I slowed down to about 25 miles an hour and sounded my horn. By this time I was close upon it, and as it did not move, I swerved sharply to the left to pass around it. Unfortunately, as I swung, the horse decided to swing also, and leaped squarely in front of my machine.
>
> I hit it with a crash, bowling it over, and, before it had a chance to recover, rolled upon it with the front wheels of my car. There I hung, with the neighing, kicking horse beneath me.
>
> I would never have been able to get off the horse, had it not been for a couple of men working on the road who came to my assistance. Our combined efforts, however, finally managed to extricate the car.
>
> Then we gave the horse our attention. An examination showed that it had its leg broken and would have to be shot. I drove down the road about a mile and waited, my hands over my eyes.
>
> I was a very sick girl by this time, and did not regain control over myself until several hours afterward. Had I not been steeled by a determination to go through with my venture at all costs, I would not have had the nerve to continue.
>
> The right front fender of the car had sustained most of the shock, and, though bent, was in shape to continue. I feared that the radiator had been sprung, but could not verify this.

Preuss reported the accident to the Pine Bluffs marshal, according to the *Motorist*, "with the result that at Kimball, Neb., some thirty miles further east, she was headed off by long distance telephone and placed under arrest. Though she was in no way responsible for the accident, she states, she was forced to pay $150 to the sheriff of Kimball before she was allowed to proceed. Having no time to argue the matter, she paid and went on, leaving the matter for her insurance company to settle afterward."[27] The $150 was for the horse owner, "whose sole defense was that the animal had been running free on the road for the last four years and that nothing had happened to it in that time," said Preuss.

Preuss Drives Day and Night

"Leaving Kimball, I drove with re-doubled speed, and, though the roads were still somewhat heavy with rain, made very good time, considering. All that day I drove, all that night, and all the next day, arriving the following evening [Tuesday] in Ames, Iowa, after having covered 765 miles of my route in one stretch."

Except for refueling, Preuss recalls, she made only two more stops in Nebraska on Monday — at Big Springs for lunch and Cozad for dinner. Driving on into the night,

I felt myself going to sleep, and, having no one in my car to keep me awake, determined to pull up along the road for a while and sleep, lest I go into a ditch. I had slept a couple of hours, I imagine, when I was roughly awakened by someone pulling at my arm and shouting, "Hey, Mister, have you got a Blue Book?"—another case of mistaken identity, due to my attire.

I informed my interrogator sleepily that I had nothing he wanted, and, my voice having proclaimed my sex, was showered with profuse apologies. It was very fortunate that he woke me, or I might have been sleeping there yet. I was sufficiently refreshed to continue the rest of the night and on until 10:30 the next morning, when I had to take another two hours' sleep in a garage at Council Bluffs.

Actually, Preuss drove through Omaha, crossed over the Missouri River and stopped in Council Bluffs, Iowa, at about noon Tuesday, August 15, according to the *Omaha Daily News.* Unaware of her nap, the *Motorist* observed that Preuss "achieved almost the physically impossible, driving on one occasion 29 hours and 20 minutes without sleep, between Cheyenne, Wyo., and Council Bluffs, Ia., a distance of 580 miles."[28]

"Touring Made Easy" is how the *Council Bluffs Daily Nonpareil*—unaware both of her nap and her collision with the horse — described Preuss' trip to that point:

She has had wonderful luck, thanks to the manufacturers of the car she is driving, who follow her with pilot cars from station to station and met her in Council Bluffs with an expert mechanician from the factory, who had repairs and accessories to meet all her needs.

Her car was placed in the Raapke Motor company's garage and given a thorough overhauling by the Raapke men under supervision of the factory expert.

Miss Preuss, who made the drive of 580 miles from Cheyenne, Wyo., to Council Bluffs in a no-stop run of a day and a night, came from her dressing room at the Raapke garage with an armful of printed statistics about her car, but the reporter said:

"Oh, please talk to me. We get all those figures from the advertising department. Have you had any adventures and what have you seen?"

"Well, I'm averaging 250 miles a day and the Olds car is the best on earth."

"But where have you been and what have you seen?"

"I drove fourteen miles in first and second speeds with my dustpan dragging. Don't you think that was a wonderful performance for my car?" and turning to the expert mechanician from the factory she inquired anxiously if the pilot car from Des Moines had arrived to set her on the way. She's just touring for pleasure, but she doesn't like it when she thinks that she's a day behind her schedule and should have been in Cedar Rapids today, where the pilot car from Chicago is to meet her.[29]

Mom Intervenes

The *Nonpareil* reporter makes no mention of what the mechanics were doing — perhaps repairing the car's fender and other parts damaged by the horse. From Council Bluffs, Preuss drove 185 miles farther east to reach Ames at 10:30 P.M. Tuesday. "I had been on the road for practically forty-one consecutive hours, with but six hours of eating and sleep sandwiched in between," Preuss said. In Ames on Wednesday, August 16, "I rose at daybreak and took to the road once more. This time I drove through to South Bend, Ind., a distance of 480 miles, driving for 23 hours and 46 minutes." Earlier Wednesday while still in Iowa, she ate breakfast in Cedar Rapids and lunch in Clinton, where she crossed the Mississippi River on the Lincoln Highway bridge into Fulton, Illinois.

> In the afternoon, just before entering Dixon, Ill., the radiator I had rammed into the horse at Pine Bluff[s] suddenly sprung a leak, and had to be replaced, an Oldsmobile owner kindly coming to the rescue with a radiator from his own car. While the change was being made, I slept for a couple of hours in a garage office.
> Arriving in South Bend at 4:45 in the morning [Thursday], I found my parents, who had come down from Chicago to meet me. They were the most welcome sight in the world to me, and I to them. I abandoned myself to their care, and was put to bed.
> In a couple of hours, however, I awoke with a start, imagining myself at the steering wheel again, flying over the road. After that, sleep was impossible, though my mother made me stay in bed a couple of hours more.
> Even before I breakfasted, I went to look after my car, and, finding there was an Oldsmobile agency in town, ordered the radiator I had borrowed at Dixon, Ill., replaced, and returned to the owner. Then I ate, and soon was ready for the road again. I bade my parents good-bye and struck for the open highway at 12:30 P.M.
> By this time I had passed the hardest part of my journey. From Ames, Ia., on the roads had constantly improved, and I expected even better.

Never Notices Alleghenies

Preuss replaced her leather driving gloves at South Bend, "the old ones having rubbed clear though. Incidentally, I had to tape my steering wheel three times, as every thousand miles or so the old tape would get so slippery it would not furnish a good grip." On this Thursday, August 17, Day 10, "I lunched at Ft. Wayne [Indiana], and dined at Lima, O.," Preuss recounted. "The same night I made Canton, O., arriving at 2 A.M. after having covered 328 miles. Early the next morning [Friday] I was on the road once more, headed for Pittsburgh." Pennsylvania's toll roads "slowed me up a lot. Every so often I'd have to stop my car and pay seven cents toll." Later Friday, while leaving Pittsburgh,

> I was warned against the Alleghenies, and, of course, looked for some bad grades. I traveled all that day and far into the night without seeing anything serious, and so, when I arrived in Gettysburg, where I was to sleep, I asked the hotel clerk when I would get into the mountains.
> "Why!" he said to me, "you are out of the mountains." I had passed through them and didn't know it.

It was thus on Friday, August 18, that Preuss first observed what she later described to the *San Francisco Chronicle* as a regional difference in Americans' outlook on life:

> Broadly speaking, Easterners are pessimists and Westerners optimists.
> In the West, when I would ask my way or the conditions of the road, I was invariably answered with a sort of sunshiny courage: "Oh, it's only a couple of miles," would be the answer. "Roads are pretty good in spots. You'll make it all right in a couple of hours. It ain't bad."
> You see, Westerners are used to heartbreaking distances and hard going. East-

Preuss (in white, back to camera) is the center of interest during a gas and oil stop at an unidentified point in Pennsylvania. (*A Girl* booklet/OHC)

erners aren't. When I asked a man in [Pennsylvania] a direction, he said: "Why, you'll never get over the Alleghenies. Grade's something terrific. 'Fraid you're going to have trouble."

Well ... I was so busy looking for the troubles he warned me of I didn't even notice the little old grade of the little old Allegheny mountains. After the Sierra they were not very much. That man was accustomed to the short distances and conveniences of the East. Easterners don't know what hardship is. Westerners like it; it builds character.[30]

Reaches Times Square "In No Mood to Chat"

From Gettysburg, Pennsylvania, on Saturday, August 19, Preuss drove 212 miles to arrive in Times Square at 2:45 P.M., ending her coast-to-coast drive but beginning her first visit to New York City. "I was met and checked in by a group of newspaper men, headed by Mr. R.L. Sykes, of the *Brooklyn Citizen*, and made and fussed over until I was glad to get away," Preuss said later. As Sunday's *New York Tribune* recounted it, "When Miss Amanda Preuss drove her Oldsmobile off the Forty-second Street ferry yesterday she completed a trip from San Francisco, which she started alone, eleven days ago. Despite the fact that she had driven the car the entire distance herself, and had cut down the women's transcontinental record by twenty-two days, she looked fresh and unwearied."[31]

With a time of 11 days, 5 hours, 45 minutes[32] over a 3,520-mile route from Oakland to New York City, Preuss actually cut not 22 but 37 days from the questionable transcontinental record of 48 days that Anita King set on her 1915 solo trip. Some observers were unsure what to make of Amanda Preuss and her performance: The *New York Times* "believed" she had set

Top: A traffic officer gives Preuss directions through Philadelphia, a mere 100 miles from Gotham. (*A Girl* booklet/OHC) *Bottom:* Driving off the ferry from Weehawken, New Jersey, Preuss arrives at her destination — New York City. (*A Girl* booklet/OHC)

a women's record; *Automobile* allowed that it was "probably" so. Preuss "has won the distinction of being the first woman to cross the continent alone by motor car," one newspaper said in error, forgetting King's 1915 solo trip. The *New York Times* erred, as well, in asserting that Preuss "spent several nights in the open and made her own repairs."[33] Except for her roadside nap in Nebraska, the record shows that she slept in hotels or garages and — in Council Bluffs, at least — had a factory mechanic at her disposal.

Preuss met her goal of traveling more than 300 miles daily — averaging 313.18 miles per day. Her average speed of 13.05 mph for the elapsed time was just slightly below the 13.75 mph that Cannon Ball Baker achieved on his 1915 coast-to-coast run. Preuss used 251 gallons of gas to average 14.02 mpg, "which was very good, I thought, considering the various altitudes, roads, and weather conditions I had passed through." Aside from mentioning repairs to the "brake mechanism" in Cheyenne, Preuss makes no accounting of any mechanical problems. Her tire troubles were limited to the blowout near Cheyenne, she said.

Though she appeared "fresh and unwearied" to the *New York Tribune* reporter, the *New York Herald*'s writer observed that Preuss showed the effects of her long trip:

> Miss Amanda Preuss, an attractive young woman clad in khaki and somewhat travel worn at that, stopped her automobile at the front entrance of the McAlpin Hotel yesterday with a sigh of relief. She had just finished a ride from San Francisco to New York over the Lincoln Highway route in what she believes to be a record for a woman driver.... She drove all the way herself and did not carry a passenger or an assistant. She said she was handicapped along the way by heavy rainfalls.
>
> Miss Preuss was not in a mood to

chat. She wanted a bath, a good dinner and then some sleep. Ever since she started on the run she has been forced to put up with about four hours' rest a night. Now she's going to try and catch up some of the lost sleep.[34]

Deep Tan, Swollen Fingers

How did she achieve her record? "It was just a matter of good driving, coolness and nerve," she said modestly in a *San Francisco Chronicle* interview some days later:

> I often drove twenty-four hours at a stretch during the hardest parts of the journey, because the nervous tension caused by bad roads, washouts, dust and mud keyed me up so that sleep was impossible. I just kept on going, so as not to waste any time.
>
> In one of those periods I made 780 miles. My average for the whole trip was 300 miles a day. When I struck decent roads again, nearing the end of my drive, I used to be afraid I would go to sleep at the wheel, it seemed so easy and monotonous after what I had been through.[35]

On Monday, August 21, "I was again in the limelight, calling at the New York city hall," Preuss said. There, she presented the letter from San Francisco Mayor James Rolph, Jr., to New York City Alderman Frank L. Dowling,[36] who was acting mayor in John P. Mitchel's absence. Added Preuss:

> As for myself, I was none the worse for wear, though I found I had lost seventeen pounds. I also found that the many days of exposure in all kinds of weather had given me a deep coat of tan, though my skin, due to the fact that I used nothing but cold cream, was in excellent condition. My ears, however, were as hard baked as a prize-fighter's, from the sun and wind.... After-effects of the trip, I

Still wearing her driving outfit, Preuss presents to Alderman Frank L. Dowling the letter she carried from San Francisco Mayor James Rolph, Jr. (*A Girl* booklet/OHC)

had none, with the exception of slightly swollen fingers, which remained puffed up for several days.

Preuss "is resting up a bit in New York, and between rests is seeing the sights of the 'big town,'" according to the *San Francisco Chronicle*.[37] As announced earlier in the *Salt Lake Tribune*, her plans upon reaching New York were "to visit some of the more important cities of the east to spread her out-of-doors gospel, particularly among the women's clubs and Y.W.C.A.'s, and then drive through to Chicago, her parents' home, via the Olds Motor Works at Lansing, Mich. Her return journey to San Francisco will be made by train after an absence of probably two months."[38] Including her coast-to-coast journey, the trip to Chicago and evidently some other driving, Preuss would put 6,000 miles on the Oldsmobile, according to the *Tribune*.

During her trip to Lansing, Preuss also visited Detroit, according to the Lincoln Highway Association's September 13, 1916, *Lincoln Highway* news sheet:

The fears of those who have anticipated hardships and dangers in driving across the Great West, via the Lincoln Highway have [been] put at rest by a little California girl, Miss Amanda Preuss, of Sacramento, who drove into Detroit today after completing the transcontinental run over the Lincoln Highway from San Francisco to New York, and thence via Albany, Buffalo, Erie and Cleveland to Detroit....

Miss Preuss stopped in Detroit at the headquarters of the Lincoln Highway Association on her way to Lansing where she will leave the Oldsmobile Eight roadster, in which she made the trip, at the factory. Except for a coating of dust and grease, the car was none the worse for its long trip and it is planned to put it on exhibition at the Automobile Show in New York City next January, where Miss Preuss will be in attendance to explain to the enthusiastic motorists who attend

Aviator Ruth Law, left, and Preuss strike a pose with the transcontinental Oldsmobile. (OHC)

the show, the ease and comfort of the transcontinental drive and outline some of her pleasurable experiences.[39]

Public: Feat Not So Neat

A publicity photo that appeared in the December 1916 *American Chauffeur* and presumably elsewhere shows Preuss and aviator Ruth Law, "the two most daring women in America." On November 19, 1916, Law set an American nonstop record by flying 590 miles between Chicago and Hornell, New York.[40] In the photo, Preuss, wearing street clothes, and sitting at the wheel of the transcontinental Oldsmobile, chats with Law, dressed in her flight suit.

According to *American Chauffeur*, Preuss and Law met at the Iowa State Fair, which was held in Des Moines from August 26 through September 1, 1916. During Law's three flights on August 28, "she sailed over the exposition grounds doing fancy stunts, looping the loop whenever the winds were steady enough to permit it," according to the *Des Moines Register and Leader*.[41] This suggests that Preuss drove a meandering route back to the Oldsmobile factory—one that took her two states to the west of Michigan. Her coast-to-coast Olds is not known to survive today.

The Johnson Company of Detroit ran a full-page ad containing photos of Preuss "driving her JOHNSON-Equipped Olds-

Miss Amanda Preuss driving her JOHNSON-Equipped Oldsmobile with which she established a transcontinental touring record for women—11 days, 5 hours and 45 minutes.

It was perhaps during her post-run visit to Detroit that Preuss posed for this photo used to promote the car's Johnson carburetor. (Oct. 19, 1916, *Automobile*)

mobile." But forget Preuss and her car, implies the ad — for the "Johnson Carburetor Sets a new Transcontinental Record[,] demonstrating remarkable consistency of performance at all altitudes, all temperatures and under widely varying atmospheric conditions."[42]

The trek earned Preuss and the Oldsmobile a measure of publicity in the news columns of auto journals and newspapers, as well. But despite slashing by three-quarters the women's coast-to-coast speed record, Preuss' dash excited less comment and raised fewer eyebrows than did those of the female drivers who preceded her. Actress Anita King had driven the Lincoln Highway a year earlier, for one thing, though at a snail's pace by comparison: 109 miles per day, or about one-third the speed Preuss achieved. Clearly, King's star status earned her transcontinental trip a greater measure of publicity that she

would have earned as a lesser-known motorist.

Further, although Preuss' time approached that of the best male drivers, she proved what had already been proven — that a woman was as capable as a man of driving an automobile across the continent. What's more, as increasing traffic on the Lincoln Highway formed a virtual "moving chain" of autos,[43] popular magazines had begun featuring articles that referred, familiarly, to "The Transcontinental Game." The novelty was gone. Ironically, as the roads got better, the cars faster and the drivers more daring, transcontinental runs received less and less attention — in part because they were over so quickly.

Returning to Sacramento, Amanda Preuss would spend her upcoming vacations in less spectacular pursuits.

Headlines tersely tell of Preuss' grueling coast-to-coast trip.

*   *   *   *

America's 1917 entry into World War I temporarily postponed the kinds of coast-to-coast automobile travel engaged in by Louise Davis, Alice Ramsey, Blanche Scott, Anita King and Amanda Preuss. Yet their remarkable feats of courage in the pioneering years of the Motor Age helped popularize the automobile, proved that women made good drivers and inspired greater numbers of ordinary women to take to the roads.

Although Ramsey received considerable recognition for her early exploits when she reached her 70s, time has generally been unkind to the memory of the first female transcontinentalists. The other pre–World War I female coast-to-coast drivers, far from household names today, receive nary a line in general histories of 20th century American life. Likewise, the exploits of the first women on wheels have also escaped detection by serious automotive historians; only as the American automotive industry enters its third century has a book — this one — appeared, a first attempt to end the long-standing neglect of the historical contributions made by five trend-setting female motorists.

As you motor forth onto the highways and byways of modern America, consider this: The next time you accuse someone — or are yourself accused — of being a "woman driver," recall the accomplishments of Louise, Alice, Blanche, Anita and Amanda. Infused by this memory, you will find it tempting to view the slur "woman driver" as an unintentional compliment.

The correct reply, of course, would be "thank you!"

Appendix:
Trips at a Glance

At-a-Glance Summary of the 1899 Davis Trip

DRIVER	John D. Davis
PASSENGER	His wife, Louise Hitchcock Davis
AUTOMOBILE	2-cylinder 5 to 7-horsepower National Duryea "touring cart"
CITY-TO-CITY	New York City to Chicago
DATES	July 13, 1899–October 1899 (exact date unknown)
DISTANCE	At least 1,132 miles
ELAPSED TIME (ET)	—
RUNNING TIME	—
AVG. SPEED (ET)	—
FIRSTS	First recorded U.S. transcontinental attempt; first woman rider to attempt a coast-to-coast trip; most likely the world's longest auto trip to date for either a man or a woman.

At-a-Glance Summary of the 1909 Ramsey Trip

DRIVER	Alice Huyler Ramsey
PASSENGERS	Margaret Atwood, Hermine Jahns, Nettie Powell
AUTOMOBILE	4-cylinder, 30-horsepower, 1909 Maxwell Model DA touring car
CITY-TO-CITY	New York City to San Francisco
DATES	10 a.m. June 9–August 7, 1909 (the exact finish time is unknown)
DISTANCE	3,800 miles
ELAPSED TIME (ET)	59 days
RUNNING TIME	42 days
AVG. SPEED (ET)	2.68 mph
FIRSTS	First woman to drive coast to coast.

At-a-Glance Summary of the 1910 Scott Trip

DRIVER	Blanche Stuart Scott
PASSENGERS	Amy Phillips (New York City to Toledo, Ohio) and Gertrude Phillips (Indianapolis to San Francisco)

AUTOMOBILE	4-cylinder, 25-horsepower, 1910 Model 38 Overland runabout
CITY-TO-CITY	New York City to San Francisco
DATES	Noon May 16–about 10:30 A.M. July 23, 1910
DISTANCE	Approximately 5,200 miles
ELAPSED TIME (ET)	68 days, 1 hour, 30 minutes
RUNNING TIME	Reportedly 41 or 42 calendar days
AVG. SPEED (ET)	3.18 mph
FIRSTS	Though the Willys-Overland Company billed Scott as the first female coast-to-coast driver, Alice Ramsey actually claimed that honor in 1909. Scott's trip nonetheless generated widespread publicity.

At-a-Glance Summary of the 1915 King Trip

DRIVER	Anita King, a silent-film star
AUTOMOBILE	6-cylinder, 31-horsepower, 1915 KisselKar 6-42 touring car
CITY-TO-CITY	San Francisco to New York City
DATES	September 1–October 19, 1915 (exact times are unknown)
DISTANCE	5,231 miles
ELAPSED TIME (ET)	48 days
RUNNING TIME	—
AVG. SPEED (ET)	Approximately 4.54 mph
FIRSTS	Possibly the first woman on record to make a solo coast-to-coast trip; King's time cut 11 days from the women's transcontinental record.*

*At the time, the press generally accepted King's trip as legitimate. But her undocumented and seemingly scripted adventures — lost in the Nevada desert, stalked by wild animals, rescued by auto-borne prospectors, and so on — raise doubts about the authenticity of this record.

At-a-Glance Summary of the 1916 Preuss Trip

DRIVER	Amanda Preuss
AUTOMOBILE	1916 Model 44 V-8 Oldsmobile roadster
CITY-TO-CITY	Oakland, California, to New York City
DATES	6 A.M. August 8–2:45 P.M. August 19, 1916
DISTANCE	3,520 miles
ELAPSED TIME (ET)	11 days, 5 hours, 45 minutes
RUNNING TIME	—
AVG. SPEED (ET)	13.05 mph
MILES/DAY AVG. 313.18	
FIRSTS	Cuts Anita King's questionable 1915 record by 37 days.

Notes

One. "Ring the Curtain Down on This Farce!"

1. "Successful Start Made," *New York Herald*, July 14, 1899, p. 3:6.

2. "Views of Coast Editors on the Great Automobile Race," *San Francisco Call*, July 19, 1899, p. 6:4.

3. "Four Thousand Miles by Automobile," *Leslie's Weekly*, Aug. 5, 1899, p. 114:1; "Across the Continent in an Automobile," *San Francisco Call*, July 2, 1899, p. 19:1; and "Will Serve a Good End," editorial, *Chicago Times-Herald*, reprinted in the *New York Herald*, June 30, 1899, p. 6:1.

4. The *Denver Times* reprinted portions of the *Chicago Tribune's* editorial in its response, "Rockies and the Automobile," *Denver Times*, July 23, 1899, n.p.

5. "The Davises Have Arrived," *Cleveland Plain Dealer*, Aug. 7, 1899, p. 10:5; and "Automobile Accidents," *Albany (N.Y.) Times-Union*, July 18, 1899, p. 5:4.

6. Hugh Dolnar, "American Automobile Notes," *Autocar*, Aug. 19, 1899, p. 743:2; and "The Davis Automobile," *Erie (Pa.) Morning Dispatch*, Aug. 7, 1899, p. 5:1.

7. *New York Herald*, July 14, 1899, p. 3:6, and "Ready to Start Automobile Trip," July 13, 1899, p. 3:6.

8. *New York Herald*, July 14, 1899, p. 3:6.

9. "To the Pacific in an Automobile," *New York Tribune*, July 14, 1899, p. 5:6; and "Automobile to Be Strengthened," *New York Herald*, July 2, 1899, I, p. 9:3.

10. *New York Herald*, July 14, 1899, p. 3:6.

11. "Thousands Witnessed the Start," *San Francisco Call*, July 14, 1899, p. 1:1.

12. H.F. Rodney, "Across the Continent on the Automobile," portion of a poem, *San Francisco Call*, July 4, 1899, p. 6:5.

13. "Go West, young man, go West!" originated in an 1851 *Terre Haute (Ind.) Express* editorial written by John L.B. Soule. But Greeley popularized the phrase, using it in various writings over the years. The version used here is from Greeley's *Hints toward Reform*, quoted in Burton Stevenson, *The Home Book of Quotations Classical and Modern*, 9th ed. (New York: Dodd, Mead, 1964).

14. Accounts of the start are from *New York Herald*, July 14, 1899, pp. 3–4; "Automobile Off for the West," *New York Times*, July 14, 1899, p. 12:2; *New York Tribune*, July 14, 1899, p. 5:6; and "The Herald Trans-Continental Motor Carriage Tour," *Horseless Age*, July 19, 1899, p. 19:1.

15. *New York Herald*, July 2, 1899, p. 9:3.

16. "Mishaps Do Not Stop Automobile," *New York Herald*, July 16, 1899, I, p. 6:1.

17. *Albany (N.Y.) Times-Union*, July 18, 1899, p. 5:4.

18. *New York Herald*, "Best Day's Run of Automobile," July 18, 1899, p. 9:5, and "Automobile Is Now in Syracuse," July 22, 1899, p. 9:6.

19. Louise Hitchcock Davis, "Automobile on the Road," *Cleveland Plain Dealer*, Aug. 6, 1899, p. 14:1.

20. *New York Herald*, "Map of Through Roads to the Pacific Coast," July 16, 1899, p. 4 of colored section, and July 13, 1899, p. 3:6.

21. "Across the Continent," *Toledo (Ohio) Blade*, Aug. 18, 1899, p. 1:8.

22. *Horseless Age* explained the cause of the collapsed wheel in "Transcontinental Tour," July 26, 1899, p. 21:2.

23. *New York Herald*, July 22, 1899, p. 9:6.

24. *New York Herald*, "One Armed Bicyclist to Wheel across Continent," July 19, 1899, p. 6:2; "He Will Wheel across the Continent," July 24, 1899, p. 4:2; "Postal Messenger Boy Making Good Time on Bicycle," July 27, 1899, p. 4:6; "Roe Well on His Journey," July 27, 1899, p. 7:2; "Messenger Speeding West," July 28, 1899, p. 10:4; and "One-Armed Bicycle Messenger Speeding toward Erie," July 30, 1899, p. 4:6.

25. "Automobilists Have Reached Bergen," *New York Herald*, Aug. 2, 1899, p. 6:5.

26. *Cleveland Plain Dealer*, Aug. 6, 1899, p. 14:5.

27. Richard P. Scharchburg in *Carriages Without Horses: J. Frank Duryea and the Birth of the American Automobile Industry* (Warrendale, Pa.: Society of Automotive Engineers, 1993), p. 153, says five horsepower. *Autocar's* July 22, 1899, edition said "between five and six brake horsepower" at 1,000 rpm. According to David L. Cole, "John D. Davis and the Transcontinental Auto Trip of 1899," *Automotive History Review* (Society of Automotive Historians), Winter 1993-94, p. 13:1, John Davis claimed the National Duryea developed seven horsepower. Two National Motor Carriage Company ads from mid–1899 do not mention a horsepower rating. Auto specifications and descriptive details are drawn from "Across the North American Continent by Motor Vehicle," *Horseless Age*, July 5, 1899, p. 10:1; "Automobile's Trip Begins Auspiciously," *New York Herald*, July 14, 1899, p. 3:6; and Hugh Dolnar, "Late American Notes," *Autocar*, July 22, 1899, p. 649.

28. National Motor Carriage Company ad, *Horseless Age*, June 14, 1899, p. 25; and Beverly Rae Kimes and Henry Austin Clark, Jr., *Standard Catalog of American Cars, 1805–1942*, 2nd ed. (Iola, Wis.: Krause Publications, 1989), p. 485:1.

29. "A Trans-Continental Automobile Trip," *Scientific American*, July 8, 1899, p. 26:3; and *New York Herald*, July 2, 1899, I, p. 9:3.

30. *Leslie's Weekly*, Aug. 5, 1899, p. 114:1.

31. *New York Herald*, July 22, 1899, p. 9:6.

32. *Cleveland Plain Dealer*, Aug. 7, 1899, p. 10:5, and Aug. 6, 1899, p. 14:3.

33. *Autocar*, Aug. 19, 1899, pp. 743-44.

34. *Erie (Pa.) Morning Dispatch*, Aug. 7, 1899, p. 5:1.

35. "New Record Made Right at Start," *New York Herald*, July 15, 1899, p. 5:2.

36. Untitled article, *San Francisco Call*, Aug. 1, 1899, p. 5:4; and "Here and There," *Automobile*, September 1899, p. 12:1.

37. *Rochester (N.Y.) Democrat and Chronicle*, "Automobile Has Arrived," Aug. 1, 1899, p. 5, and "Traveled by Night," Aug. 2, 1899, p. 7.

38. "Think Troubles Are Now Ended," *New York Herald*, Aug. 4, 1899, n.p.

39. *Cleveland Plain Dealer*, Aug. 6, 1899, p. 14:1.

40. *Cleveland Plain Dealer*, Aug. 7, 1899, p. 10:5.

41. "The Coming Automobile," editorial, *San Francisco Call*, Aug. 14, 1899, p. 4:2.

42. "Transcontinental Tour Abandoned," *Horseless Age*, Aug. 23, 1899, p. 8:1.

43. *Toledo (Ohio) Blade*, Aug. 18, 1899, p. 1:8.

44. *Toledo (Ohio) Blade*, Aug. 18, 1899, p. 1:8.

45. "The Transcontinental Tourists," *Horseless Age*, Aug. 16, 1899, p. 6:2.

46. Untitled editorial, *Horseless Age*, Oct. 18, 1899, p. 7:2; and *Scientific American*, "A Transcontinental Automobile Vehicle," July 29, 1899, p. 75:1, and "Automobile News," Oct. 7, 1899, p. 231:3.

47. Van Tassel Sutphen, "A Transcontinental Automobilist," *Harper's Weekly*, July 22, 1899, p. 731:1.

48. "Journey Delayed," *Toledo (Ohio) Blade*, Aug. 19, 1899, p. 7:4.

49. Who owned the car? The various accounts cited in this paragraph are from the *Toledo (Ohio) Blade*, Aug. 19, 1899, p. 7:4; "From Atlantic to the Pacific by Automobile," *New York Herald*, June 29, 1899, p. 3:6; "Automobilists in [Town]," *Rochester (N.Y.) Herald*, Aug. 1, 1899, p. 7; *Autocar*, Aug. 19, 1899, p. 743:2; and *Toledo (Ohio) Blade*, Aug. 18, 1899, p. 1:8.

50. "Continued Trouble," *Motor Vehicle Review*, Sept. 5, 1899, p. 8:1.

51. "Automobile News," *Scientific American*, Sept. 2, 1899, p. 153:3.

52. "The Davises Still Repairing," *Motor Age*, Oct. 3, 1899, p. 71:2.

53. "The Davises Still Traveling," *Motor Age*, Oct. 17, 1899, p. 113:1.

54. Julian Pettifer and Nigel Turner, *Automania: Man and the Motor Car* (Boston: Little, Brown, 1984), p. 71.

55. "Sharp Criticisms by the Editors/Automobile Trip across the Continent May Result in a Revolution in Traveling," editorial, *San Francisco Call*, reprinted in the *New York Herald*, July 6, 1899, p. 8:6; and *New York Herald*, July 13, 1899, p. 4:1.

56. The 275-mile figure is according to mileages given in the "Shortest Motor Distances Via the Transcontinental Trails" section of *Best Roads of All States: Across the Continent Motor Atlas* (Chicago: Clason Map, undated but uses 1920 population figures). A table on p. 4 and the Ohio map on p. 15 were also used for the calculations made in this paragraph.

57. According to "Automobile Ends 1,050 Mile Trip," *New York Herald*, Aug. 6, 1899, p. 13:1, the autoists' Kokomo–New York City distance was in question because the auto's odometer malfunctioned for a time.

58. *Scientific American*, Sept. 2, 1899, p. 153:3.

59. "Automobile Awaits the New Cylinder's Arrival," *San Francisco Call*, July 26, 1899, p. 2:6; and a *Chicago Times-Herald* editorial reprinted in the *New York Herald*, June 30, 1899, p. 6:1.

Two. "A Reliable Car and a Woman Who Knows It"

1. Alice Huyler Ramsey, *Veil, Duster, and Tire Iron* (Pasadena, Calif.: Castle Press, 1961), 104 pp.; and "They Are Plucky," *Wyoming Cheyenne Tribune*, July 15, 1909, p. 5:3.

2. Ramsey book, p. 1. From this point onward, unattributed quotations are from Ramsey's 1961 book, and to avoid clutter they will run without citations.

3. "From New York to Golden Gate/Four Hackensack Women Start on Record Auto Trip," *Hackensack (N.J.) Republican*, June 10, 1909, p. 1:4. This is evidently from a Maxwell press release, since the wording appears nearly verbatim in several other early accounts of the trip.

4. "Iowa's Roads Disgust Women Automobilists," *Sioux City (Iowa) Daily Tribune*, July 2, 1909, p. 4:1.

5. This biographical information comes from the *Hackensack (N.J.) Republican*, June 10, 1909, p. 1:4; Ramsey's book, p. 9; "1st Woman to Drive across U.S. Revisits City of Initial Stopover," *Poughkeepsie (N.Y.) Journal*, July 3, 1966, n.p.; and Mary Freericks, "Alice Huyler Ramsey, 1886–1983," in The Women's Project of New Jersey Inc., *Past and Promise: Lives of New Jersey Women*, (Metuchen, N.J.: Scarecrow Press, 1990), pp. 183–85.

6. "Mrs. Ramsay [*sic*] Plans Transcontinental Tour," *Automobile*, May 20, 1909, p. 841:1.

7. "Two-Day Automobile Run to Montauk Point and Return," *New York Times*, Sept. 20, 1908, IV, p. 4:3.

8. John S. Hammond II, "First Lady Transcontinental Driver," *Antique Automobile*, September–October 1979, p. 23:1.

9. "Women Motorists Finish Their Run," *New York Times*, Jan. 13, 1909, p. 1:4. Other *New York Times* articles on this run appeared Dec. 20, 1908, IV, p. 4:3; Jan. 11, 1909, p. 7:5; Jan. 12, 1909, p. 7:1; Jan. 15, 1909, p. 7:4; and Jan. 16, 1909, p. 9:2.

10. "Women Have a New York–Philadelphia Endurance Run," *Automobile*, Jan. 14, 1909, p. 125:1; "Motors and Motorists," *Kansas City (Mo.) Star*, Aug. 29, 1909, p. 10A:2; and Ramsey book, p. 9.

11. "Taking Time for Pink Teas," *Motor World*, July 1, 1909, p. 553:1.

12. "Four Women and an Auto," *Automobile*, June 24, 1909, p. 1044:1; and "Long Auto Ride by Women Motorists," *Deseret Evening News* (Salt Lake City), July 21, 1909, p. 2:3.

13. "Mrs. 'Maxwell' Ramsey Reaches Omaha," *Automobile*, July 1, 1909, p. 37:2; and "What a Thrill to Take the Wheel," *Ms.*, February 1975, p. 17.

14. Beverly Rae Kimes and Henry Austin Clark, Jr., *Standard Catalog of American Cars, 1805–1942*, 2nd ed. (Iola, Wis.: Krause Publications, 1989), p. 900:2.

15. "Women Autoists Reach Salt Lake," *Salt Lake (City) Herald*, July 21, 1909, p. 10:1.

16. Specifications are from "The 1909 Maxwell Line," *Cycle and Automobile Trade*

Journal, November 1908, pp. 153–54; "Details of the 1909 Cars," *Automobile*, Dec. 31, 1908, p. 927; and from Ramsey's book.

17. "Women's Tour from Coast to Coast," *Automobile*, June 17, 1909, p. 973:1.

18. "Four Women in Car," *Cedar Rapids (Iowa) Daily Republican*, June 25, 1909, p. 7:4; and John S. Hammond II, "Woman Motorist of the Century," *NRTA (National Retired Teachers Association) Journal*, May-June 1978, pp. 32:3.

19. "New Woman a Freak, Says Bishop Doane," *New York Times*, June 9, 1909, p. 7:3.

20. "Woman Makes St. Louis–Chicago Record," *Automobile*, Oct. 31, 1903, p. 465:1.

21. An unidentified June 29, 1950, newspaper article, quoted in the "Teape, E.E." section of History of Bonner County History Book Committee, *Beautiful Bonner: The History of Bonner County, Idaho* (Dallas: Curtis Media Corp., 1991).

22. "Women to Be Transcontinentalists," *Automobile*, May 7, 1908, p. 630:2.

23. "Current Comment," *Motor Age*, June 4, 1908, p. 11:2.

24. *Motor Age*, June 4, 1908, p. 11:3; and "Local Paragraphs," *Northern Idaho News* (Sandpoint), June 23, 1908, p. 6:4. Details of their trip are from two dozen press accounts in auto journals, the *Northern Idaho News* and newspapers along the route Teape and McKelvie followed.

25. *Motor Age*, "Four Women Touring," July 23, 1908, p. 28:1, "Women Tourists Reach New York," Aug. 6, 1908, p. 25:2, and "Women Finish Tour," Aug. 27, 1908, p. 6:3.

26. "Motor Car Literature," *Motor Age*, Jan. 16, 1908, p. 20:2; "Mrs. Cuneo's New Records," *Automobile*, Oct. 14, 1909, p. 664:1; and M.M. Musselman, *Get a Horse! The Story of the Automobile in America* (Philadelphia: J.B. Lippincott, 1950), pp. 242–43.

27. Mrs. Andrew Cuneo, "Why There Are So Few Women Automobilists," *Country Living in America*, March 1908, pp. 515–16.

28. *Automobile*, Jan. 14, 1909, p. 125:2, and "Do Women Make Safe Auto Drivers?" Sept. 30, 1909, p. 579:1; and "Women on Long Tour," *Motor Age*, June 10, 1909, p. 37:2.

29. *Antique Automobile*, September–October 1979, p. 20:2.

30. "Auto Run to Coast," *New York Tribune*, June 10, 1909, p. 5:3; and "Women Motorists Start Tour," *Motor Age*, June 17, 1909, p. 35:1.

31. Alice H. Ramsey, "Transcontinental Automobile Trip/Mrs. Ramsey Tells of Her Ocean to Ocean Drive," *Hackensack (N.J.) Republican*, Aug. 19, 1909, p. 1.

32. "Mrs. Ramsey, Woman Driver from New York to Pacific Coast, Starts Out of Toledo in Rain," *Toledo (Ohio) Blade*, June 17, 1909, p. 10:3.

33. "Maxwell Tourists Arrive in the City," *Chicago Inter Ocean*, June 20, 1909, p. 10:2.

34. "Women Off to Coast in Auto," *Chicago Daily Tribune*, June 22, 1909, p. 9:1.

35. *Hackensack (N.J.) Republican*, Aug. 19, 1909, p. 1.

36. *Cedar Rapids (Iowa) Daily Republican*, June 25, 1909, p. 7:4.

37. *Sioux City (Iowa) Daily Tribune*, July 2, 1909, p. 4:1.

38. *Sioux City (Iowa) Daily Tribune*, July 2, 1909, p. 4:1.

39. "Women on a Long Auto Tour," *Boone (Iowa) News-Republican*, June 28, 1909, p. 4:4.

40. *Hackensack (N.J.) Republican*, Aug. 19, 1909, p. 1.

41. "Woman Auto Driver on Cross Country Trip to Stop Here," *Sioux City (Iowa) Daily Tribune*, July 1, 1909, p. 5:2.

42. *Sioux City (Iowa) Daily Tribune*, July 2, 1909, p. 4:1.

43. *Sioux City (Iowa) Daily Tribune*, July 2, 1909, p. 4:2.

44. *Hackensack (N.J.) Republican*, Aug. 19, 1909, p. 1.

45. "Fair Tourists/Party of Ladies Pass through for Golden Gate," *Grand Island (Neb.) Daily Independent*, July 10, 1909, p. 1:4.

46. "Quartet of Fair Motorists Break Road Record for Women in Trying Trip from New York to Cheyenne," *Cheyenne (Wyo.) State Leader*, July 15, 1909, p. 1:3.

47. *Wyoming Tribune* (Cheyenne), July 15, 1909, p. 5:3.

48. *Wyoming Tribune* (Cheyenne), July 15, 1909, p. 5:3.

49. *Hackensack (N.J.) Republican*, Aug. 19, 1909, p. 8:3.

50. *Salt Lake (City) Herald*, July 21, 1909, p. 10:1.

51. "Reaches City in Automobile from Buffalo, N.Y.," *Salt Lake (City) Evening Telgram*, July 21, 1909, p. 3:4.

52. *Salt Lake (City) Evening Telegram*, July 21, 1909, p. 3:4.

53. *Deseret Evening News* (Salt Lake City), July 21, 1909, p. 2:3.

54. "Daring Woman Who Is Making Trans-Continental Trip in Auto Expected to Arrive in Reno Tonight," *Reno (Nev.) Evening Gazette*, July 28, 1909, p. 5:2.

55. *Hackensack (N.J.) Republican*, Aug. 19, 1909, p. 8:3.

56. Charles Kuralt, *On the Road with Charles Kuralt* (New York: G.P. Putnam's Sons, 1985), p. 73.

57. "Trans-Continental Drive Made on Dare," *Omaha (Neb.) Daily News*, Aug. 29, 1909, II, p. 7B:4; and "Women Auto All Way from Jersey," *San Francisco Examiner*, Aug. 9, 1909, p. 62:4.

58. *Hackensack (N.J.) Republican*, Aug. 19, 1909, p. 8:3.

59. *Hackensack (N.J.) Republican*, Aug. 19, 1909, p. 8:3.

60. "Ramsey Party Reaches City," *Sacramento (Calif.) Union*, Aug. 6, 1909, p. 2:1.

61. *Hackensack (N.J.) Republican*, Aug. 19, 1909, p. 8:3.

62. Unnamed San Francisco newspaper account reprinted in the *Hackensack (N.J.) Republican*, Aug. 19, 1909, p. 8:4.

63. Beverly Rae Kimes, "Cadwallader Washburn Kelsey: The Spirited Career of an American Pioneer," *Automobile Quarterly*, vol. 13, no. 2 (1975), p. 139:2.

64. R.R. L'Hommedieu, "Women Motorists End Long Tour," *San Francisco Call*, Aug. 8, 1909, p. 29:1.

65. *San Francisco Examiner*, Aug. 9, 1909, p. 62:4.

66. W.H.B. Fowler, "Pretty Women Motorists Arrive After Trip across the Continent," *San Francisco Chronicle*, Aug. 8, 1909, p. 36:1.

67. Letter reproduced in Ramsey book, p. 103.

68. *San Francisco Chronicle*, Aug. 8, 1909, p. 36:1.

69. Maxwell ad, *San Francisco Chronicle*, Aug. 8, 1909, p. 36:1.

70. *San Francisco Chronicle*, Aug. 8, 1909,

p. 36:1; and Splitdorf ad, *San Francisco Chronicle*, Aug. 8, 1909, p. 36:6. E.A. Kelley made similar assertions in the article "Splitdorf Does Some Noteworthy Work," *San Francisco Chronicle*, Aug. 8, 1909, p. 36:1.

71. "An Ajax Transcontinental Record," *Automobile*, Aug. 26, 1909, p. 376:2.

72. *Hackensack (N.J.) Republican*, Aug. 19, 1909, p. 8:3.

73. Percy F. Megargel, "Megargel on Way West," *Motor Age*, Aug. 31, 1905, p. 9:2.

74. This background is from the *Standard Catalog of American Cars, 1805–1942*, 2nd ed., pp. 292:2, 901:1; and Richard M. Langworth and Jan P. Norbye, *The Complete History of Chrysler Corporation, 1924–1985* (New York: Beekman House, 1985), pp. 16–17.

75. Alice Huyler Ramsey, "Veil, Duster, and Tire Iron," *Vassar Quarterly*, June 1962, p. 8:2; and Alice Huyler Ramsey, as told to Tom Mahoney, "I Was the First Woman to Drive Coast to Coast," *Family Weekly*, Sept. 27, 1964, p. 17:3.

76. *Poughkeepsie (N.Y.) Journal*, July 3, 1966, n.p.; and *Family Weekly*, Sept. 27, 1964, p. 17:3.

77. Joseph C. Ingraham, "'From Hell Gate to Golden Gate'— in 1909," *New York Times*, June 7, 1959, XII, p. 53:1.

78. Mrs. R.S. Bruns, Jr., "Still on the Road," *New York Times*, June 28, 1959, II, p. XX5:4.

79. Patricia Rusch Hyatt, *Coast to Coast with Alice* (Minneapolis: Carolrhoda Books, 1995), 72 pp.

80. Information about these awards comes from Ramsey's book, pp. 102–3; and an undated clipping, "Alice Huyler Ramsey Dies; 1st Trans-con Woman Driver," *Old Cars Weekly*, from a file on transcontinental auto travel at the Smithsonian Institution's National Museum of American History, Washington, D.C.

81. Cited in Burt A. Folkart, "1st Woman to Drive across U.S. Dies," *Los Angeles Times*, Sept. 13, 1983, II, p. 2:6.

82. *Past and Promise: Lives of New Jersey Women*, p. 185:1.

83. *On the Road with Charles Kuralt*, p. 73.

Three. "The Car, the Girl and the Wide, Wide World"

1. Blanche Stuart Scott, "as told to William J. Adams," *Not on a Broom*, undated 127-page typewritten manuscript in the Blanche Stuart Scott biographical files (CS 326000-01, -02, -03, -22 and -40) at the Smithsonian Institution's National Air and Space Museum, Washington, D.C., p. 2.

2. "Woman to Drive Auto to Frisco," *New York Times*, May 17, 1910, p. 11:6.

3. "Woman Motorist Enjoys Journey," *Des Moines (Iowa) Register and Leader*, June 18, 1910, p. 2:2; and "Overland Transcontinentalists Rapidly Nearing Their Goal," *Automobile*, July 21, 1910, p. 82:2.

4. "Two Women Auto Enthusiasts Meet Unawares in Salt Lake," *Salt Lake (City) Tribune*, July 12, 1910, p. 10:4.

5. *Not on a Broom*, p. 2. Unattributed quotations in the remainder of this chapter are from Scott's *Not on a Broom* manuscript, and to save space will run without individual citations.

6. Gertrude Phillips, *5000 Miles Overland/Wonderful Performance of a Wonderful Car/The Story of Miss Scott's Journey Overland* (Toledo, Ohio: Willys-Overland Company, 1910), 51 pp., quoted in *Not on a Broom*, p. 7. The booklet's title and other publishing information comes from Carey S. Bliss, *Autos Across America: A Bibliography of Transcontinental Automobile Travel: 1903–1940* (Austin, Texas: Jenkins & Reese, 1982), pp. 14–15.

7. "Overland Girl Reaches Bluffs," *Council Bluffs (Iowa) Sunday Nonpareil*, June 19, 1910, p. 6:2. Tuttle was evidently referring to an organization of Iowans that was promoting the state's all-dirt River-to-River Road, created in 1909, as an official transcontinental route through Iowa.

8. "Long Auto Ride by Women Motorists," *Deseret Evening News* (Salt Lake City), July 21, 1909, p. 2:3.

9. "Girl Autoists Reach City," *Cleveland Plain Dealer*, May 27, 1910, p. 9:7; and "Girl Autoist on Long Trip," *Des Moines (Iowa) Evening Tribune*, June 17, 1910, p. 4:3.

10. "Woman to Drive Auto to Frisco," *New York Times*, May 15, 1910, IV, p. 4:2.

11. "Woman Motorist Crossing Continent," *Motor Field*, June 1910, p. 32:1.

12. "Reaches Omaha in Auto Journey," *Omaha (Neb.) Sunday World-Herald*, June 19, 1910, II, p. 7N:1; and Paul Herpolsheimer ad, *Seward (Neb.) Independent-Democrat*, June 23, 1910, p. 1:6.

13. "Overland Is Away with Woman Driver," *Chicago Inter Ocean*, June 12, 1910, p. 8:2.

14. "Plucky Girls Cross Continent in Auto," *Ely (Nev.) Weekly Mining Expositor*, July 21, 1910, p. 5:4; "Boost for Better Roads," *San Francisco Examiner*, Aug. 21, 1910, p. 45:1; and "Girl Motored across Continent," *New York Morning Telegraph*, July 31, 1910, p. 8:2.

15. "The Overland Girl," *Overland Scout*, vol. 1, no. 5 (1910), from the Toledo–Lucas County Public Library, Toledo, Ohio, back cover.

16. "Woman Starts across Continent," *Automobile*, May 5, 1910, p. 857:2; and Bill Adams, "Rochester's Remarkable Flying Redhead!" undated typewritten manuscript in the Blanche Stuart Scott collection at the Smithsonian Institution's National Air and Space Museum, Washington, D.C., p. 2. The same figure appears in William J. Adam's, "Blanche Stuart Scott, (1892–1970)," in David Wallechinsky and Irving Wallace, *The People's Almanac #2* (New York: William Morrow, 1978), p. 674:1.

17. "Girl Driving Overland from New York to Frisco," *Overland Scout*, vol. 1, no. 5 (1910), pp. 45–46.

18. Consolidated Wagon & Machine Co. ad, *Salt Lake (City) Evening Telegram*, July 9, 1910, p. 7:3; *Overland Scout*, vol. 1, no. 5 (1910), p. 46:2; *Cleveland Plain Dealer*, May 27, 1910, p. 9:7; and "Tourists Coming Here," *Toledo (Ohio) Daily Blade*, May 30, 1910, p. 1:2.

19. "Rochester's Remarkable Flying Redhead!" p. 2.

20. "Resume Western Trip," *Toledo (Ohio) Daily Blade*, June 7, 1910, p. 6:2.

21. "Nervy Women Driving Auto across Continent," *Cheyenne (Wyo.) State Leader*, July 1, 1910, pp. 1:5, 5:2; "Girls Crossing the Continent by Auto," *New York Morning Telegraph*, July 10, 1910, p. 6:4; and "Miss Scott Reaches Toledo," *Overland Scout*, vol. 1, no. 6 (1910), p. 11:1.

22. *Council Bluffs (Iowa) Sunday Non-*

pareil, June 19, 1910, p. 6:2; and "The Overland Lady," *Blue Valley Blade* (Seward, Neb.), June 22, 1910, p. 1:4.

23. "Rochester's Remarkable Flying Redhead!" p. 2.

24. "'The Car, The Girl and the Wide, Wide World,'" *New York Morning Telegraph*, May 15, 1910, IV, part 2, p. 1:6.

25. "Young Women Start on Tour to Coast," *New York Herald*, May 17, 1910, p. 12:4.

26. "Miss Scott on Long Auto Run," *New York Morning Telegraph*, May 17, 1910, p. 7:4.

27. "Off on a Long Jaunt," *New York Tribune*, May 17, 1910, p. 8:5.

28. "Characteristics of Model 38 Overland," *Automobile*, May 19, 1910, p. 944; and *Overland Scout*, vol. 1, no. 5 (1910), p. 47:2.

29. "Long Trip for Young Girl," *Motor Age*, May 12, 1910, p. 14:3; and *Des Moines (Iowa) Register and Leader*, June 18, 1910, p. 2:2.

30. *Overland Scout*, vol. 1, no. 5 (1910), p. 48:2.

31. *Cleveland Plain Dealer*, May 27, 1910, p. 9:7; and *Motor Age*, May 12, 1910, p. 14:3.

32. Valerie Moolman, *Women Aloft*, Epic of Flight series (Alexandria, Va.: Time-Life Books, 1981), p. 18, says Scott was born "about 1890." Two sources give Scott's birthday as April 8, 1889: "Aviation's Bloomer Girl," *FAA Aviation News*, April 1970, p. 12:1; and "Blanche Stuart Scott: Early American Aviatrix," 4-page typewritten manuscript in the Blanche Stuart Scott collection at the Smithsonian Institution's National Air and Space Museum, Washington, D.C., p. 1. In this same collection, a date on the back of Photo A-1041 says Scott was born April 8, 1891. *The People's Almanac #2*, p. 673:2, gives the year of her birth as 1892. But in "Rochester's Remarkable Flying Redhead!" p. 1, Scott claims she was born in 1894.

33. *Des Moines (Iowa) Register and Leader*, June 18, 1910, p. 2:2.

34. No enrollment records exist for Scott, according to Barbara Hoeft, Alumnae House, Vassar College, in a Jan. 23, 1995, telephone interview with the author. The quoted obituary is "Blanche Stuart Scott, 84, Dies; Made First Solo Flight in 1910," *New York Times*, Jan. 13, 1970, p. 45:1. Though not quoted directly, the *Omaha (Neb.) Sunday World-Herald*, June 19, 1910, II, p. 7N:1, provided biographical information for this section.

35. "'Overland Girls' Arrive in Town After Tiring Trip," *Toledo (Ohio) Daily Blade*, June 3, 1910, p. 16:3; and *Overland Scout*, vol. 1, no. 6 (1910), p. 12:1.

36. "Miss Scott Plows through Swamps," *Horseless Age*, May 25, 1910, p. 806:2; and "Miss Scott Is Confident," *Cleveland Leader*, May 29, 1910, p. 6:3.

37. *Des Moines (Iowa) Register and Leader*, June 18, 1910, p. 2:2.

38. "Young Woman in Omaha Today, Drives Car Over Continent," *Omaha (Neb.) Daily News*, June 19, 1910, V, p. 4:1; *Toledo (Ohio) Daily Blade*, June 3, 1910, p. 16:3; *5000 Miles Overland*, quoted in *Not on a Broom*, p. 7; and *Overland Scout*, vol. 1, no. 6 (1910), p. 11:1.

39. Specifications are from "Number of Cylinders and Bore and Stroke of American Cars," *Motor Age*, March 3, 1910, p. 3:1; *Automobile*, May 19, 1910, pp. 931, 944; Overland ads in the *Chicago Inter Ocean*, June 12, 1910, p. 8:4; *Des Moines (Iowa) Register and Leader*, June 17, 1910, p. 3:1; and *Salt Lake (City) Evening Telegram*, July 9, 1910, p. 7:3. Production figures are from Beverly Rae Kimes and Henry Austin Clark, Jr., *Standard Catalog of American Cars, 1905–1942*, 2nd ed. (Iola, Wis.: Krause Publications, 1989), p. 1053:2.

40. "Women Autoists Meet in Salt Lake," *Salt Lake (City) Herald-Republican*, July 12, 1910, p. 2:1; and *Toledo (Ohio) Daily Blade*, June 3, 1910, p. 16:3.

41. "Two Girls Cross Continent," *Nebraska State Journal* (Lincoln), June 20, 1910, p. 3:4; and "Lady Autoists Arrive in Town," *Deseret Evening News* (Salt Lake City), July 12, 1910, p. 5:1.

42. *Cleveland Plain Dealer*, May 27, 1910, p. 9:7.

43. *Cleveland Leader*, May 29, 1910, p. 6:3.

44. "Miss Scott Visits Harmon," *Cleveland Leader*, June 5, 1910, II, p. 3:4.

45. "Notable Overland Trip," *Columbus (Ohio) Sunday Dispatch*, May 29, 1910, II, p. 2:4. In the early going, Scott talked of tackling Death Valley, as Jacob M. Murdock had done in 1908. She actually crossed into California at Lake Tahoe, farther north.

46. Ohio Automobile Co. ad, *Dayton (Ohio) Journal*, May 29, 1910, p. 30:2.

47. According to "Two Ships in Air at the Same Time," *Dayton (Ohio) Daily News*, May 30, 1910, p. 8:2, Orville Wright — not Wilbur, as Scott asserts — was flying one of the two planes.

48. *Toledo (Ohio) Daily Blade*, June 3, 1910, p. 16:3.

49. "Motor Records Go by Board," *Chicago Daily Tribune*, May 31, 1910, p. 15:6.

50. Scott is evidently mistaken about driving one of the Peerless Motor Car Company's Green Dragon racers. Hired in mid–1904 to drive the first 60-horsepower Green Dragon, Oldfield "stormed twenty tracks and won sixteen races out of sixteen starts, besides leaving in [his] wake a phenomenal string of broken records and defeated opponents," according to historian John Bentley, quoted in Marion George, "The Fearless Men in the Peerless Green," *Automobile Quarterly*, vol. 11, no. 1 (1973), p. 109:2. Oldfield failed to start in one of the four remaining races; crashes and a broken axle prevented him from finishing the other three. But Oldfield and Peerless parted company "soon thereafter," the article states. Press accounts of the 1910 Indianapolis Motor Speedway races that Scott witnessed report that Oldfield alternately drove two racers: a Knox and a "big Benz" — not a Green Dragon.

51. *Toledo (Ohio) Daily Blade*, June 3, 1910, p. 16:3.

52. *Overland Scout*, vol. 1, no. 6 (1910), p. 13:2.

53. *Chicago Inter Ocean*, June 12, 1910, p. 8:2.

54. *New York Morning Telegraph*, May 15, 1910, IV, part 2, p. 1:5.

55. "Take Trans-Continental Trip in Search of Pleasure," *Milwaukee Journal*, June 14, 1910, p. 9:3.

56. "Woman in Cross Country Run Here," *Council Bluffs (Iowa) Daily Nonpareil*, June 18, 1910, p. 7:4.

57. Untitled article, *Cedar Rapids (Iowa) Daily Republican*, June 16, 1910, p. 6:2.

58. Ideal Auto Co. ad, *Des Moines (Iowa) Register and Leader*, June 17, 1910, p. 3:1.

59. *Des Moines (Iowa) Register and Leader*, June 18, 1910, p. 2:2.

60. "Woman Driver Says Iowa Roads Great," *Des Moines (Iowa) Capital*, June 17, 1910, p. 8:1.

61. *Des Moines (Iowa) Capital*, June 17, 1910, p. 8:1; and *Nebraska State Journal* (Lincoln), June 20, 1910, p. 3:4.

62. *Council Bluffs (Iowa) Sunday Nonpareil*, June 19, 1910, p. 6:1.

63. *Omaha (Neb.) World-Herald*, June 19, 1910, II, p. 7N:1.

64. *Nebraska State Journal* (Lincoln), June 20, 1910, p. 3:4.

65. "The Auto, the Girl and the Wide, Wide World," *York (Neb.) Republican*, June 22, 1910, p. 5:3.

66. "Triumph for Miss Scott," *Motor Age*, June 30, 1910, p. 32:1.

67. "From New York to Frisco by Auto," *Seward (Neb.) Independent-Democrat*, June 23, 1910, p. 1:4.

68. *Blue Valley Blade* (Seward, Neb.), June 22, 1910, p. 1:4.

69. "A Fine Trip," *York (Neb.) Times*, June 22, 1910, p. 3:4.

70. *York (Neb.) Republican*, June 22, 1910, p. 5:3.

71. "Additional Local," *Hamilton County Register* (Aurora, Neb.), June 24, 1910, p. 6:3.

72. "Local Overrun," *Aurora (Neb.) Sun*, June 24, 1910, p. 8:2.

73. "Miss Scott and 'Lady Overland,'" *Hastings (Neb.) Daily Republican*, June 21, 1910, p. 1:1; and "Waiting for Camp Outfit," *Hastings (Neb.) Daily Tribune*, June 21, 1910, p. 4:2.

74. *Hastings (Neb.) Daily Republican*, June 21, 1910, p. 1:1.

75. *Hastings (Neb.) Daily Tribune*, June 21, 1910, p. 4:2; and *Hastings (Neb.) Daily Republican*, June 21, 1910, p. 1:1.

76. "Lady Autoists Arrive in Kearney on Trip to San Francisco," *Kearney (Neb.) Morning Times*, June 30, 1910, p. 1:3.

77. "Not Much of a Feat," *Keith County News* (Ogallala, Neb.), June 30, 1910, p. 1:1.

78. *Cheyenne State Leader*, July 1, 1910, pp. 1:5, 5:2.

79. "Miss Scott Reaches Frisco," *Overland Scout*, November 1910, p. 35:2.

80. *New York Morning Telegraph*, July 10, 1910, p. 6:4.

81. *Deseret Evening News* (Salt Lake City), July 12, 1910, p. 5:1.

82. "Miss Scott Motors across Continent," *New York Morning Telegraph*, July 17, 1910, p. 8:3.

83. *Ely (Nev.) Weekly Mining Expositor*, July 21, 1910, p. 5:4.

84. "Rochester's Remarkable Flying Redhead!" p. 3.

85. *Automobile*, July 21, 1910, p. 83:2.

86. "Woman Transcontinentalist Nearing 'Frisco,'" *Automobile Topics*, July 23, 1910, p. 1035:2; and *Wyoming: A Guide to Its History, Highways, and People* (New York: Oxford University Press, 1941, reprinted Lincoln: University of Nebraska Press, 1981), p. 258.

87. *Automobile*, July 21, 1910, pp. 82:2.

88. *Automobile Topics*, July 23, 1910, p. 1035:2.

89. Consolidated Wagon & Machine Co. ad, *Salt Lake (City) Evening Telegram*, July 9, 1910, p. 7:3.

90. *Salt Lake (City) Tribune*, July 12, 1910, p. 10:3.

91. *Deseret Evening News* (Salt Lake City), July 12, 1910, p. 5:1.

92. "Sunbrowned Girls Making a Long Overland Journey," *Salt Lake (City) Evening Telegram*, July 12, 1910, p. 3:6; and *Salt Lake (City) Tribune*, July 12, 1910, p. 10:4.

93. Though she wrote her book as "Harriet White Fisher," most newspapers called her Harriet Clark Fisher, Clark being the first name of her deceased husband. "Woman Meets Adventure in Motor Tour of the World," *New York Times*, Aug. 21, 1910, V, p. 2:1, neglects to mention it but Fisher's maid shares the honor of being the first woman to complete a driving tour of the world. The headline is from the *Salt Lake (City) Tribune*, July 12, 1910, p. 10:3.

94. *Salt Lake (City) Herald-Republican*, July 12, 1910, p. 2:1. In a 1911 book, Fisher told her "plain unvarnished tale ... [of] the trip of a woman who had grown a little weary of the details of a useful but somewhat heavy business" — running Eagle Anvil Works, a Trenton, New Jersey, anvil and vise factory. Setting sail from New York City to France on July 17, 1909, with her car aboard, Fisher "sought recreation under India's burning sun, in Ceylon, China, Japan, in many places where no motor-car had

ever taken man or woman before." (Harriet White Fisher, *A Woman's World Tour in a Motor* [Philadelphia: J.B. Lippincott, 1911], p. 8.)

From Yokohama, Japan, she returned to the United States by ship, arriving at San Francisco June 17, 1910. Fisher began her transcontinental trip June 26, accompanied by her Italian maid, an English servant, and her nephew and driver — Harold Fisher Brooks.

In making what was reportedly a $25,000 round-the-world tour, Fisher spent just 50 cents at Salt Lake City for her first repair, the *Salt Lake Evening Telegram* remarked, "but it grieved her because she had become hopeful of making the entire trip without a break." ("Woman Completing Remarkable Tour," *Salt Lake [City] Evening Telegram*, July 16, 1910, II, p. 7:3.) Fisher's four-passenger Locomobile runabout reached New York City on Aug. 16, 1910, after a trip estimated at between 18,000 and 20,000 miles.

95. *Deseret Evening News* (Salt Lake City), July 12, 1910, p. 5:1.

96. *Ely (Nev.) Weekly Mining Expositor*, July 21, 1910, p. 5:4.

97. W.H.B. Fowler, "Miss Scott in Her 'Lady Overland' Arrives," *San Francisco Chronicle*, July 24, 1910, p. 35:1.

98. *San Francisco Chronicle*, July 24, 1910, p. 35:1.

99. *San Francisco Chronicle*, July 24, 1910, p. 35:1.

100. A search of several newspapers for late June and early July 1910 failed to locate the Associated Press article to which Scott refers.

101. "First Woman Pilot Helping Air Force Save Aviation's Past for Future," *U.S. Flying News*, Sept. 12, 1955, p. 1:1.

102. *Women Aloft*, pp. 9, 18.

103. *Women Aloft*, pp. 9, 18–19; and Claudia M. Oakes, *United States Women in Aviation through World War I*, Smithsonian Studies in Air and Space, Number 2 (Washington, D.C.: Smithsonian Institution Press, 1978), p. 17:2.

104. *New York Times*, Jan. 13, 1970, p. 45:2; and *United States Women in Aviation through World War I*, p. 19:1.

105. *Women Aloft*, p. 18.

106. "A Woman Is Seen as First on Moon," *New York Times*, Feb. 28, 1960, p. 22:3; and *The People's Almanac #2*, p. 674:2.

107. *New York Times*, Jan. 13, 1970, p. 45:2. Though not quoted directly, the Bill Adams articles cited earlier provided details on Scott's aviation background.

108. Norman E. Borden, Jr., "The Car, the Girl and the Wide, Wide World," *Bulb Horn*, November–December 1965, p. 10.

109. "Miss Blanche Scott's Tour a Success," *Toledo (Ohio) Daily Blade*, July 30, 1910, p. 14:5.

110. These estimates are from *The Complete Official Road Guide of the Lincoln Highway*, 5th ed. (Detroit: Lincoln Highway Association, 1924, reprinted Tucson, Ariz.: Patrice Press, 1993), p. 109.

Four. King Kruises "Koast to Koast in a KisselKar"

1. "Girl to Cross Continent Alone," *Motor West*, Sept. 1, 1915, p. 23:1; and Stuart Gayness, "Woman Sets Auto Record," *San Francisco Examiner*, Aug. 27, 1915, p. 19:8.

2. *San Francisco Examiner*, Aug. 27, 1915, p. 19:8.

3. Leon J. Pinkson, "Fair Autoist Sets Intercity Mark for Women," *San Francisco Chronicle*, Aug. 27, 1915, p. 13:7; "Movie Actress to Drive across U.S.," *San Francisco Chronicle*, Aug. 29, 1915, p. 42:7; and *Motor West*, Sept. 1, 1915, p. 23:1.

4. "Film Star Is Now Making Long Trip in Kissel-Kar," *Salt Lake (City) Herald-Republican*, Sept. 5, 1915, p. 9:2.

5. The distance is from the *San Francisco Chronicle*, Aug. 27, 1915, p. 13:7. Details on the various other record-setting runs mentioned in this paragraph come from "A New San Francisco–Los Angeles Record," *Automobile*, Nov. 15, 1906, p. 636:2; "Cadillac Makes San Francisco to Los Angeles in 12 Hours 10 Minutes," *Automobile*, June 17, 1915, p. 1097:1; and "Another Record Is Made on Coast Run," *Reno (Nev.) Evening Gazette*, May 20, 1916, p. 2:5.

6. Specifications are from "Passenger Cars for 1915 Listed with Their Principal Specifications," *Automobile*, Dec. 31, 1914, pp. 1224–25; the National Automobile Chamber of Commerce's *Hand Book of Automobiles, 1915*; and "Movie Star Reaches Chicago," *Motor Age*, Sept. 30, 1915, p. 21:3. The *Hand Book of Automobiles* lists the 1915 6-42's tire size as 34 × 4 inches.

7. "Paramount Girl Here on Her Long and Solitary Trip," *Wyoming Tribune* (Cheyenne), Sept. 16, 1915, p. 2:3.

8. An untitled article in the *Grand Island (Neb.) Daily Independent*, Sept. 20, 1915, p. 8:3, names the siren brand. The two quotations are from the *Wyoming Tribune* (Cheyenne), Sept. 16, 1915, p. 2:3; and "Local and Personal," *North Platte (Neb.) Semi-Weekly Tribune*, Sept. 21, 1915, p. 4:2.

9. *Motor West*, Sept. 1, 1915, p. 23:1; and "Anita King to Drive across Continent Alone," *Los Angeles Times*, Aug. 22, 1915, VI, p. 7:2.

10. "Paramount Girl at the Majestic Today," *Nevada State Journal* (Reno), Sept. 3, 1915, p. 4:4; Charles K. Field, "A Little Mother of the Movies: Screening the Screen-Struck Girl from the Perils of the New Rialto," *Sunset: The Pacific Monthly*, September 1916, p. 33:2; and M.M. Musselman, *Get a Horse! The Story of the Automobile in America* (Philadelphia: J.B. Lippincott, 1950), p. 246.

11. "Anita King of Movies Here in Motor Monday," *Omaha (Neb.) Daily News*, Sept. 19, 1915, p. 11C:2; *San Francisco Chronicle*, Aug. 29, 1915, p. 42:7; and "Girl Driver Out for New Record," *San Francisco Examiner*, Aug. 29, 1915, p. 32:5.

12. "Movie Star, Alone on Desert, Kills Pet When Water Is Gone," *Omaha (Neb.) World-Herald*, Sept. 21, 1915, p. 9:2.

13. *Sunset*, September 1916, p. 33:2.

14. Stuart Gayness, "Woman Will Drive Motor across U.S.," *San Francisco Examiner*, Sept. 1, 1915, p. 11:1.

15. "Cross Continent Trip in KisselKar," *Hartford (Wis.) Press*, Aug. 27, 1915, p. 1:7.

16. "Pretty Motorist Will Travel Alone from Los Angeles to New York," *Los Angeles Examiner*, Aug. 22, 1915, VII, p. 3:4.

17. "Movie Star Begins Long Trip," *Hartford (Wis.) Press*, Sept. 3, 1915, p. 1:5.

18. In a June 24, 1995, letter to the author, Kissel historian Val V. Quandt said company records date King's car as a 1915 model. It would be impossible to identify the model year from surviving photos, Quandt said: "There were no visible external changes from the 1915 to the 1916 models."

19. "Pretty Anita King, Heroine of Many Adventures on Long Auto Trip, in Omaha," *Omaha (Neb.) Daily News*, Sept. 21, 1915, p. 9:4; and "News from the KisselKar Factory," *Hartford (Wis.) Press*, Sept. 17, 1915, p. 4:1.

20. Robert Connelly, *The Motion Picture Guide: Silent Film, 1910–1936* (Chicago: Cinebooks, 1986), p. 44:1. Farrar's years at the Met are from Ephraim Katz, *The Film Encyclopedia*, 2nd ed. (New York: HarperPerennial, 1994), p. 435:2.

21. Rolph's background comes from the *New York Times*, "Turns Movie Actor," Aug. 30, 1914, VI, p. 6:3, "Nebraskan Brings Greetings to City," Sept. 9, 1914, p. 18:1, and "Frisco Phones A.N.P.A. Greetings," April 23, 1915, p. 5:1; and Melvin G. Holli and Peter d'A. Jones, eds., *Biographical Dictionary of American Mayors, 1820–1980* (Westport, Conn.: Greenwood Press, 1981), pp. 256–57, 310–11.

22. Photo and cutline, *Los Angeles Times*, Aug. 26, 1915, III, p. 2:2; and *Nevada State Journal* (Reno), Sept. 3, 1915, p. 4:4.

23. "Paramount Girl Is Local Visitor," *Sacramento (Calif.) Union*, Sept. 2, 1915, p. 2:3.

24. *Sunset*, September 1916, p. 32:2.

25. Paramount's history is from Anthony Slide, *The American Film Industry: A Historical Dictionary* (New York: Greenwood Press, 1986), p. 256.

26. Grace Kingsley, "All-Around Anita: Auto or Aviation Stuff, No One Needs to Double for Anita King," *Photoplay Magazine*, August 1916, pp. 144–45.

27. Quoted in *Sunset*, September 1916, p. 32:2.

28. *Sunset*, September 1916, p. 32:2; and Virginia Scharff, *Taking the Wheel: Women and the Coming of the Motor Age* (Albuquerque, N.M.: University of New Mexico Press, 1991), p. 29.

29. "'Movie' Actress Reaches Chian After Hard Trip," *Cheyenne (Wyo.) State Leader*, Sept. 17, 1915, p. 5:1.

30. These findings are from researcher Walt Jayroe of Phoenix, who searched 1908–15 race reports in the *Arizona Republican* and *Phoenix Gazette*.

31. According to "First Accident at Motordrome," *New York Times*, April 11, 1910, p. 8:4.

32. *Sunset*, September 1916, pp. 32–33.

33. *Sunset*, September 1916, p. 33:2; and *Motion Picture News'* semiannual *Studio Directory*, April 12, 1917, n.p.

34. *Photoplay*, August 1916, p. 143:1.

35. *Omaha (Neb.) World-Herald*, Sept. 21, 1915, p. 9:2.

36. Patricia King Hanson and Alan Gevinson, eds., *The American Film Institute Catalog* (Berkeley: University of California Press, 1988), p. 751–52.

37. *The Motion Picture Guide: Silent Film, 1910–1936* (Chicago: Cinebooks, 1986), p. 226:1.

38. *Motor West*, Sept. 1, 1915, p. 23.

39. *Omaha (Neb.) Daily News*, Sept. 21, 1915, p. 9:2.

40. *Omaha (Neb.) Daily Bee*, Sept. 22, 1915, p. 7:2. Many other newspapers joined the *Daily Bee* and *Daily News* of Omaha in printing versions of this story.

41. "Anita King, Paramount Girl, Finishes First Lap in Trip," *Reno (Nev.) Evening Gazette*, Sept. 3, 1915, p. 8:3.

42. "Auto Parties Pay Brief Visits Here," *Nevada State Journal* (Reno), Sept. 4, 1915, p. 4:6.

43. "A Regular Girlie, Is Little Anita King, Movie Miss, Alone on Coast to Coast Auto Trip," *Cedar Rapids (Iowa) Evening Gazette*, Sept. 25, 1915, p. 10:4.

44. *Grand Island (Neb.) Daily Independent*, Sept. 20, 1915, p. 8:3; and *Omaha (Neb.) Daily News*, Sept. 21, 1915, p. 9:3.

45. "Ocean-to-Ocean Trails Well Worn," *MoTor*, December 1915, p. 56:2; and *Photoplay*, August 1916, p. 145:1.

46. *Omaha (Neb.) World-Herald*, Sept. 21, 1915, p. 1:5.

47. *Get a Horse!* p. 247.

48. "Paramount Girl Motors from Pacific to Atlantic," *Salt Lake (City) Herald-Republican*, Sept. 7, 1915, p. 4:4 of sports section.

49. "Miss Anita King Writes of Her Interesting Trip," *Hartford (Wis.) Press*, Sept. 17, 1915, p. 1:4.

50. "Miss Anita King Reaches City, Worn and Weary," *Deseret Evening News* (Salt Lake City), Sept. 8, 1915, p. 5:1.

51. "Woman Motorist to Arrive in Salt Lake This Afternoon," *Salt Lake (City) Tribune*, Sept. 8, 1915, p. 3:3.

52. "Photoplay Artiste Encounters Coyote," *Salt Lake (City) Tribune*, Sept. 9, 1915, p. 4:1. of sports section.

53. *Deseret Evening News* (Salt Lake City), Sept. 8, 1915, p. 5:1; and "News from the Kissel-Kar Factory," *Hartford (Wis.) Press*, Oct. 1, 1915, p. 4:1.

54. "Paramount Girl Arrives in City," *Salt Lake (City) Herald-Republican*, Sept. 9, 1915, p. 10:4.

55. "Anita King, Heroine of Movies, Driving Auto to New York," *Salt Lake (City) Evening Telegram*, Sept. 8, 1915, II, p. 1:3.

56. "A Cat May Look Upon a King — But —," *White Pine News* (East Ely, Nev.), Sept. 12, 1915, p. 1:5. So imposing was Copper Flat, west of Ely, that the H.M. Gousha Co.'s 1941 Nevada highway map alerted travelers that they were passing "one of the largest man-made holes on earth."

57. "Paramount Girl Visits at Factory," *Hartford (Wis.) Press*, Oct. 29, 1910, p. 1:1; and "Plucky Actress Nearing Chicago," *Hartford (Wis.) Times*, Sept. 24, 1915, p. 1:2.

58. "The Paramount Girl Reaches the City," *Laramie (Wyo.) Republican*, Sept. 16, 1915, p. 6:4.

59. *Laramie (Wyo.) Republican*, Sept. 16, 1915, p. 6:4.

60. *Cheyenne (Wyo.) State Leader*, Sept. 17, 1915, p. 5:1.

61. *Omaha (Neb.) Daily Bee*, Sept. 22, 1915, p. 7:2. This verbatim account also ran in the *Hartford (Wis.) Press*, Oct. 1, 1915, p. 4:1.

62. *Hartford (Wis.) Press*, Oct. 1, 1915, p. 4:1.

63. *Sunset*, September 1916, p. 33:2.

64. *Sunset*, September 1916, p. 68:3.

65. *North Platte (Neb.) Semi-Weekly Tribune*, Sept. 21, 1915, p. 4:2; and "Miss Anita King Is Delayed in Voyage," *Omaha (Neb.) Daily Bee*, Sept. 20, 1915, p. 7:7.

66. *Kearney (Neb.) Daily Hub*, Sept. 20, 1915, "Movie Star Passes Through," p. 3:4, and "Road Condition on Highway Bad," p. 3:3.

67. *Omaha (Neb.) Daily Bee*, Sept. 22, 1915, p. 7:2.

68. *Grand Island (Neb.) Daily Independent*, Sept. 20, 1915, p. 8:3.

69. Untitled article, *Columbus (Neb.) Telegram*, Sept. 24, 1915, p. 7:5; and "Paramount

Girl Was in Columbus," *Columbus (Neb.) Journal*, Sept. 23, 1915, p. 7:6.

70. Estimates from the *American Motorist* are quoted in "Touring the Continent Becoming More Popular," *Hartford (Conn.) Times*, May 13, 1911, p. 12:1. AAA figures are quoted in "Tourists to Spend over $1,000,000," *New York Times*, April 21, 1912, VIII, p. 13:1.

71. Reo ad, *Collier's*, June 19, 1915, pp. 22–23; *MoTor*, December 1915, p. 56:1; and Hamilton M. Laing, "The Transcontinental Game," *Sunset: The Pacific Monthly*, February 1917, p. 72:1.

72. *Omaha (Neb.) World-Herald*, Sept. 21, 1915, p. 9:2.; and *Omaha (Neb.) Daily News*, Sept. 21, 1915, p. 9:2. A studio directory says King had auburn hair and hazel eyes, which clashes with the *Daily News* description.

73. *Omaha (Neb.) World-Herald*, Sept. 21, 1915, p. 1:4.

74. *Omaha (Neb.) Daily News*, Sept. 21, 1915, p. 9:2; and *Omaha (Neb.) Daily Bee*, Sept. 22, 1915, p. 7:2.

75. *Omaha (Neb.) Daily News*, Sept. 21, 1915, p. 9:3.

76. "Paramount Girl Pays Visit to the Bluffs," *Omaha (Neb.) World-Herald*, Sept. 22, 1915, p. 2:4; and *Omaha (Neb.) Daily Bee*, Sept. 22, 1915, p. 7:2.

77. *Omaha (Neb.) World-Herald*, Sept. 22, 1915, p. 2:4.

78. *Hartford (Wis.) Times*, Sept. 24, 1915, p. 1:2.

79. "The Paramount Girl in Boone," *Boone (Iowa) News-Republican*, Sept. 23, 1915, p. 1:4.

80. "Real Movie Queen in Ames Yesterday," *Des Moines (Iowa) Register and Leader*, Sept. 24, 1915, p. 2:1.

81. *Cedar Rapids (Iowa) Evening Gazette*, Sept. 25, 1915, p. 10:3.

82. *Motor Age*, Sept. 30, 1915, p. 21:3; and "Anita King Reaches Town," *Chicago Daily Tribune*, Sept. 27, 1915, p. 15:4.

83. "Anita King Receives Welcome in Chicago," *Hartford (Wis.) Press*, Oct. 1, 1915, p. 1:4.

84. "The Paramount Girl Completes Her Drive," *Hartford (Wis.) Press*, Oct. 22, 1915, p. 1:2.

85. "Movie Star at Her Journey's End," *Hartford (Wis.) Press*, Oct. 8, 1915, p. 1:3.

86. *Hartford (Wis.) Press*, Oct. 8, 1915, p. 1:3.

87. *Motor Age*, Sept. 30, 1915, p. 21:3.

88. *Hartford (Wis.) Press*, Oct. 8, 1915, p. 1:3.

89. *Hartford (Wis.) Press*, Oct. 22, 1915, p. 1:2.

90. "Actress Drives across Continent," *New York Herald*, Oct. 20, 1915, p. 12:3.

91. *New York Herald*, Oct. 20, 1915, p. 12:3.

92. *Hartford (Wis.) Press*, Oct. 22, 1915, p. 1:2. An identical account ran in the same day's *Hartford Times*.

93. *MoTor*, December 1915, p. 56:2; *Hartford (Wis.) Press*, Oct. 8, 1915, p. 1:3; and a Kissel ad, *Motor Age*, Oct. 21, 1915, p. 75.

94. "Paramount Girl Completes Drive," *Hartford (Wis.) Times*, Oct. 22, 1915, p. 1:4.

95. *Hartford (Wis.) Press*, Oct. 8, 1915, p. 1:3.

96. "News from the KisselKar Factory," *Hartford (Wis.) Press*, Oct. 29, 1915, p. 4:1.

97. *Hartford (Wis.) Press*, Oct. 29, 1910, p. 1:1.

98. "Hartford People Have Pleasure of Meeting Movie Actress," *Hartford (Wis.) Times*, Oct. 29, 1915, p. 1:3.

99. "Anita King Now Has King Eight," *Omaha (Neb.) World-Herald*, May 21, 1916, p. 10E:6.

100. *Photoplay*, August 1916, p. 145:2.

101. *Sunset*, September 1916, p. 32:2; and *Photoplay*, August 1916, p. 145:2.

102. *Sunset*, September 1916, p. 68:3.

103. Information for this paragraph comes from "Early Day Film Star Anita King McKenna Dies," *Los Angeles Times*, June 11, 1963, n.p.; Jeane Hoffman, "Anita King McKenna Top Woman in Racing," *Los Angeles Times*, Feb. 20, 1952, n.p.; and "Anita King, Star of Silent Films, Dies," *Los Angeles Herald-Examiner*, June 10, 1963, n.p.

104. Val V. Quandt, *The Classic Kissel Automobile* (Hartford, Wis.: Kissel Graph Press, 1990), pp. 86, 94, 110–12.

105. "Anita King of Silent Screen; Actress Turned to Racing," *New York Times*, June 11, 1963, p. 37:2.

Five. "Just a Matter of Good Driving, Coolness and Nerve"

1. Amanda Preuss, *A Girl — A Record and an Oldsmobile* (Lansing, Mich.: Olds Motor Works, 1916), 24 pp. While the *Sacramento Bee* and *Sacramento Union* claim Preuss as a local resident, a smattering of newspaper accounts give her residence as San Francisco. One such *San Francisco Chronicle* article from Sept. 3, 1916, plays up her ties to the Bay City: "Miss Preuss said that at one time she had been a stenographer in San Francisco. Later on she worked for a while on a San Francisco newspaper." Another *Chronicle* piece, however, calls Preuss a Sacramento resident.

2. "Would Interest Women in Transcontinental Touring," *Salt Lake (City) Tribune*, Aug. 13, 1916, p. 6:2 of auto section.

3. Ursinus Erhard, "San Francisco Girl Rests After Auto Run to Gotham," *San Francisco Chronicle*, Sept. 3, 1916, p. 29:2.

4. Preuss booklet, pp. 3–4. Hereafter, unattributed and uncited quotations are from this booklet.

5. Frank Herman, "Lone Woman to Drive across Continent in 'Olds,'" *San Francisco Call and Post*, Aug. 5, 1916, p. 9:2.

6. *Salt Lake (City) Tribune*, Aug. 13, 1916, p. 6:3 of auto section; *San Francisco Call and Post*, Aug. 5, 1916, p. 9:2; and *Salt Lake (City) Tribune*, Aug. 13, 1916, p. 6:3 of auto section.

7. *San Francisco Call and Post*, Aug. 5, 1916, p. 9:1. Specifications are from "1916 Passenger Automobiles Listed with Their Technical Specifications," *Automobile*, Dec. 30, 1915, pp. 1250–51.

8. *San Francisco Chronicle*, Sept. 3, 1916, p. 29:2; and *Salt Lake (City) Tribune*, Aug. 13, 1916, p. 6:2 of auto section.

9. Aug. 17, 1995, letter to the author from Elizabeth D. Norris, YWCA of the U.S.A. historian, who also enclosed a photocopy of the 1919 poster.

10. "Girl Completes Automobile Tour from San Francisco to New York," *New York Herald*, Aug. 20, 1916, III, p. 9:2.

11. *San Francisco Call and Post*, Aug. 5, 1916, p. 9:1.

12. "Crossing Continent to Demonstrate That Women Can Make Transcontinental

Tours," *Salt Lake (City) Telegram*, Aug. 13, 1916, p. 6:5 of automobile and motorcycle section.

13. "Woman Drives across County Alone," *Rock Springs (Wyo.) Rocket*, Aug. 18, 1916, p. 5:3.

14. *Salt Lake (City) Tribune*, Aug. 13, 1916, p. 6:5 of auto section.

15. *Salt Lake (City) Telegram*, Aug. 13, 1916, p. 6:5 of automobile and motorcycle section.

16. *Salt Lake (City) Tribune*, Aug. 13, 1916, p. 6:2 of auto section.

17. *The Complete Official Road Guide of the Lincoln Highway* (Detroit: Lincoln Highway Association, 1916; reprinted Sacramento, Calif.: Pleiades Press, 1995), p. 21.

18. *San Francisco Call and Post*, Aug. 5, 1916, p. 9:1; and *Salt Lake (City) Tribune*, Aug. 13, 1916, p. 6:3 of auto section.

19. Frank Herman, "Woman Driver Is After New Record," *San Francisco Call and Post*, Aug. 8, 1916, p. 7:1; and "Woman Crosses Continent in 11.23 Days," *Automobile*, Aug. 24, 1916, p. 335:3.

20. *San Francisco Call and Post*, Aug. 8, 1916, p. 7:1.

21. "World's Longest Causeway," *MoTor*, June 1916, p. 80; and "Giant Causeway Shortens Lincoln Highway Route in California," *Lincoln Highway*, March 8, 1916, p. 1:1.

22. *San Francisco Call and Post*, Aug. 5, 1916, p. 9:1.

23. In saying "I negotiated three snowsheds," Preuss evidently is referring to the wooden walls and roofs that the Southern Pacific Railroad built around sections of track to repel snow in the Sierra Nevada. Where the Lincoln Highway intersected such snowsheds, the railroad provided doors that motorists could open — and close behind them — to cross the tracks.

24. *A Complete Official Road Guide of the Lincoln Highway*, 5th ed. (Detroit: Lincoln Highway Association, 1924; reprinted Tucson, Ariz.: The Patrice Press, 1993), p. 43.

25. *Salt Lake (City) Telegram*, Aug. 13, 1916, p. 6:3 of automobile and motorcycle section.

26. "Society Woman Makes Lone Tour," *Cheyenne (Wyo.) State Leader*, Aug. 13, 1916, p. 8:3.

27. "Woman Drives across Country in Eleven Days," *Motorist*, September 1916, p. 45:2.

28. "Woman Is Motoring across Country Alone," *Omaha (Neb.) Daily News*, Aug. 16, 1916, p. 3:6; and *Motorist*, September 1916, p. 45:1.

29. "Woman Crossing Continent Has Her Way Made Easy," *Council Bluffs (Iowa) Daily Nonpareil*, Aug. 16, 1916, p. 5:4.

30. *San Francisco Chronicle*, Sept. 3, 1916, p. 29:3.

31. "Girl Breaks Women's Automobile Record," *New York Tribune*, Aug. 20, 1916, p. 14:3.

32. *Automobile*, *Motor Age* and the *New York Herald* say 11 days, 5 hours, 30 minutes — instead of 45 minutes. But many more newspapers and auto journals agree with the 45-minute figure Preuss uses in her booklet.

33. "Woman Motors 3,000 Miles," *New York Times*, Aug. 20, 1916, I, p. 9:3; *Automobile*, Aug. 24, 1916, p. 335:3; "Woman Goes over Continent in Record Time of 10 Days," *Erie (Pa.) Dispatch*, Sept. 17, 1916, p. 14:5; and *New York Times*, Aug. 20, 1916, I, p. 9:3.

34. *New York Herald*, Aug. 20, 1916, III, p. 9:2.

35. *San Francisco Chronicle*, Sept. 3, 1916, p. 29:2.

36. In her booklet, Preuss mistakenly names "Victor Dowling" as the acting mayor. The *New York Times*, however, confirms that Frank L. Dowling, president of the Board of Aldermen, was acting mayor when Preuss arrived.

37. *San Francisco Chronicle*, Sept. 3, 1916, p. 29:2.

38. *Salt Lake (City) Tribune*, Aug. 13, 1916, p. 6:4 of auto section.

39. "Woman Driver Sets Record on Lincoln Highway," *The Lincoln Highway*, Sept. 13, 1916, p. 1:1.

40. Photo and cutline, *American Chauffeur*, December 1916, p. 558:1. Valerie Moolman, *Women Aloft*, Epic of Flight series (Alexandria, Va.: Time-Life Books, 1981), pp. 32–33, details Law's nonstop flight.

41. "State Fair Crowd Near 50,000 Mark," *Des Moines (Iowa) Register and Leader*, Aug. 29, 1916, p. 2:3.

42. Johnson Co. ad, *Automobile*, Oct. 19, 1916, p. 99.

43. Hamilton M. Laing, "The Transcontinental Game," *Sunset: The Pacific Monthly*, February 1917, p. 72:1.

Index

Page numbers in italics have photographs